The More Fun You Have Selling Real Estate, the More Real Estate You Will Sell!

The Sequel to Sell with Soul

Jennifer Allan-Hagedorn, GRI

Charlie Kem
9/7/2017

bluegreenbooks

D0843694

ISBN: 978-0-9899326-2-2

Cover, Interior Design and Illustrations by Sheryl Evans, Evans Studios,
www.evans-studios.com

First Printing 2016
Printed in the United States of America

Published by Bluegreen Books
Publisher@Bluegreenbooks.com

Dedication

This book is dedicated to my ~~groupies~~ ~~fans~~ ~~stalkers~~ readers who have been a tremendous source of inspiration to me over the years. You've cheered me on when I was on a roll; ~~slapped me out of my pity party~~ cheered me up when I was down and brought tears to my eyes with your effusive letters of gratitude. In fact, I've said more than once that everyone should write a book so that they can experience the joy of receiving fan mail.

From the bottom of my heart (and soul), I thank you.

This one's for you!

acclaim for Jennifer Allan-Hagedorn's

"The More Fun You Have Selling Real Estate, the More Real Estate You Will Sell!"

"What an inspiring, fun and informative book! Great for newer agents and those needing some new motivation—or even a kick in the pants (done gently, of course!). A perfect companion to my resource Up and Running in 30 Days."

— *Carla Cross, CRB, MA*
> *Best-selling author of 6 real estate production resources, National Realtor Educator of the Year, named 50 Top Women in Real Estate 2008*

"While in any walk of life, we must sell ourselves as competent professionals, no one wants to be 'sold to.' If you've ever dreamed of guiding, advising and consulting with your clients rather than simply hunting them down, Jennifer's approach is spot on and this book is a must-read for you."

— *Mollie W. Wasserman*
> *Founder of: The Accredited Consultant in Real Estate® Course and Coaching Program. Author of "Ripping the Roof off Real Estate - How a Multi-Billion Dollar Industry Came to Have an Identity Crisis"*

"Once again, you nailed it. You give a voice to all the great agents who love what they do and wake every morning ready to be of service to their clients. We help people achieve home ownership; 'The American Dream.' And we do it with respect and a servant's heart. Yes, you bet it's fun."

— *Trish Kraus,*
> *Training and Development, Prudential California Realty*

"Selling real estate requires skill, knowledge, character, ethics and heart. Jennifer leads the way in showing Realtors® how to exemplify exactly that!"

— *Stefan Swanepoel, 15-time Author, Speaker and Visionary*

"If every real estate professional would read Jennifer Allan-Hagedorn's 'The More Fun You have Selling Real Estate' and actually follow her guidance, there would be a lot more real estate professionals having a lot more fun (and making a lot more money.)"
— *Dr. Kenneth W. Edwards, GRI*
Real Estate Broker/Author/Educator, Author of "Your Successful Real Estate Career" (Fifth Edition)

"Throw out all the old-fashioned notions about how to sell real estate! Forget cold-calling, warm-calling, farming, pestering, and other outdated methods. Jennifer Allan-Hagedorn gives us permission to go with our instincts and do what we do best: finding out what people need, and helping them get it in ways that are comfortable for us, and therefore comfortable for our clients. Networking is the key, and Jennifer's guidance makes it easy and productive. Every new and experienced real estate agent will be pleasantly amazed by this book!"
— *Madge Walls*
Author of "Paying the Price", an award-winning novel of real estate in Hawaii and "Hawaii Real Estate Exam Book, A Study Guide for the Hawaii Real Estate Exam"

"As a real estate agent, author and professor and as someone who has read virtually every real estate agent success book out there, I can say, unequivocally, that Jennifer Allan-Hagedorn has written THE BEST book on the topic. All real estate agents, seasoned and new, who want to create a successful practice they actually enjoy, must read this book!"
— *Tamara Dorris, MA*
Author of "Think & Get Rich in Real Estate Sales"

"Jennifer takes a no-nonsense approach to our business and has hit the nail on the head by stating the obvious...if you're not having fun selling real estate, you're not doing it right! Whether you're a rookie or seasoned veteran, you need to read her new book. I give it two thumbs up!"
— *Phyllis Staines,*
Realtor of the Year 2004 Northeast Florida, Co-Author of "Get the Best Deal When Selling Your Home"

"Finally, a book that says it's okay to have some fun again! Jennifer Allan-Hagedorn's book celebrates the good times in real estate that many of us have forgotten about during the tough times. Her buyers are not liars, and most of her clients are friends or personal acquaintances.

But the book offers more than just feel-good motivational words – there's meat in this stew. Jennifer offers tips on subjects ranging from negotiation skills to 'convincing' a buyer that now is the time to buy to listing presentations to how to develop and maintain your sphere of influence as your main source of business.

'Making gobs of money is fun. Getting steady streams of referrals is fun. Being a master negotiator is fun. Solving problems is fun, Being an exceptional real estate agent is fun.'

And reading this book is fun too because it doesn't sound like a textbook, but rather more like advice from a friend."
— *Jim Adair, Editor*
   REM Magazine

"When you love what you do, you never have to work. Jennifer shows you can have it all AND become successful. Not only does she give you great tips and techniques, she presents it in and enjoyable way. A very pleasant business-building strategy book!"
— *Tom Gosche, The Business Strategist, Executive Director*
   BNI Marketing

Special Thanks to...

The CLSWS (and Ed), Susan, Rockin' Kim, Heather, Sue, Ronda, Stacie, Carin & Ed - you ladies (and Ed) really, really GET IT. It's a joy having you in my world and I can't tell you how many times I've ROTFLMAO at your soulful (yet often snarky) observations of the ridiculousness preached as gospel in our industry. Someday we'll write a book...

Active Rain – The Sell with Soul message probably would never have reached beyond the walls of my office without Active Rain (www.activerain.com). What an incredible community of real estate professionals! Thanks a gazillion for all your support.

Sue Gabriel – Sue, you've been my lifeline these last few years! And I better never p*ss you off because you know more about me than probably any other human bean on the planet. Thanks for always being there to vent to, to brag to, to brainstorm with and to help keep the SWS engine moving smoothly. You da' best! Xoxo

My Family – Thanks Mom, Janice, Julie, Tom & Lynn for your enthusiastic support of my writing career and of SWS. I hope I've made you proud!

Mom – Mom never quite figured out how on earth I could run a business on my computer, but she still thought I was awfully darn clever for doing it. Every time she read one of my newsletters, she wrote me back with something like "You're so smart." Gotta love that.

Of my mother's many brilliantly-stated Mom-isms, here's my favorite:
<regarding Sell with Soul, the book> "Well, Jennifer, it's awfully well-written, but what's the big deal? It all seems so sensible."

Dorothy Seacat Allan, May 16, 1926 – August 15, 2010

Julie Baswell – Julie is my sister and biggest fan. She hasn't the slightest interest in selling real estate, but never hesitates to let me know how proud she is of me and how much she enjoys my writings. Contrary to popular belief, writing books does not a mortgage payment make, so her frequent feedback and encouragement is more appreciated than she knows...

Baba, Zigger, Barton & Lucy – Thank you for your undying love, support and companionship. There's nothing quite like having a dog (or four) snoring at your feet (or nuzzling at your elbow) to make you smile -- just when you're ready to throw the computer thru the nearest window. Love you!

My Beloved SWS'ers – I'm oh, so tempted to make a list of the faithful readers who buy my stuff, participate in my forum, show up for my teleseminars, comment on my blogs, subscribe to my newsletters, ask me for advice and share their personal stories with me... and then thank ME for being there. No, my friends, THANK YOU. I won't make that list, much as I'd like to, because I'd surely leave someone off and then kick myself for being so careless.

You know who you are... and yes, I mean YOU!

The More Fun You Have Selling Real Estate, the More Real Estate You Will Sell!

THE SEQUEL TO SELL WITH SOUL

table of contents

Acclaim for Jennifer Allan-Hagedorn's "The More Fun You
Have Selling Real Estate"   iv

Special Thanks   viii

Dedication   iii

(Re)INTRODUCTION to Selling Real Estate with Soul   *1*

CHAPTER ONE
What's Fun Got to Do with it?   *5*
"The More Fun You Have Selling Real Estate, the More Real Estate
    You Will Sell!"   6
About Me   8
JENNIFER'S BLOG: Be Yourself... Have More Fun...   11

CHAPTER TWO
The Reluctant Prospector   *13*
    Do You Worry if You're Too Nice... or Too Thin-Skinned to be
    a Real Estate Agent?   14
    Stop Trying to Cure us!   15
    Are You a Salesperson? Are You Really?   16
    Dear Jennifer...   18
    Introverts are Special!   19

CHAPTER THREE
Prospecting with Soul   *21*
Stop Wasting Your Time (and Money) Marketing to Me!   24
    JENNIFER'S BLOG: How Can a Lender Earn my Business?   24
    Promise me...   26
    JENNIFER'S BLOG: I'm Too Sexy for Your Script   27

CHAPTER FOUR
The Seduction of Your SOI   *29*
    Seduction?   30
    JENNIFER'S BLOG: SOI & the Single Gal   30
    Just Be You, courtesy of John MacArthur   33
    No Harm in Asking? Au Contraire!   34
    Dear Soulful Ones...   35
    The Best Way to Ask for Referrals--Don't!   37
    JENNIFER'S BLOG: 10 Ways SOI is like Dating   38

CHAPTER FOUR - continued

(RE)Defining SOI 39
Who is Your SOI? 41
    How Many in Your SOI? 41
How Much Business Does Your SOI Have to Give? 40
Attracting Business to You 42
The $10,000 Paycheck 43
The Most Important Thing to Do to Succeed in an SOI-Based Business 43
Being Worthy of Referrals 44
"But Everyone I Know Already Knows Five Real Estate Agents!" 46
Is SOI Right for You? 47
Creating an SOI Business Model 49
Other Prospecting Techniques 52
    Web Marketing 52
    Floor Time 53
    Farming 53
For Sale by Owners 54
    Expired Listings 54
    Newspaper Advertising and Real Estate Magazines 55
BE the Person Your Boyfriend Wouldn't Dream of Cheating On 55

CHAPTER FIVE

Playing the Numbers Game (or not, as the case may be) 57
The Numbers Game of SOI 58
JENNIFER'S BLOG: Bringing in Business... One Warm Body ... 60
Touching versus Impressing 61
JENNIFER'S BLOG: Treat Every Buyer Like the Gold Mine He ... 64
Antenna Up for Follow ups 65
Some More Compelling Numbers from the Numbers Game 67
Don't Oversystematize Your Prospecting Efforts 68

CHAPTER SIX

Our Buyers Aren't Liars! 71
How to Chase Away Your Perfectly Qualified, Perfectly Loyal Buyers
Turning the Reins Over to Your Buyers 73
Selecting the Right Homes to Show 74
Are Buyers Really Liars? 75
Most Fix-up Buyers Aren't 77
Let Your Buyer's Emotions Make the Decision, Not Yours 78
When Your Buyer Wants to Purchase a "Fatally-Flawed" Property 81
Special Buyers 83

CHAPTER SIX - continued
    Amateur Investors   83
        Finding Projects for Your Amateur Investor   85
        Bad Projects for Amateur Investors   86
        The Benefits of Working with Investors   88
        Considerations when Selling Fixed-n-Flipped Properties   90
    Out-of-Town Buyers   90
        Types of Out-of-Town Buyers   92
    "I Sell Real Estate Every Day... Sometimes I even get paid for it!"   94

CHAPTER SEVEN
    Rethinking the List(en)ing Presentation   *97*
    Words of Wisdom from the Trenches   99
    Pricing it Right with a Persuasive CMA   99
    Confidence Envelopes You When You Care Enough to
        Make a Difference, courtesy of Meyer Leibovitch   100
    Do You Want the Listing?   103
    JENNIFER'S BLOG: I Got the Listing by Being Soulful!   105

CHAPTER EIGHT
    The New "Three-P's" of Selling Houses   *107*
    The Old "3P's" Of Selling Houses   107
    JENNIFER'S BLOG: "I'm the Best Listing Agent I know. Are you?"   108
    The New "3P's"   109
    P1—Preparing the Relationship   111
    Be Upfront with Your Commission   112
    The Market Value of the Home   113
    JENNIFER'S BLOG: Houses Aren't Pet Rocks!   114
    P2—Preparing the Product   116
    Pricing   116
JENNIFER'S BLOG: Two Types of Seller's Regret   118
    The Importance of the First Impression   119
    Unseen is Unsold   121
    Dear Jennifer...   122
    Why the Seller Must SCRAM for Showings   123
    Seller-Imposed Showing Restrictions   123
    P3—Putting it on the Market   125
    How Do You Reach the Real Estate Community?   127
    Solve the Problem Instead of Reducing the Price   128
    Under-promise and Over-deliver   131
    Open Houses   132

CHAPTER NINE
Pricing Difficult Properties   135
Pricing Flawed Properties   135
Fatally-Flawed Properties   136
    Locational Fatal Flaws   136
    Property-Specific Fatal Flaws   140
    Communicating the News   142
Fixable Flaws   144
    Maximize the First Impression   144
    Force the Issue   145
    Photos   145
    Open Your Checkbook   145
    Staging   145
    Price   146

CHAPTER TEN
Getting What You Want—the Art of Persuasion & Negotiation   147
Negotiation   147
    Commission Negotiation   148
    Other Commission Considerations   151
       Offering Sellers a Menu of Services   151
JENNIFER'S BLOG: Sex, Lies and the Assumptive Close   152
The Art of Persuasion   153
The Power of Reverse Psychology   157
Please please don't bury my deal yet! Courtesy of Bryant Tutas   159
How to Convince a Buyer that NOW is a Great Time to Buy!   160
Seven Bonus Negotiation Tips   161

CHAPTER ELEVEN
Real Estate Offers the ILLUSION of Controlling Your Time   163
My New Buyer Calls at 7:30 am on Sunday Morning...   165
"I'm a Professional and My Time is Extremely Valuable"
    courtesy of Kim Brown   166

CHAPTER TWELVE
Career Development and Quandaries   169
When to let a buyer or seller go   170
    Letting Buyers Go   171
    Letting Sellers Go   171
    Energy Vampires   173

CHAPTER TWELVE - continued

Discount Brokerage—Can it Work for You?   173
JENNIFER'S BLOG: Are You a Ritz? Or a LaQuinta?   174
Real Estate in Jammies?   178
Help! Help! I'm Drowning! Successfully Teaming up   180
    Before Partnering, Search Your Soul   181
    Agent Hires a Licensed Assistant   182
    Agent Hires an Unlicensed Assistant   183
    Agent Takes on a Partner   183
Leaving the Business   185
    Burn Out   185
    Taking it Down a Notch   186

CHAPTER THIRTEEN

In Conclusion…Are You in This Business for the Long Haul?
Or just another few months?   191

EPILOGUE

Lessons from a Recession (a collection of blogs)   195
    Where'd My Money Tree Go?   196
    I Cannot Tell a Lie… It's Tougher Today   197
    What I Love About This Market   198
    The Realities of Today's Less-than-Vibrant Real Estate Market   200
    Today's Market Realities II - Old Fogies Agents—
    Consider Living a Bit less large…   200
    Seriously, is it Time to Hit PAUSE on Your Real Estate Career?   202
    Is it Okay to Blame the Market for Your Lower Production?   203

APPENDIX

Sample Competitive Market Analysis (CMA)   209
Sample Reconnection Letters   216
"What to Expect When on the Market"   222
Contributors   231
Resources   232
Excerpt from Prospect With Soul: The Story of Joe   235

The Secret of Joy in work is one word—excellence. To know how to do something well is to enjoy it.

Pearl S. Buck

(Re)Introduction to Selling Real Estate with Soul

*S*ell with Soul: v. [sĕl wǐth sōl] *To enjoy a wildly successful career selling real estate by treating clients and prospects respectfully, as you yourself would like to be treated.*

To those of you joining us from *Sell with Soul, Creating an Extraordinary Career in Real Estate without Losing Your Friends, Your Principles or Your Self-Respect*...welcome back! I'm thrilled that you've chosen to continue your journey with me! If this is your first venture into Soulful Selling, let me congratulate you on taking a big step toward improving both your professional life, as well as the public's perception of the real estate sales community.

Selling with Soul has nothing to do with new-age philosophies, holier-than-thou attitudes or learning to dance. It's really just a catchy phrase for following the Golden Rule in your day-to-day practice of real estate. For treating your clients and prospects respectfully, as you would like to be treated. For being competent, reliable and fair. For appreciating the commissions paid to you directly by your sellers, and indirectly by your buyers, and for not taking these hefty paychecks for granted. For truly wanting to earn your commission, not just showing up at closing with hand outstretched.

But there's more! If you Sell with Soul, not only will you be a breath of fresh air to the home-buying and -selling public, you can also make gobs and gobs of money while sleeping soundly at night. You make all this money because you're good at your job. You are a Good Real Estate Agent!

You find your buyers the right homes, not just because you know your market, but also because you listen to your clients and strive to meet their needs for a home, not just your need for a commission. (See Chapter Six)

Your sellers' homes sell, not just because they're priced right, but because you've helped them recognize and correct any obstacles to sale...instead of just bullying them for a price reduction. (See Chapters Seven, Eight and Nine)

You know how to hold your sales together. You usually get through inspection periods, even difficult ones, not just because you're a good negotiator, but also because you have great resources for getting repairs made.

Your listings appraise because you are prepared for the appraiser and know how to defend your sales price. Throughout the transaction, you strive for a win/win whenever possible and you don't antagonize the other team, just because they're sitting on the other side of the closing table. (See Chapter Ten)

And of course, as an agent who Sells with Soul, you will be rewarded with plenty of repeat business and referrals. You won't have to spend thousands of dollars on personal promotion, or pester strangers to ask for their business; no, your friends and past clients will be your own personal marketing department. You'll be proud of the business you've developed and will have no problem selling yourself at listing appointments or social encounters.

But lest you believe that soulful real estate agents are simply nice guys and gals who smile sweetly and then get trampled over by the rest of the real estate community, that just ain't so. You don't have to be a "natural" salesperson to be a soulful one; your natural instincts to protect your client will ensure that you are not a pushover. Instead of protecting that client by blustering and posturing and setting up unnecessary confrontations, you do it with creativity, good negotiating skills and old-fashioned good manners. Oh, and throw in a healthy serving of competency.

Neither are soulful real estate agents simply For Sale Signs For Hire or Tour Guides for the Unmotivated Buyer. We don't knowingly take overpriced listings, because that would mean we misled our seller with regards to market value. We don't waste energy that should be devoted to our other clients or take time away from our families to entertain unmotivated clients with no real need to buy or sell. (That may sound a bit un-soulful to you, but it isn't. We treat the business of real estate with respect and have every right to expect the same in return from those people we choose to work with. We are not afraid to walk away from overly difficult or unmotivated clients who are draining our personal energy that is needed and appreciated elsewhere.)

* * *

This all sounds pretty rosy, doesn't it? As in, Be Nice and They Will Come? Real Estate in Utopia? I read over the above and smile...because, well, it's not that easy, of course. Selling real estate is a tough business, and the staggering failure and dropout rates can attest to that. Every client, every sale, every situation is unique and it's not always easy, or even possible (for us human types, anyway) to play by the Golden Rule perfectly, every time.

But it's not impossible or even difficult to be a soulful real estate agent most of the time. If you are a basically decent person who wants to make a fantastic living, sleep well at night and respect yourself in the morning, read on!

A Special Message for Newly Non-Rookies (agents just through their first year) As you near the end of your first year, you may feel as if you've been selling real estate forever. Hopefully you're enjoying the ride. If you're still in the game (i.e. you're not one of those first year casualties), congratulations! The majority of new licensees never make it this far. You have a lot to look forward to!

The next few years will be even busier, certainly more lucrative and far more challenging. New dilemmas and interesting roadblocks will challenge your creativity and sharpen your skills. Now that you have a grasp on the day-to-day realities of life as a real estate professional, you will really start to develop your own business philosophy. When people ask you for your opinion of the real estate market, you'll actually have one...a good one even. It's a lot of fun.

Again, congratulations on making it to your second year!

The More Fun You Have Selling Real Estate, the More Real Estate You Will Sell!

The Sequel to Sell with Soul

> *People rarely succeed unless they have fun in what they are doing.* **99**
> Dale Carnegie

Chapter One

What's Fun Got to Do with it?

Selling real estate can be a blast. All day, every day? Uh, no. There will be days you long for the stability and security of a steady paycheck and regular hours. There will be nights you lie awake tossing and turning, unable to forget that scathing criticism you received from your unhappy seller. You'll have weeks—maybe even months—when you have no idea where your next mortgage payment is coming from. That's definitely not fun... and, unfortunately, something most real estate agents can relate to at some point in their careers.

But you'll also enjoy the euphoria of successfully negotiating a tough inspection. Of beating out five other agents for that primo listing without budging on your commission. Of picking up the phone to find a $1.5M buyer on the other end who found you as a result of your blog. Of hearing from your new referred client that your mutual friend said you were "the best." Of being too busy to breathe and then, when you finally come up for air, realizing that you just had a $50,000 month.

Making gobs and gobs of money is fun. Getting steady streams of referrals is fun. Being a master negotiator is fun. Solving problems is fun.

Being an exceptional real estate agent is fun.

This book is going to show you how to have more fun selling real estate by being exceptional at what you do and making lots of money doing it. Yes, you can mix business and pleasure...and have a heck of a good time doing it.

First, we'll revisit and expand upon the Sphere of Influence (SOI) business philosophy introduced in *Sell with Soul*, because having lots of friends is fun, even for introverts like me. Getting business and referrals from your friends is even more fun—more fun than cold-calling, door-knocking, mass-mailing and advertising combined! We'll discuss how the traditional Numbers Game is not much fun at all and how you can change the rules and beat 'em at their own game.

Moving on, we'll jump into the car with your buyers and debunk most of the nonsense that real estate trainers have been pushing at us since time began. The way we've been trained to "manage" and "handle" and "protect ourselves from" our buyers is a bunch of hooey! Relax, enjoy your buyers, trust your buyers, respect your buyers and they'll be a joy to work with.

Next, we'll spend some time discussing some advanced strategies for marketing, selling and closing your listings, with a particular emphasis on pricing. Trust me, being an outrageously effective listing agent—that is, one who knows how to actually sell houses—is buckets of fun. Being good at turning your listings into paychecks gives you an intoxicating sense of power over your business.

We'll also discuss some of the finer points of being an exceptional real estate agent—covering topics such as win/win negotiating, the right use of systems and effective communication skills.

Finally, we'll wrap things up with some fresh ideas on time management, taking your career to the next level (or conversely, down a notch), firing your clients and much more.

"The More Fun You Have Selling Real Estate, the More Real Estate You Will Sell!"

Who says that your career can't be profitable and a heck of a lot of fun? Not me. In fact, I proclaim that the more fun you have selling real estate, the more real estate you will sell.

Okay, sure, that sounds nice, Jennifer, but what do you mean exactly? How do I have FUN?

Well, first, you need to enjoy working for a living! I mean this in a general sense—that you have a reasonably strong work ethic...that you get up early in the morning or work past 5 p.m. at night. Or both. That the idea of earning lots of money makes you smile. Note, I didn't say "being handed" lots of money; I said "earning" lots of money. There's a difference.

I love to work. I love making money. I get a real thrill out of doing something a little better or a little smarter than I did it last week and seeing an increase in my compensation as a result. Not to say I haven't had jobs I hated; no, I've had my share of those, just like you. But I've never considered leaving the working world altogether; in fact, I'll bet there hasn't been one day in the last 20 years that I haven't worked, even if just for ten minutes. I doubt I'll ever retire. What on earth would I DO all day?

Now, if the idea of working for a living is distasteful to you, you may not get much out of this book at all. Just so you know.

Anyway, back to fun.

One of the primary impediments to fun in a real estate career is Other People. There are certainly lots of unpleasant Other People in this industry. My advice is simple: stay away from them. Let them go. Refer. Delete. NEXT! Find someone new to play with. Open your mind to the idea that you can choose your friends, clients, associates and service providers.

Another way to kill your fun is to do things that make you feel icky. A lot of agent training programs require you to knock on doors and pester For Sale by Owners (FSBOs). If these activities make your stomach churn, don't do them. Truly, there are dozens of ways to drum up business besides these traditional methods, and you'll learn about many of them here. If you're worried your broker will disagree, come up with your own plan that suits your personality and present it to him or her. Because, yes, you need to be doing something! And the quicker you figure out what works for you, the quicker you'll start having FUN. (And making money.)

I'm a big fan of staying in my comfort zone. I don't see any need to stress myself out over a marketing activity I don't want to do, just because some guru tells me I should. I think I'm pretty wonderful the way I am, and I feel just fine about accommodating my own personality when planning my business activities and initiatives. And you know what? Maybe one day I'll wake up and decide that I want to pursue FSBOs or Expired Listings and at that point, I'll do it. Before then...nah. I have other things to do that are fun for me. As I described in *Sell with Soul*, I ran a nearly 100% SOI business (that is, all my business came from people I knew or people I met, instead of through overt prospecting to strangers). Now let me tell you...THAT is fun.

In short, make your career work for you. YOU. Part of the joy of this career is the freedom to be YOU and do it YOUR way.

Have fun!

About Me

I was a "real" real estate agent. As in...I wasn't mega-producing superstar in a blue suit with a million-watt smile and an ego the size of Montana. I made mistakes and am not embarrassed to tell you all about them. I was fired by clients, sometimes even deservedly so, and I dropped the ball on occasion. I showed up at the wrong title company for a contentious closing; I mis-measured houses; I offended prospects with politically incorrect jokes.

But I was also a Very Good real estate agent. I was successful by just about anyone's definition of success, and I believe I made more people happy than unhappy over the course of my career. I pulled off miracles and changed people's lives. I made a whole bunch of money and gave back a fair share to my community.

I never intended to be a real estate agent. And once I was, I certainly didn't expect to be a top-produc-

I remember a conversation with an Old School agent in my office that still makes me laugh. I was telling him a story of a time I was accused by a client of doing something I truly did not do. There was not even a little smidgeon of uncertainty that I might have been in the wrong. I told this agent that it was "so nice to defend myself without that little niggle in the back of my mind worrying that maybe I could have handled it better." He arrogantly stated that he'd "never done anything in his career that he second-guessed; that he always did the right thing by his client." Oh puh-lease! That's up there with the inherently false statement "I never lie." C'mon, we've all screwed up—just admit it so others can learn from our mistakes!

ing one. As described in *Sell with Soul*, I got my real estate license so that I could get rich buying and selling investment properties. And, yes, that did happen eventually, but not before I fell in love with the career of selling houses in Denver, Colorado.

I'm not really a people-person. I'm not anti-social, just uncomfortable making small talk with strangers. I don't enjoy parties (the best I can say is that I tolerate them), and I'd lose sleep the night before I met a new client, worrying about the stupid things I might say during any awkward silences. While I rarely doubted my own competence and professional value, I almost always doubted my ability to carry on a decent conversation and build that oh-so critical rapport with a new buyer or seller.

Hard to believe I went into real estate, huh? Yeah, seems weird to me, too. Although, at the ripe old age of 29, when I got my license, I wasn't self-aware enough to recognize that my lack of social skills might make a sales career a little painful; I just assumed that everyone felt apprehensive about meeting new people and that they just conquered their nerves. In fact, it wasn't until I was 37 that I realized most people in the world actually look forward to, and enjoy, social events!

But I digress. My point is that because I was naturally introverted, I created a way to sell real estate that worked for me and my personality—a way to market myself without pushing myself. Because I was too embarrassed to role-play the traditional sales and closing techniques, I created ways to sell and close that did not involve any techniques at all! And I experienced wild success in spite of my reluctance to actually "sell."

How do I define Wild Success? To me, success means making enough money to do what I want to do, when I want to do it. Of course, what I want to do will be different from what you want to do. Me? I want to be able to buy an investment property I run across that is priced under-market. I wanna re-do my kitchen when the mood strikes. I wanna plan a vacation to Mexico and not fret over whether the airfare is $300 or $450. I wanna buy a new elliptical machine when mine starts squeaking too loudly. I wanna dream about living on a catamaran in the Virgin Islands and actually put the wheels in motion to make it happen.

Wild Success also means loving what I do every day. Yes, every day. Sure, some days suck, but not because I hate my job. Any job worth doing is going to be challenging sometimes. But to wake up every morning excited to go to work—anxious to check my messages after a two-hour closing to see what new business opportunities and challenges have arisen while I was unavailable, to actually look forward to earning my continuing education credits because I love learning more about my craft—that's what Wild Success means to me. And I experienced it, fairly early in my career. I'd like to help you do the same.

I've done it all. Started fresh...and burned out. Retired...and came back blazing. I've hired an assistant, fired an assistant, even was an assistant. I owned a home-staging company and I owned a real estate company. I've worked 60 hours a week...and worked 60 hours a month. Been rich, been broke. Loved my job, hated my job. But throughout the fluctuations of my real estate career, one thing that has never varied (okay, this is going to sound really sappy) is a commitment to serving my clients to the best of my ability. Seriously.

And that's what this book is about.

JENNIFER'S BLOG: *Be Yourself...Have More Fun...Sell More Real Estate*

"The more fun you have selling real estate, the more real estate you will sell!"

I believe this with all my heart. When I'm having fun and feeling good, my business explodes. Have you ever noticed that one great phone call begets another...and another? When you're rolling in MoJo and you know you're hot stuff...the whole world seems to think so, too. And that phone RINGS!

So, how to keep the MoJo Risin'? By ramping up your cold-calling and door-knocking efforts? By signing up for yet another expensive monthly postcard campaign?

Uh, no. Not for me at least.

If I were to force myself to make phone calls to strangers on a regular basis, I'd be a mess. Because that's not ME, and it's not FUN. And I can guarantee you it would be incredibly UNproductive time for me, in more ways than one. Not only would I be utterly wasting my time during my stranger-pestering activities, but I'd also be one depressed, MoJo-less real estate agent. Which is bad for my mood...and therefore my business.

So, what's FUN for you? Do that. Often. Okay, well, if the only fun things you can think of are sleeping and reading, those might not work, but otherwise...what makes you smile? What would you do more of "if you only had the time?"

Chances are, most of the things you enjoy doing involve being out in the world where other people happen to be. And if you're out there, too, being yourself, having fun, you'll be magnetic. And it's REAL EASY to let people know you're a kick-a$$ real estate agent (assuming you believe that yourself) when you're in a good mood and feeling foxy.

Don't tell me you don't have time to have fun. Puh-leeeeaze! Life's WAY TOO SHORT for that attitude, doncha' think? GO HAVE SOME FUN!

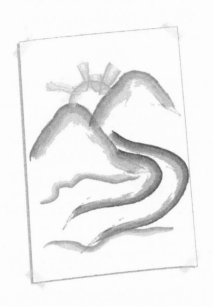

> *I've had smarter people around me all my life, but I haven't run into one yet that can outwork me. And if they can't outwork you, then smarts aren't going to do them much good. That's just the way it is. And if you believe that and live by it, you'd be surprised at how much fun you can have.*
>
> *Woody Hayes*

Chapter Two

The Reluctant Prospector

I'm naturally rather shy. Not wallflower shy—I'm not afraid to speak in public and I was even a cheerleader in high school, but shy as in... socially uncomfortable. Small talk is a foreign language to me. I've faked more than one twisted ankle to get out of attending a wedding or baby shower, and in college, I was placed on "social probation" by my sorority because I didn't attend enough parties.

So in 1996, I made the obvious career choice and entered the world of real estate sales. Funny, huh? No, actually, I did it because, like many other budding real estate moguls, I planned to buy and sell my own properties and get rich. Perhaps, if I had time, I would try to squeeze in a few clients here and there to make sure the bills were paid while I was building my own empire.

> ### What's the Difference Between an Extrovert and an Introvert?
> *An extrovert is someone who gets his or her energy from being around others; an introvert is someone who is energized by being alone. When an extrovert is left alone for long periods of time, he becomes lethargic. Conversely, an introvert will be exhausted and drained after a day of social interaction.*

But I never planned to be a real estate agent. No, I knew I was too shy to succeed in a business dominated by charismatic extroverts.

It's funny that no one ever admits to hiring a salesperson based on their ability to B.S. their way to a sale. Yet high-pressure, can't–be–bothered–with–the –details salespeople get hired every day because they're likeable. Bully for them. There are plenty of sexy programs and glitzy seminars out there for the extrovert to develop their natural skills of prospecting and networking. If you're shy like me, don't waste your time or money. The strategies directed at extroverts won't work for you. You might even be discouraged from a career in real estate if they convince you that you can't succeed without putting their high-pressure tactics into play.

Contrary to popular belief, you can succeed in a real estate career, even if you're not an extrovert. In fact, you can be great, but only if you're GOOD. Good at the details, good at the paperwork, good at negotiating, good at the follow up. If you can't distract and dazzle them with your charm, you can still blow them away with your competency. And isn't that more rewarding anyway?

If you, too, are an introvert, you are probably already a bit of a stickler for details. You are probably already reliable, organized and efficient. These skills will take you much farther than you might suspect in your real estate career. And you know what? Your introversion might actually be a big factor in your success. If you consider traditional real estate prospecting and closing techniques too invasive and assumptive for your personality, you will develop your own style that, as a by–product, shows respect for your prospects and clients. You will treat them as if they are intelligent human beings, which they will truly appreciate and find refreshing.

Do you worry if you're too nice...or too thin-skinned...to be a real estate agent?

A lot of introverts do. We're sensitive and easily hurt. Because we tend to put ourselves in the other guy's shoes, it's normal that we might be sensitive to others' reactions to us.

But that's okay! Sure, you might cry into your pillow every once in a while (literally or figuratively), but overall, your sensitivity will serve you well. Can you imagine a life where you truly didn't care how you appear to others? When I meet someone who only cares about ME, ME, ME, I'm turned off. I bet you are too. *So are your customers and potential customers.* Those who worry about what other people think of them are more likely to make the effort to ensure that other people think WELL of them! Nothing wrong with that.

Yes, the thicker-skinned may outshine us in some areas, specifically in their more aggressive self-promotion and pushy closing techniques. They may even sleep better at night. But I wouldn't trade my thin skin for anything.

If you're new to real estate, you may find yourself upset a lot of the time. The good news is that as time goes by, you will naturally become less sensitive as you realize that someone who hurts your feelings does so unintentionally—that is—it isn't personal. At first, you may fret for 24 hours or more, but later, maybe 15 minutes.

Don't try to change too much...you're wonderful the way you are.

Stop Trying to Cure Us!

How old are you now—25? 32? 47? 65? It doesn't really matter; I'll assume that if you're reading a book about selling real estate successfully, you're old enough. Old enough for what? Well, to know who you are, what you like to do, where you like to do it, and how often, right?

In other words, you are who you are, and you'll probably not change all that much. Agreed?

I read a lot of sales training material—not just real estate sales training; stuff by other gurus as well. What I often see is how the gurus advise salespeople to "get over their fear" or "stop wasting time on pretty brochures" or "suck it up and do it" (whatever "it" is that the salesperson doesn't want to do).

This annoys me. Why? Because it assumes that there is only one personality or approach that will work when one is trying to find customers and persuade them to part with their hard-earned money; that if you don't do it "this way," you'll fail miserably. *And I don't believe that.*

I think that if you're great at creating fabulous brochures, that's part of your personality, and you're far better off finding a way to harness that energy in your sales efforts. If you suck at networking events, there's no reason to torture yourself by attending—but I'll bet there's something else you would enjoy that would allow your natural wonderful-ness to shine through. If you cringe at the thought of begging your friends for referrals (on the first Monday of every month), then it's perfectly fine not to do it—and to use that natural reluctance to pester to your advantage.

You don't have to become someone you aren't...someone you don't recognize...someone you don't even like much to succeed in a real estate career. In fact, you'll sell a lot more once you abandon the notion that you have to change, and work on capitalizing on the gifts and talents God gave you. There is a natural salesperson in there...but it's probably NOT that person you read about in the last **"How To Sell"** book you bought!

Are You a Salesperson? Are You REALLY?

Let's deal with the idea that just because we work on commission, we are automatically "salespeople." Nonsense. To my way of thinking anyway, and since this is my book, I'll continue with...well...my way of thinking.

To me, a professional salesperson is someone who sells something all day long. Whether it's medical supplies, copy machines, mutual funds, encyclopedias or whatever, that's his job—to sell, to facilitate the exchange of a product or service for money. This is not to say that professional salespeople don't have customer service skills or aren't knowledgeable about their product; oh no, but simply that their job is to create a need for their widget and then fulfill that need. And then to move on to the next widget-buying prospect. This is what they do all day, figuratively speaking, anyway, and they love it. They love prospecting. They love networking. They'd be in salesperson heaven if they could simply spend their days pursuing the next target for their well-rehearsed sales pitch.

Fair enough, but I don't think that's the job description of a real estate agent. What, exactly, do we sell?

Houses? Uh, no. We don't actually sell the house.

Ourselves? Well, yes, but so do a lot of other self-employed professionals and we don't call them salespeople. When you visit your accountant and he helps you through a complicated process (e.g. filing your tax return) and gives you professional advice, is he selling? When your general contractor manages all the moving pieces and parts of your construction project, is he a salesperson? When your dentist uses his professional expertise to do your root canal and oversees the process from start to finish...is he selling?

No, and neither are we when we help our clients buy or sell homes.

Sure, we need some sales-type skills. We need to be able to write appealing copy for our marketing materials; we should be good negotiators and have some systems in place to stay in touch with the people we know and a plan to meet new people, but I don't think one needs "natural sales ability" (whatever that is) to be a good real estate agent.

Yes, while we need to sell ourselves in order to bring business in the door, it's not our primary job. We sell ourselves so that our clients hire us and agree to pay for our services, which are not related to the process it took to get those clients sitting on the other side of our desk.

Of course, there are those within our ranks who are professional salespeople whose role is to GET the business and then hand it off to their team of assistants and processors. There's an urban legend in the real estate industry about a guy in Southern California who claims to prospect 14 hours a day and make a gazillion dollars a year from his efforts. When I first heard of this gentleman and his business strategy, the first question that came to my mind was, "When does he take care of his clients?" One has to assume that he doesn't, which I dare to say is why he's still prospecting 14 hours a day after a number of years in the business!

Back to the question that headlines this section...are you a salesperson? Are you REALLY? Well, if your primary role in your business is to go out into the world and hunt down your prey, kill it, drag it home and then head right back out to do it all over again, then yes, you are a salesperson. However, if you also are responsible for, well, processing the "kill" (sorry, all this killing isn't quite the metaphor I was hoping for, but it seems to fit), then, in my opinion, you are not so much a salesperson as you are an advisor, a consultant or a provider of service.

That said, and here's the point of even declaring yourself to be (or not to be) a salesperson—you need to honor your preference and your personality when creating your business model.

What do I mean by that?

I mean that you must stay true to who you are. If you are not a natural salesperson, by the traditional definitions at least, you will very likely fail if you attempt to follow the teachings of traditional sales trainers. If aggressive sales-pitches and hard-core closing techniques go against your natural instincts, your discomfort at implementing them will be crystal clear to your prospect or client. Not only will your audience feel uncomfortable as they're being pitched or closed, but you'll be a basket-case of misery each and every time you do it.

....

Dear Jennifer,
Your advice on prospecting really rings true for me—I can't imagine myself cold-calling strangers and asking them for business. But my mentor insists that I try it, even though I've told him I don't want to. And, maybe he's right. After all, he's very successful and he's built his business by cold-calling. Who am I to argue with success?
Robert

Dear Robert,
Excellent observation and question!
Here's the thing. Your mentor has a completely different personality from you. Aggressive prospecting comes naturally to him. He probably enjoys it and, frankly, he may be pretty darn good at it. If you had the same personality, we probably wouldn't be having this conversation right now. But you don't. So, unfortunately, even if you wanted with all your heart to duplicate his success, using his methods, they wouldn't work for you. You need to find your own style that meshes with your less-aggressive personality.
And there's NOTHING WRONG WITH THAT!
Jennifer
....

Introverts are Special!

Contrary to popular belief, we're not shy or withdrawn, anti-social or unfriendly, although we've lived our lives thinking we are. No! We're creative...intelligent...thoughtful...empathetic...imaginative. We're organized, efficient and reliable. We do what we say we're going to do, when we say we're going to do it. We have the ability and DESIRE to put ourselves in the other fellow's shoes and see things from their perspective. Our personality is to be celebrated, not overcome. And yes! We CAN sell circles around the social butterflies, as long as we stay true to ourselves.

> *If you're not having fun—I don't care what you're doing, don't do it. Move on. Find something else, life's too short.*
>
> Jerry Doyle

Chapter Three

Prospecting with Soul

All rightee...let's get the ball rolling with a topic near and dear to every real estate agent's heart. Generating business. Good business. Loyal business. Consistent business. And, if you're anything like me, you'd prefer to generate this good, loyal and consistent business using methods that don't force you too far out of your comfort zone or make you feel...well...icky. Methods that don't make you dread getting up in the morning!

The official term for generating business is "prospecting." I found several different definitions of the word, but one of the most succinct was: "The process of identifying and qualifying potential customers." Sounds harmless enough, doesn't it? So why does the word "prospecting" get such a bad rap among all but the most outgoing, aggressive salespeople?

Well, I can't speak for the rest of the world, but for me, the term "prospecting" has become synonymous with "pestering." When I'm prospected to, I'm usually annoyed by it. Or, at the very least, indifferent. I hang up on telemarketers; I throw away junk mail; I hide when the doorbell rings. When I'm taken to lunch or out for coffee by a mortgage broker, title representative or insurance agent, I'm in full armor waiting for the inevitable sales pitch (and I confess that I'm often tempted to cancel in anticipation of it).

As real estate agents, we're trained to prospect religiously! Every day! To make room on our calendars for our daily prospecting and not let anything interfere with it! If we don't prospect on a regular basis, our businesses are doomed to failure! And it's our own fault for allowing anything (even our pesky clients) to distract us from our sole purpose in life—to find new targets for our well-rehearsed sales pitches!

Blech.

I got into the real estate business because I thought I might enjoy selling houses. I didn't know much about the actual process of selling houses, but from what I'd seen, it looked like fun. Frankly, it had never occurred to me that I would be responsible for finding people to sell houses to; like many new agents, I just figured I'd get my real estate license and, well, start selling houses!

So, it came as a surprise to me when my first broker informed me that I was responsible for drumming up business for myself. That wasn't anything I'd given much thought to. What was an even bigger surprise was when my broker told me that not only was I responsible for finding my own business, but that the best way to do that was to call up strangers on the phone and knock on my neighbors' doors asking for business. Oh, and spend a bunch of money mailing postcards and newsletters to my chosen "farm" area.

This didn't sound like much fun to me. But not only did it not sound like fun, it didn't sound like something that would actually work. I can't remember the last time I bought anything from a cold-caller or hurried to the phone to respond to a mailed marketing piece. So, why would I promote myself to other people using techniques that don't work on me? It seemed kind of silly.

This was back in 1996, before I could even spell "Google." If it sounded kind of silly then, it's outrageously ridiculous today.

I have reached the conclusion that an awful lot of traditional marketing doesn't work. Even if it used to work, it doesn't anymore. Oh, sure, people are being paid very well to create marketing products and strategies and systems, but are these products and strategies and systems actually reaching the end consumer?

I don't fancy myself any sort of economic analyst, so I won't pretend to have done much research into the matter; I can only speak for myself and for the people I know with whom I've had this conversation. Our consensus is that, no, the vast majority of marketing that crosses our radar on a daily basis does not persuade us to make a purchase we wouldn't otherwise be tempted to make. I suppose the argument can be made that we don't realize the impact marketing has on our brand awareness, and I'll buy that. I'm sure there's a reason I prefer one brand over another that has something to do with a marketing effort, but that's not what we're talking about here.

We're talking about YOU. YOU, the small business owner/real estate agent who doesn't have even a fraction of the budget necessary to implement a powerful-enough marketing campaign to create a nationally recognizable brand. Or even a city-wide recognizable brand.

Here's the thing. No one particularly likes being marketed to. We open our mail over the trash can; we put No Solicitors signs on our doors; we hang up on telemarketers and we take a bathroom break during commercials. I got loads of junk mail in my real estate office mailbox, and I never bothered to go through it- it got sent straight to the recycle bin. When a loan officer or title representative knocked on my office door asking if I'd give him a chance to "earn my business," I smiled politely, sent him on his way and promptly forget about him. I get dozens of emails every day from people I'm vaguely familiar with, asking me to try their new products (for free!)—and I delete them, even though I'm sure many of the products are actually worth looking at.

Heck, the other day, I was looking through my local neighborhood newspaper for an ad I thought I'd seen for a new hair salon and I had to actually force myself to see the advertising instead of automatically skipping over it looking for a news item of interest. I found it incredibly difficult to acknowledge the ads because I've trained myself to ignore them.

You're probably the same way, am I right?

When I want information about something, I go to the Internet. I don't need a salesperson at my door, on my computer screen or in my mailbox to provide information on their product. I can look it up myself, thank you very much, and get the details I need, including non-partisan opinions of said product!

Stop Wasting Your Time (and Money) Marketing to Me!

I once initiated an online discussion between mortgage brokers and real estate agents as to the best way for a mortgage broker to attract business from agents. Basically, I advised mortgage brokers that all their fancy marketing was utterly wasted on us real estate agent-types and that all we want from our go-to-mortgage guy or gal was exceptional service when they're working on one of our deals. Get me to the closing table, make me look good to my client, and you're golden. Especially in today's crazy mortgage environment, there's no way some fluffy marketing piece is going to convince me to entrust my precious buyer deals to someone I've not worked with before.

JENNIFER'S BLOG: *How Can a Lender Earn My Business?*

Because I teach real estate agents how to build a business based on their Sphere of Influence (SOI = the people they know and the people they meet) as opposed to marketing-to-strangers, I'm often approached by new or newer lenders asking how they can successfully persuade us (the real estate community) to give them a shot.

Frankly, I'm always stumped by the question. Traditional lender prospecting techniques simply don't work—at least not my experience. Offering daily rate sheets or open house brochures won't do it. Nor will weekly newsletters—printed or emailed. Sure, I appreciate (and will use) the information, but it's not going to get a lender on my preferred vendor list.

Even lender-modified SOI techniques probably won't work. Take me to lunch or coffee? Great! But I can't promise you a return on your investment. Pop-by my office to chat? Eh, please don't. Especially if your "chat" has anything to do with "earning" my business.

How about sending me buyers? Well, that sounds fabulous, but I've yet to have a lender do that, so I can't speak to the effectiveness of it. Hmmmmm...well, stay tuned—I'll share my thoughts on that in a sec.

So, how do I find my favorite lenders? Ah, that's an easy question. There are two ways I've found my lenders-of-choice:

- *My buyer brought his lender to the deal and the lender impressed the heck out of me.*
- *The lender on the other side of the deal (when I'm the listing agent) impressed the heck out of me.*

So, I guess my not-so-helpful answer to lenders seeking real estate agent loyalty is to...well...impress the heck out of the agents you have the opportunity to get in front of. Do your job, do it exceptionally well and then stay in touch with the agent without ever pestering her for business or referrals. Once you have an impressed real estate agent, then you're free to implement your other loyalty-inspiring activities—newsletters, lunch dates, rate sheets, etc., but without that first step—proving your competence—it's probably wasted effort.

Speaking of lender-to-agent referrals...I don't expect my lender to send me referrals, and I certainly don't make it a requirement of my loyalty. A great lender (who is what I want on my team) probably has dozens of agents he works with, and it's far more important to me that he take care of my business than that he send me business. However, I will say that if a fledgling lender does send me a referral and then impresses the heck out of me with his handling of the deal, well, then he has a good shot at making my preferred list!

The mortgage community seemed startled by my assertion that their marketing was a waste of time and money. I found this interesting on many levels. First, something that utterly perplexes me about those involved in the real estate industry is our apparent inability to consider the effect of our marketing techniques on the marketee—that is—the person we're assaulting with our sales pitch. Those who detest telemarketers and were first in line to sign up for the Do Not Call list rabidly defend their own cold-calling campaigns. And those who complain about the mountain of advertising that appears in their office mailbox often generate plenty of their own and fill others' inboxes with it. But that's a soapbox for a different chapter.

Second, it just seems so obvious that performance will far outweigh prospecting as an effective self-promotion technique. But I guess it's not (obvious). One of the mortgage brokers who participated in the conversation made the statement—"Well, shouldn't you give us a chance before you just dismiss us as incompetent?" Uh, no. Not saying that you are incompetent, but I'll admit to a level of Guilty Until Proven Innocent when it comes to my mortgage business. The ability to put together (or pay someone to put together) a pretty brochure just isn't going to convince me of your getting-the-deal-to-closing abilities. Not even a little tiny bit. In fact, I might worry that you're spending all your time marketing and not enough time getting-your-deals-to-closing!

Okay, so if we agree that marketing doesn't work the magic it used to... or any at all... then what? WHAT can you do to bring business your way? (Stay tuned—we'll get to that shortly)

Promise me...

Before I continue, let me make a disclaimer here. There are many paths to success in a real estate business, and I'm not so arrogant as to believe that mine is the only "right" path. In fact, I'll go so far as to proclaim that while MY way is perfect for me, YOUR way (not mine) will be perfect for you. And here's what I mean by YOUR way:

Commit to me that you will build your real estate business using techniques and strategies that feel right to you. That feel natural and comfortable. That strike you as... intelligent. Before you commit to a new prospecting approach, ask your gut how it feels about it. Are you excited to expose your world to this latest technique? Are you proud of it? Would it work on you? Or... are you mentally arguing with your gut, trying to convince it that you're doing the right thing, even though you're flooded with misgivings?

Trust those misgivings. If you're not proud of what you're getting ready to do, something is wrong. Maybe you just need to make a little tweak, or maybe you need to start all over from scratch. But it's worth the effort to discover YOUR way. And running a real estate business YOUR way is a lot of fun!

Traditional sales trainers will tell you to ignore your gut, buck up and Just Do It. Don't let your fear get in the way of your paycheck! Remember, real estate is a Numbers Game, so even if you're rejected over and over again, be assured that eventually you'll reach that one golden "yes" that will make all those people you irritated irrelevant! Thicken your skin or you'll never succeed!

Again, BLECH.

If I'm scared to do something, I figure there's a good reason I'm scared. And even if there isn't, unless I really, really, really want to overcome that fear, I'll look for alternatives so I can stay in my comfort zone. Why not? I like being comfortable!

So, with that said, I'll share with you how I built a successful real estate career without ever thickening my skin, venturing out of my comfort zone or pestering a soul. MY way.

JENNIFER'S BLOG: *I'm Too Sexy for Your Script*

Let's talk about scripts. I think they have a place in the human experience. We all use scripts every day, in both our personal and business lives. "Hi, how are you?" is a script, as is "Hi, this is Jennifer Allan with RE/MAX City Horizons; I'd like to set a showing…" I use essentially the same script every time I go through a purchase contract with a buyer or a listing agreement with a seller. When I finish up a day of showing, I always say "So, that's our show for today—how did we do?"

If we didn't use the same words over and over again when performing essentially the same task or activity, our brains might fill up and explode from overwork!

But here's where I don't like scripts… during the prospecting process. Effectively prospecting to someone is a delicate balancing act between subjecting someone to an unwanted sales pitch and inspiring them to actually care about whatever it is you're selling. And I think we can all agree that most salespeople err toward the side of the aggressive pitch (not you or me, of course, but everyone else).

There are probably a gazillion sales scripts out there for your consideration. Most are pretty awful, especially in the hands of an amateur, but occasionally I'll run into one that almost sounds sincere.
Almost.

Lately I've been prospected to by some pretty slick operators. I almost missed the fact that the sales pitches were well-rehearsed scripts.

Almost.

But once I realized I'd been scripted to, I was annoyed and even a little bit hurt. I thought I was special. I thought that my appointment with this sales dude or dudette was the highlight of his or her day. I thought that this person really cared whether or not he or she earned my trust and my business. But no, I was just another prospect, just another sales call… on the road to the next prospect. I was a number.

I don't like being a number. And that's how being scripted to makes me feel.

Wanna sell me something? Leave the scripts and the sales pitches at home. Make me care about you because you care about me. Open up. Be YOU. Make me feel special. There might be a sale in it for ya!

You've achieved success in your field when you don't know whether what you're doing is work or play. **"**

Warren Beatty

Chapter Four

The Seduction of Your Sphere of Influence

If you, like me, shudder at the thought of thickening your skin, playing the Numbers Game and scheduling at least three hours a day to ~~pester people~~ prospect, I have great news for you. You don't have to! There is a whole community of people out there, some of them you already know; many you don't (yet), ready and willing to send business and referrals your way!

In real estate, we call this community your Sphere of Influence ("SOI") and it includes your friends, your family, your acquaintances, your friends' friends, your friends' families, your family's friends and your family's families. Every living, breathing person you know (or will know) has the potential to become your biggest cheerleader and to bring business your way without you even asking for it.

Your own personal Sphere of Influence can be responsible for most or even all of your business, if you approach it right. However, if your SOI strategy includes any sort of pestering, obligating or generally making a nuisance of yourself, not only will the business model fail, but you'll probably lose some friendships in the process.

Rest assured, I won't let you do that. Just keep reading.

Seduction?

When you saw the title of this chapter, did you wonder why on earth I used the term "Seduction" in conjunction (hey, that rhymes, sorta) with generating business and referrals from the people who know you?

Oh, lots of reasons. First, I like it because it's fun, it's sexy, it's provocative and it grabs your attention. Having been single at various stages of my adult life, I also tend to see lots of analogies between the dating world and the business one, (keep reading; you'll find more). But on a deeper level, it's quite appropriate. While the term "seduction" may have negative connotations for some, overall, I think it's quite a positive word. Personally, I LOVE to be seduced, don't you?

JENNIFER'S BLOG: *SOI and the Single Gal*

It occurs to me that running an SOI business is a lot like dating. Trying to figure out where Mr. Right might be hanging out that day. Pondering who among my friends will give me that magic referral to the man who was The One. Trying to find the elusive balance between approachable friendliness... and aloof hard-to-get-ness. The roller coaster ride of euphoric highs followed by crushing lows.

When you're dating, you'll get lots of advice, such as: It's a good idea for a marriage-minded woman to ask a man on the first date if he's similarly-inclined. If no, NEXT! If you see children in your future, you should make sure every man you have coffee with feels the same way—before the second cup. How about announcing to all your friends that you are now Single and Available, and demand that they find you a mate?

When you begin a Sphere of Influence (SOI) business (that is, generating business and referrals from the Very Important People Who Know You), you are also given all sorts of advice, most of which makes little sense if you evaluate it from your gut. You are advised to tell everyone you meet that you Sell Real Estate and that you Love Referrals. Over and over again. That you should remind your friends constantly of that fact. That you should push your business card on anyone within shouting distance. That you should categorize your friends in order of importance—that is, how likely they are to refer to you—and socialize with them accordingly.

In short, PUSH your agenda on your SOI instead of allowing things to unfold and develop naturally.

If you interrogate a typical guy about his plans for your future together on your first (or tenth) date, he'll likely run for the hills, regardless of his feelings on the matter. The same thing will probably happen if you assault every new acquaintance with your business card and elevator speech.

If you beg your friends to play matchmaker, they may silently wonder why you're so desperate, and be unwilling to subject their USDA Prime Choice male friends to that desperation (after all, matchmaking often backfires on the matchmaker!). Similarly, when you frequently remind your friends that you love referrals, they may question your professionalism and wonder why you don't already have all the business you need. Yeah, people think this way; I do, don't you?

Of course, there's that fine line between enthusiastically letting your SOI know you're open for business...and putting your friends on the spot, both in your professional and personal life.

Finding that balance may be an ongoing struggle, but here are some tips:

1. Don't attend a party or function with the sole intent of handing out your business cards. Attend with the idea that you will meet lots of nice people, and may have enough rapport with a few to pursue a relationship. Leave your business cards in the car and just relax.

2. If a friend hasn't referred you, there may be a reason. Drop it—if you want to keep the friendship alive.

3. Wait for people to ask you what you do for a living. Answer enthusiastically and see if there's any interest. If not, talk about the weather or the shrimp kabobs.

4. Don't send a letter to your SOI simply asking for referrals. In fact, don't ask for referrals at all. There are much better ways to get that point across than flat-out asking.

5. Your friends will be happy to refer you (or hire you) if you seem to be a Reasonably Competent Human Being who enjoys selling real estate. You can't tell people this, you have to show them. Show up on time (with a smile on your face!), return phone calls promptly and do what you say you're going to do.

6. Don't ever whine about the real estate market. To anyone. Ever.

Being a positive, upbeat, confident person who believes in her heart that She's All That will attract plenty of business from both friends and strangers.

Oh, and this strategy works well with men, too.

Even when I'm aware I'm being seduced, I certainly enjoy the ride. If my husband came home tonight and outright announced he was expecting some action, I might be put off by his approach. I might feel a little used. However, if he came home with roses, gave me a big hug and kiss, helped me clear the table and then took out the trash, his chances of getting lucky would dramatically increase, wouldn't they? So what if I know what he's up to?

Or imagine a young man takes a young woman out on a date. If he were to ask her up front if he's going to get lucky that night, she would probably be offended, even though it's likely she realizes it's in the back of his mind. Yeah, we women are aware of such things. So, the smart young man takes a different approach. He is charming. He is friendly. He is appreciative. He is attentive. He is complimentary. He is respectful. In short, he's good company and makes her feel special. He's fun to be around.

Will his seduction efforts pay off? Who knows? But he's sure a whole lot closer than if he had just announced his intentions upfront. Again, the young woman probably knows she's being "seduced," but she's enjoying it.

So, let's compare a romantic seduction to the process of seducing your Sphere of Influence. Fact is you want something from your SOI. You want their business and referrals. You want to be invited to their parties. You want to be their favorite real estate agent, don't you?

Well, you could always call up everyone you know and tell them, couldn't you? Remind them on the first Monday of each month that You ♥ Referrals!? Ask them if they know of anyone needing your services this week? Maybe even ask them for an invitation to their next social gathering?

But do you think they'd look forward to hearing from you? Do you think they'd appreciate your approach? Probably not; in fact, they might start avoiding your calls.

Conversely, what if you were to call up your friends every month or two and ask how they're doing and really listen? Maybe even offer to help or send out periodic informative emails or newsletters of interest to **them** instead of **all about you**. What if you invited your friends to your Super Bowl party or sent them a postcard from your vacation in Cancun?

Would your friends realize you want their business and referrals? Maybe, but they won't care—you are making them feel special and cared about.

Seduction works in a romantic arena; it also works in a prospecting one. If we are charming, friendly, appreciative, attentive, complimentary, respectful and fun to be around (and also reliable and competent), we'll get our friends' business and referrals. We don't have to beg for it; we really don't even need to ask for it.

In fact, we shouldn't ask for it.

HUH?

Just Be You
By John MacArthur (http://www.jmacsays.com/)

I have been a proponent of "be yourself, do your job, be available and they will come" since my very first days in real estate. I don't care what sales trainers have to say about this - a practiced scripted call sounds just like a practiced scripted call. But a phone call made with the intent of developing or continuing a relationship sounds like it is a call from a friend or associate.

When I contact my sphere of influence, real estate does not come up from my side of the conversation. I am calling to keep in touch, find out what's new in their life, mention something of common interest and reinforce that I am in their life. I keep track of birthdays, anniversaries and other special dates. I know the religion of many in my SOI and acknowledge special days. I keep notes. (I don't trust my memory!)

If my friend brings up real estate, I share the information they request. End of subject. It is done in the same friendly tone that I might share the results of the raffle held at the fair. I am convinced that if you believe you are the expert, you won't have to beat people over the head with the "I am the neighborhood expert" game plan.

If, at a party, someone asks, "what do you do?" I answer..."I am a real estate agent. In my spare time my wife and I enjoy creating art with painting and photography." I always give them an out so they don't feel like they have to walk through the mine field of "who do you know?" They came to enjoy a party. If they wanted to hear a sales presentation, they would have gone to an Amway or Partylite get-together where they expect to get sandbagged!

If you begin (or end) every (or any) phone call with "If you know anyone that is looking to buy or sell...blah blah blah," caller ID will cut down on your number of completed calls in short order. Instead of "It's Jennifer on the phone!" it will soon become "Oh, crimeny, it's Jennifer again, bugging you about real estate. Let it go to voicemail."

If every chance meeting begins (or ends) with "Oh, by the way, if you know anyone...blah blah blah," you will begin to notice people crossing the street so they don't have to put up with your "elevator pitch." You might find yourself convinced you saw someone across the room who vanished before you could reach them.

For the love of pizza, just be yourself. It is okay to be you. If you work hard at your job, referrals will come. Rather than sitting in front of a mirror practicing what you will say, focus on the skills that will make you good at your profession. Once you learn to carry yourself with an air of self-confidence, people will know who you are and what you do.

Here's a fact most trainers and brokers will not share with you — that you are more attractive and approachable with spinach stuck in your teeth than you are when you leave people feeling as if they are nothing more than a stepping stone to your next deal.

No Harm in Asking? Au Contraire!

Contrary to popular belief (and the advice of most sales trainers), you should never ever ask, bribe or beg for business. See, here's the thing: A lot of people who hear about an SOI-based business model assume that it means that they're simply supposed to shift their marketing-to-strangers methods to their friends. So, they should mass-mail to their friends instead of to strangers. They should cold-call their friends instead of strangers, except that they call it "warm-calling," since the person knows who they are. They should put all their friends on their monthly newsletter distribution list. And of course, they should contact their friends on a regular basis, subject them to their sales pitch and smoothly ask them for business.

And on the surface, this makes sense. Because, after all, your friends do care about you and they probably do want to support your business, so isn't it okay to ask for that support?

Well, no. It's not. Because you know what? None of us likes being prospected to, but at least when strangers do it, we can ignore it. We can enroll in the Do Not Call list or hang up on telemarketers. But when our friends market to us, we can't hang up on them; we can't ignore them; we might even feel bad if we throw away that monthly doo-dad they send us. If our friend drops by our home or office to chat about their business, we feel we have to let them. We can be rude to strangers; we can't be rude to our friends. So when you impose your sales pitch on a friend, it's actually even MORE annoying to them than being marketed to by a stranger.

....

(Here are some nuggets of brilliance taken from a question posed on my Sell with Soul Forum)

Dear Soulful Ones,
I confess, I've been "prospecting" to my SOI. I have always felt gross doing it and haven't had good results from it anyway. In fact, I think I may have pushed some great people away because of only and always calling asking for referrals. Is there any way to recover from this and re-implement my SOI model?
Anxiously awaiting your counsel,
Joannie

Dear Joannie,
All is not lost. People are pretty savvy, and lots of them know that "begging for referrals" has gone hand-in-hand with real estate salespeople for decades. Depending on your relationships with various folks, you may find that an honest approach with them will work best.

In other words, come clean...let them know that you feel terrible that you may have sacrificed a friendship in the name of building your business, and furthermore, let them know that you hated doing it and have realized that it is not really your style, nor was it your intent to annoy, pester or drive them away. Then ask them about their lives. Listen to them, forget you are a real estate agent and rebuild the friendship.

If they ask you about real estate, by all means share your thoughts, but don't make it the entire focus of the conversation. Most folks appreciate being listened to more than anything else. You may not win them all back, but that could be for any number of reasons that really have nothing to do with you.

Re-establish the friendships you can (coffee, lunch dates, girls' night out, etc.) and work on expanding your SOI. Stay true to yourself and true to your friends...you'll surely sleep better at night, and you may well start to see referrals come your way as a result of just being genuine.

Or you could move to another state, change your name, dye your hair and open up a dog grooming business. But I'd try rebuilding the friendships first.
Yours,
Kim

Joannie,
How exactly you "fix" this with your friends and acquaintances will be determined by the nature of your relationship with them, whether it's in person, by phone, by letter, by email. A heartfelt "mea culpa" may fit your style or something humorous may work—"oy, vey, what have I done? Can you ever forgive me? I promise never to do it again"—whatever fits *your* style and personality.

For me, it would be something along the lines of, "I fell in with the

wrong crowd and did some really bad things. Can you forgive me?"
Then go on to explain how being the good little diligent agent you
were, you tried your best to do what you had been taught to do (ask
for referrals), etc...you knew it was wrong while you were doing it, yet,
everyone kept urging you to go on and keep doing it. Anyway, you get
the drift. Always leave 'em laughing, I say.

But my best advice is to just stop doing it. I sincerely believe that asking
for referrals not only does not work, it drives away potential business.
Yes, people who ask for referrals may get business from it, but it is
business that may have been referred to them ANYWAY. It's hard to
tell how many referrals and friendships have been lost, though, due to
other people feeling totally put off by it. Quite frankly, I would!

The subject of real estate ALWAYS comes up. It just does. I run into
people in my neighborhood, out in public, everywhere, and somehow,
they always end up asking me about the market. I don't bring it up—I
don't need to...and I never will. If you're equipped with helpful info
about the market, about what is selling, what is not, what so-and-so got
for their house and so on, you don't need to ask for business because you
will already be viewed as the knowledgeable, competent agent you are.

To me, when someone doesn't ask for business it says to me that they
HAVE business and aren't desperate enough to beg me to help them
find it. And that makes them much more attractive in my eyes. As soon
as they ask, bleeecchhhh...not gonna happen.
Best,
Susan

....

The Best Way to Ask for Referrals... Don't!

You should not abuse your friendships with constant requests for referrals. It's unprofessional and unnecessary, and, frankly, it makes you look desperate. It's like having that chronically single girlfriend who is always asking you to set her up with one of your single guy friends. You start to wonder why she can't find her own man and you might even feel a bit used. You may not be comfortable "referring" her to your male friends because you're not sure she's all that refer-worthy! If she's so great (as she keeps telling you), then why aren't suitable men already knocking down her door?

When someone I know asks me for referrals, it puts me on the spot, and I don't like that. If I think she's great at what she does, I'll happily refer people to her, without her asking. If I don't think she's great, or I doubt her professionalism, I probably won't, no matter how often she begs me to, or even if she bribes me.

Bribery
Never "bribe" your friends or family for business. Bribery includes offering financial incentives for referrals (illegal in most cases), gifts for referrals or even contributions to charity. When you offer incentives for referrals, it makes you look somewhat desperate and unprofessional. Doing a great job for someone who is referred to you is reward enough, although there's certainly nothing wrong with giving the referrer a gift after the fact. Just don't make it your prospecting strategy.

Think about your own referral patterns: Do you refer because you feel sorry for the person? Or because you think they're great at what they do?

So, how do you inspire the people you know to send business to you without asking or bribing? Stay tuned—I'll answer that soon. But first, let's cover some of the basics of "SOI."

JENNIFER'S BLOG: *10 Ways SOI'ing is like Dating*

1. When you leave the house, you never know who you might meet. So put on lipstick, comb your hair and put on some sexy jeans. If you feel good about yourself, others can't help but notice and be drawn to you. Conversely, if you're slouching around Wal-Mart in your baggy sweats, bed-head hair and morning breath, people will most certainly keep their distance!

2. Be nice to everyone you meet. You never know if their brother or sister or aunt or uncle or mother or father needs someone just like you, right now!

3. Be nice to everyone you meet, Part II. Even though this person may not appear to be Your Type at first glance, you never know where it might lead if you give it a chance.

4. Be nice to everyone you meet, Part III. Get in the habit of being pleasant to everyone who crosses your path and you'll be READY when you come face to face with THE ONE.

5. Get out of the house. Sure, online prospects are low-risk and plentiful, but nothing beats that rush of physical chemistry and intellectual rapport.

6. Go where other people are. Preferably to places where people talk to each other and feel good. The dog park, concerts in the park, happy hour, Water World, high school football games...

7. Play it cool. Don't put all your (business) cards on the table until the other person asks to see them.

8. Don't put your friends on the spot asking them to match you up. Okay, maybe ask ONCE if you must, but never mention it again. Feel free, however, to discuss your life (in a positive, upbeat, confident voice) with your friends, including all the great fun you're having meeting new people!

9. Be ready for the roller coaster. Euphoria and despair will be your companions on a daily basis. It's part of the fun!

10. Strive for that elusive balance between overly eager and underly responsive. Playing a little hard-to-get can make you appear more desirable, as long as you're WORTH waiting for!

(RE)Defining SOI

When I ask real estate agents to define what Sphere of Influence means to them, I typically get one of two responses—either: "Everyone I know" or "My Friends, Family and Past Clients."

Close, but not quite right.

To assume that your SOI is made up of Everyone You Know is dangerous and will lead you to a false sense of security (or, conversely, a false sense of rejection—see below). The problem is that in order for someone to be considered SOI, for business purposes anyway, they need to know two things about you. WHO you are and WHAT you do. Don't laugh! The people in our lives aren't keeping track of us on a regular basis, and if they haven't heard from us in a while, they may very well have forgotten we exist or, at least, forgotten our occupation.

I once worked with a 3rd year real estate agent named Laurie. Laurie contacted me for help generating more business. When I suggested we approach her Sphere of Influence, she immediately objected, claiming that she'd already done that and that her SOI had never sent her any business. I convinced her to trust me, and we crafted an interesting, relevant, non-salesy reconnection letter and followed it up with an interesting, relevant, non-salesy email. Lo and behold, the vast majority of Laurie's SOI had no idea she was still selling real estate, and the calls of good wishes and support came flooding in. Within a month, Laurie had three new clients from her SOI. (You can see samples of interesting, relevant, non-salesy reconnection letters in the Appendix.)

At the other extreme, "My friends, family and past clients" is way too limiting. Unless you just got to town yesterday, you know a whole lot more people than that, and every single person you know has the potential to bring or send business your way. Just because someone isn't a best friend doesn't mean they won't be your biggest fan.

So, what's my definition of Sphere of Influence?

"Everyone Who Knows You and Knows that You Sell Real Estate"

When you see it in black and white, it seems obvious, doesn't it?

Okay, So WHO Is Your SOI?

Let's start with the obvious suspects. Your friends, family, current clients, past clients, current prospects and past prospects. Don't forget about your spouse's family, your spouse's work associates, your dog-groomer, your house-cleaner, the nurse at your chiropractor's office, your Spanish tutor, your pest-control guy, your renters and your landlord.

Never discount someone because you can't imagine they would ever have a need for you; you never know who they know and what social or professional circles they run around in. They might just be married to, best friends with or chiropractor to your biggest client ever!

Your SOI also potentially includes everyone you meet in your day-to-day wanderings. No, you don't have to (nor should you) accost everyone who crosses your path, but if you're open to friendly encounters with strangers, you'll be surprised how many new friends you can make in a week. What if you met one new person every day? Or even one a week?

HOW MANY in Your SOI?

Shoot for an SOI of around 200 warm bodies, although more is perfectly fine. As we'll discuss shortly, you aren't depending on your 200 friends to hire you; you're actually not even after their business, although you'll certainly take it. No, your 200 friends are the gatekeepers to thousands of potential clients for you, both directly from their enthusiastic referrals, and indirectly through your social encounters with them.

What's so special about 200? Well, I'd like to blow you away with some complicated, yet oh-so-sensible mathematical formula to explain why 200 is the magic number, but I can't, really. It's just been my experience (and, frankly, a gut feeling) that if there are 200 people in the world who know who you are and know what you do, then that's enough to: 1) spread the word about your fabulousness, and 2) offer you enough social opportunities to spread the word yourself.

How Much Business Does Your SOI Have to Give?

One of the first objections real estate agents raise when presented with the idea of depending on one's SOI for business is that "I don't know anyone who wants to buy or sell a house right now! What if none of my friends has a real estate need? What then?"

Great question! However, as we alluded to above, you're not depending on your SOI to spoon-feed you their business—that would be a lousy business model. No, you're depending on your SOI to offer you opportunities to get your smiling face in front of everyone they know—either literally, with personal introductions, or figuratively with their referrals. This does not mean that you will need to bombard your SOI with aggressive sales pitches, or become a pest at their parties (if you do, you'll soon enough find yourself no longer invited!), but rather that you nurture the relationships you have with the intent of being someone your friends trust, like and are proud to be associated with.

There's a big difference.

Anyway, back to the question, "How much business does my SOI have to give me?"

Let's do some simple math.

If you know just 50 people on this planet, and all 50 of those people know 50 other people, that's a pool of over 2,000 potential clients for you. And what if those 2,000 each know 50 people? What if you know 100 people? 200 people? The numbers add up quickly.

Or how 'bout this? What if everyone you know, knows just one person who will have a use for your real estate expertise this year? I think that's probably a reasonable expectation, so your goal is become the go-to real estate agent in your social circles. And it's much easier than you might think to become that person.

The people you know have the potential to generate tons and tons of business for you, as long as you approach them, and their social network, correctly.

So how do you do that? It's pretty easy, actually—much easier and more common-sensical than most SOI trainers will have you believe.

Attracting Business to You

If you love being a real estate agent and you know your market, you'll attract business left and right, as long as you're out there in the world with your antenna up and a smile on your face. You don't need to shove your business card at everyone you meet, or dazzle them with a fantastic elevator speech—no, if your enthusiasm and expertise shine through in your casual conversations, the people you know and the people you meet will want to do business with you, if they have business to do.

So, the trick is to always be doing a couple of things:

First, always be mastering your market. The more intelligently you can speak about the local real estate market, the more magnetic you'll be when you're talking to people. For example, when I was invited to a party, I'd try to check out the market in the area of the party ahead of time so that when I was mingling at the party, if the subject of real estate came up, I could talk about that house down the block that's been on the market for 9 months, and I knew why it hadn't sold. I also knew about the one around the corner that just came on the market last week. Even if I didn't use the knowledge I obtained during my pre-party previewing, karma seemed to work with me and would put me in a position to use it soon.

Seriously, a real estate agent who knows his market exudes a confidence that will draw people to him.

The second thing to be doing is related to the first, in that you should always be looking for opportunities to put your smiling face and your market expertise in front of other people. Now when I say this, I don't mean that you should make a nuisance out of yourself in public on a regular basis—do that and you might find yourself avoided—but rather open up room in your calendar for casual socializing. Accept invitations you might normally decline. Make a concerted effort to go to lunch with friends two or three times a week. Pick up the phone to ask a friend a question instead of shooting off a text message. Go into the bank instead of the drive-thru.

The $10,000 Paycheck

You know what I love about this business? Every single person you meet every single day has the potential to bring you a $10,000 paycheck. And you have no idea who that person will be—it could be your mailman, it could be your hairdresser, it could be your dog-sitter. It could be the lady you sat next to at the nail salon. Every time you venture out into the world with your antenna up and a smile on your face, you could meet your next biggest client.

But, that probably won't happen if, when you venture out into the world you don't come across to people as someone who loves and is good at her job. And that's not the impression you leave when you're always in sales-pitch mode. So, leave the sales pitch at home, focus on being a great real estate agent who loves her job and knows her market and stays in touch with the people she knows without ever pestering them for business and referrals. I think you'll find that you'll attract far more business than you have in the past, and have a heck of a lot more fun doing it.

The Most Important Thing to Do to Succeed in an SOI -Based Business

There are a lot of misunderstandings out there about running a real estate business based on the personal relationships in your life. One of the more popular myths of an SOI-based business is that the most important thing you need to do to ensure business and referrals from the people you know is to stay in touch with them. So, in line with that thinking, there are whole industries created to help us real estate types keep our names, numbers and smiling faces in front of the people we know. Spring Forward and Fall Back postcards, football schedules, recipe cards, template email newsletters and lots of cute little trinkets designed to be personally dropped off once a quarter to your Group A SOI.

Fair enough.

Certainly, making sure that your SOI can find you is important. After all, if someone wants to hire you or refer to you, they probably won't go out of their way to figure out how to get a hold of you, unless they really, really love you. And that's probably not a chance you want to take.

But, as important as staying in touch is, it's not the most important thing. Any thoughts as to what might be more important than staying in touch?

Being Worthy of Referrals

Be someone your SOI feels comfortable hiring or referring to. When people make a hiring or referring decision, they rarely do it based on how much they think the person they're referring to *needs* that business. No, when we hire or refer, we're looking for the person we think will do the best job for us or our friend. Especially when we refer others, we take great pride in a referral that goes well...but we're mortified when a referral goes poorly. No matter how much I like someone, or how many marketing postcards I've received from him, there's no way I'm going to risk my reputation referring someone to him if I don't think he'll make me proud.

So, how do you demonstrate to your SOI that you are refer-worthy?

Well, within your SOI there are two groups of people: those who have used your services and those who haven't. If you're new to the business, there's only one group—and none of them have had the pleasure of knowing whether or not you are good at what you do yet. But that doesn't mean you can't demonstrate your worthiness to them. I'll get back to that in a minute.

But those who have been in the business a while probably know what a valuable resource satisfied past clients are. Once I was up and rolling, the vast majority of my business came from that segment of my SOI who had used my services in the past and thought I was a great real estate agent. Note: I didn't say they thought I was a great real estate prospector or stay-in-toucher—they thought I did a great job when we worked together.

Therefore, I give agents the permission to knock themselves out serving their current clients. Don't ask what your client can do for you; ask what you can do for your client. DO that open house, even if you don't want to. Attend your buyer's inspection, even if inspections bore you to tears. Call your seller every single week, even if you have nothing much to report. Cheerfully take your buyer back to the house for the third time so he can measure the windows before writing an offer. Follow up with your buyer a few days after closing to see if any problems arose during move-in that you can help with.

Seriously, if you take great care of your current clients, they will take great care of you for years to come. Conversely, if you abandon your current clients in favor of pursuing new ones, it's likely they'll forget your name, no matter how nice a closing gift you give them or how many Happy Anniversary cards you mail them after the closing!

For newer agents who don't yet have any satisfied past clients, how can you demonstrate your refer-worthiness? By being what I call an RCHB—a Reasonably Competent Human Being—every time you have contact with the people you know. Fortunately or unfortunately, the general public doesn't think our job is all that hard, so if the people you know think you're a generally intelligent, reliable and ethical guy or gal, they'll assume you're a great real estate agent, too. This means that you show up on time for appointments, whether business or personal. That you return phone calls promptly. That your written materials, even emails, are mostly error-free. That you do what you say you're going to do, when you say you're going to do it. You pay back the money you owe and return the book you borrowed. You don't whine and complain about the market, your husband or your hangover.

In short, you realize that when you're self-employed and dependent on the good will and trust of your friends, you're always on display. Does that mean you have to be boring? Not at all; just not flaky! Strive to be an RCHB at all times and most of the people you know and meet will assume that you're capable of handling their real estate business.

"But Everyone I Know Already Knows Five Real Estate Agents!"

I'm certainly not the only sales trainer on the planet who espouses an SOI business model - there are a lot of us out there. Most have distinctly different philosophies from mine; in fact, many of my students appear on my virtual doorstep after trying these other methods and realizing they're not a good fit.

And that's fine, of course. As I said earlier, there are many paths to success, and mine is only one of them.

A common principle in many relationship-based approaches is that you should categorize your SOI based on the likelihood that they will generate business for you. It is recommended that in order to determine someone's category, you should outright ask that person if he or she is willing to refer real estate business to you. Your "A" group is made up of people who would most certainly be a business or referral source; someone who might refer would be a "B," and "C" is someone who probably won't. As you can imagine, your prospecting efforts with each category vary in intensity. You'll hit those A's hard; the B's sort of hard and pretty much ignore the C's. I've even seen some in my industry (who are rather too full of themselves, in my humble opinion), claim that they fine-tune their categories based on the number of times someone has referred! Until someone has performed for you at least ten times, they are not entitled to the honor of being in your "A" group.

Blech.

Besides, it's really dumb.

Here's the thing. Referral patterns can and do change. And y'know what? You have the power to change those patterns, starting today. There may be a whole bunch of people in your SOI who probably wouldn't hire you or refer to you today, but they might tomorrow or next month, as you change your behavior toward them. However, if you were to implement a policy of treating them according to your expectation that they'll hire or refer you, you've almost certainly cemented their position in your Category C group (which is not where you want them).

I change my opinions of the people in my world all the time, both positively and negatively. You probably do, too. Someone I thought walked on water two years ago might have hurt my feelings and is now off my radar. Someone who I barely gave a thought to might have done something really nice for me and is now my go-to source for whatever it is they do.

One last thought on the topic of "But everyone I know already knows five other real estate agents."

It's a safe assumption that you're not the only real estate agent your SOI knows. You may very well be one of five or ten or even more. 'Specially during boom times, it seems that every other warm body on the planet has a real estate license and would sure like to do something with it (that is, sell a house and get a paycheck).

However, I never felt in competition with the thousands of other real estate agents in my community, even if they were friends of my friends. Why? Because I was a better real estate agent than they were. And not only was I better than my competition, I was way better at staying in touch with my SOI. Now that's a rare combination—a great real estate agent who does a great job of staying in touch. I'm serious—if you do both, you'll have no problem filling your pipeline and keeping it full. It really is (almost) that simple.

Is SOI Right for You?

While a Sphere of Influence business model can be a beautiful alternative to the more traditional methods of pursuing business, it's not right for everyone.

SOI Will Work for You If...
- You are darn good at being a real estate agent, and
- The people you know perceive you to be a Reasonably Competent Human Being, and
- You know people, or are willing to meet some, and
- You take good care of your clients, and
- You enjoy what you do.

SOI May Not Work for You If...
- You aren't darn good at selling real estate, or
- The people you know think you're a flake, or

- You don't know anyone and like it that way, or
- You'd rather hunt for new clients than take care of the ones you have, or
- You're unhappy with your career path.

1. **Are you really good at managing a real estate transaction?** As we just discussed, you need to be refer-worthy to succeed with your Sphere of Influence. If your past clients wouldn't use you again and don't recommend you to others, you'll always have to be on the prowl for new clients. If you don't take good care of the referrals you receive from your friends, those referrals will eventually stop coming in. Which is not only bad for business, it's also bad for your friendships.

2. **Are you an RCHB (a Reasonably Competent Human Being)?** If your friends perceive you to be a generally reliable, ethical, organized, dependable person, they'll be delighted to send business your way, even if they have no personal experience with your service. However, if your social circle sees you as a bit of a flake, you may have some repair work to do before you'll see much success with your SOI.

3. **Do you have a reasonably robust circle of friends or acquaintances, or are you willing to pursue one?** Depending on one's Sphere of Influence requires that one has a Sphere of Influence. That is—that you know people. It doesn't mean that you must have a wide circle of friends, but it is necessary that there are people in your community who know who you are! If this is not the case today, are you willing to make an effort to change that?

4. **Are you committed to taking great care of your current clients?** If you make taking care of your current clients your priority, they will take care of you the rest of your days. However, if you focus your efforts more on pursuing tomorrow's business than taking care of today's, it doesn't matter how "good" you are at your job; your clients won't feel loved... and will express that sentiment in their referral patterns!

5. **Do you enjoy what you do? Do you really?** There's something magical about sincere enthusiasm. When someone loves their job, you almost can't help but want to work with them—it's magnetic. And y'know what? If you radiate enthusiasm about what you do, others will assume that you're good at what you do. Sweeeet.

Creating an SOI Business Model

I offer an online program called "SOI with SOUL" where I guide you through the entire process of creating a Sphere of Influence business model from scratch. You can visit my bookstore to learn more (www.SWSStore.com). But here's a quick summary of the process.

It's not rocket science, but it can be a bit labor intensive upfront. Getting an SOI business model up and running takes about a month and includes the following steps:

- Make a list of everyone you know and enter it into a contact management system
- Write an interesting, relevant, non-salesy announcement or reconnection letter to everyone on your list
- Create an SOI business plan and set goals
- Implement your plan

Step One

The first step – making a list of everyone you know – is probably something you have done at least once in your career. Whether or not you've kept up that list is another story. Most agents don't, so if you haven't, don't feel bad. However, that list is a gold mine for you, especially if you keep it updated. In fact, if you make your list and keep it maintained through the years, you may never have to prospect for business again.

As you're putting together your very first list, or reorganizing the one you have, you will probably notice that there are two general categories of contacts in your Sphere, the first being those in your social network and the second being, well, everyone else who knows you and knows that you sell real estate. The first group, which I call (very cleverly) my Group One, is made up of the people I'd probably invite to my wedding. The "everyone else" group, which I call Group Two, includes clients, prospects, work associates, service providers—anyone I don't necessarily consider a "friend," but who would recognize my name if I called them up. I define my Group One as those I'd be comfortable asking out for coffee; my Group Two are those I wouldn't. But don't underestimate the power of your Group Two – just because someone isn't your best friend doesn't mean they don't respect your abilities as a real estate agent. I got a lot of business from my Group Two.

Step Two

The second step, writing your reconnection letter, can be a turning point in your career, as long as your letter is interesting, relevant and non-salesy. If you use one of the boiler-plate, corporate-inspired (or referral-begging based) letters, you'll be wasting your time, money and energy.

Even if you've been around the real estate block a time or two, that's no excuse to bore your readers to death. Believe me, our friends have lots and lots of choices when it comes to real estate agents. Don't count on their loyalty just because you send them boring, scripted letters on a regular basis thanking them for their support and begging for their referrals.

Most real estate agents have great personalities that shine through when they speak out loud. But put them in front of a keyboard or hand them a pen and paper...and apparently they freeze up. At least, that's how it seems when I read the nonsense they create when communicating in written form.

There's no reason your written communication should be any less exciting and interesting than you are in person. Even if you aren't the world's most gifted writer, that's no excuse. If you can speak intelligently and usually hold your listener's interest, then you can transfer that ability to paper. You can see samples of effective reconnection letters in the Appendix.

Step Three

The next step is to create a business plan for yourself. Now, don't worry. It's not complicated or complex or tedious; it'll probably take you less than an hour to do. All you need to do is sit down and think of activities you enjoy that include people you already know or increase the likelihood that you'll meet new people. And then decide how many times a week, a month, a quarter or a year you're going to do these activities.

For example, here are some items you might include:
- Lunch/coffee/margarita/dinner dates
- Personal phone calls
- Personal emails
- Handing out business cards
- Collecting business cards
- Adding names to your SOI
- Floor time
- Monthly get-togethers

- Mass emails
- Postal mailings
- Thank you cards
- Join a new group
- Blog about your neighborhood
- Get Out There in the World
- Go to the office
- Open houses
- Attend PTA meetings
- Attend neighborhood meetings

Next, you put the activities into a simple spreadsheet and create goals for yourself as to frequency.

Here's an excerpt from my own SOI business plan:

ACTIVITY	TARGET AUDIENCE	GOAL
Lunch/coffee/dinner date	Group One	2 per week
Personal phone calls	Group One	2 per week
Personal emails	Group One	3 per week
Monthly get-together	Group One	1 per month
Add names to SOI	Groups One and Two	3 per week
Mass emails	Groups One and Two	1 per month
Postal mailings	Groups One and Two	2 more this year
Thank you cards	Anyone	3 per week
Join a "group"	n/a	1 per month
Attend a community event	n/a	2 per month
Hand out business cards	Anyone	5 per day
Collect business cards	Anyone	1 per day

Step Four
Once you've made your list and sent out your letter to everyone on your list and created your business plan, it's time to implement that plan.

It's pretty easy—just follow the plan! Schedule lunch dates, look for opportunities to pick up the phone and call people you know (without a hint of a sales pitch), spend half an hour every morning sending out personal emails. Keep your antenna up for opportunities to thank people. Think of creative ways to hand out your business card without being a pest about it. Accept invitations to parties and have a few of your own. Go inside the bank instead of through the drive-thru. When you're at Walmart, smile at people instead of avoiding eye-contact.

The good news is that after a month or two of consciously following your plan, you won't really need the plan anymore. You'll be doing it naturally and you'll be seeing results from it that will inspire you to keep it up. My SOI business plan pretty much ran itself so the only reminders I needed were to do my two-to-three-times-a-year postal mailings and my monthly mass-emails. Otherwise, I just did this stuff naturally.

So, the big picture... if you are a great real estate agent who stays in touch with the people you know without ever making a nuisance of yourself, you're WAY ahead of your competition. Your competition is made up of other great real estate agents AND other real estate agents who stay in touch with their clients, but very few Great Agents Who Do a Good Job of Staying in Touch.

Other Prospecting Techniques

(excerpted with revisions from *Sell with Soul*)
I'm not going to waste your time describing prospecting methods I don't know anything about. You can find plenty of resources with information about cold-calling, door-knocking and leads-for-purchase programs. In fact, I'm certain that your broker has material for you to read on such strategies. Following are the prospecting strategies I tried; some successfully, others not-so. Some of these methods fall under my overall SOI model, of course, since that's where the vast majority of my real estate business came from.

Web Marketing
I did very little web marketing for my real estate business, so please don't

expect much from me on the topic! However, let me just encourage you to consider blogging.

If you're a reasonably good writer, you might want to consider starting a blog about your real estate market. A "blog" is simply an online journal, visible to the world, about whatever you want it to be about! It's not necessarily your regular website, although your blog can be incorporated into your site or even function as your primary web presence. Successful real estate bloggers write about their local market, as well as tidbits about their personal observations and experiences selling real estate. The more personable and interesting you make your online persona, the more likely it is that you will attract like-minded clients to your door.

How do buyers and sellers find your blog? Well, that is a topic that is beyond the scope of this book, but for now, just know that if your blog is well-written, interesting and consistent (that is, you contribute to it regularly), you will eventually be rewarded with online inquiries.

Floor Time

Floor time is the opportunity to respond to inquiries that come into your office from advertising and For Sale signs. When you are on your floor time shift, you must be available to answer phone calls and talk with walk-in prospects and hopefully convert them into clients. To be effective on "floor" (as it's called), you'll need to be familiar, at a minimum, with the listings in your office. Of course, the more familiar you are with the market in general, the more productive your floor time will be. Some offices have tremendous floor activity; some have very little. If your office requires you to take floor time, well, then I guess you'll do it! If it's voluntary, I recommend that you give it a fair shot to see if it works for you. Many floor calls are time wasters, but certainly not all. If you take floor time a few times a month, you'll probably have three or four closings a year as a result. If your average commission is $5,000, that's not a bad use of your time!

Farming

"Farming" refers to targeting a specific area and bombarding it with your marketing material. Some agents swear by it, others lose their shirts doing it. I did a little half-hearted farming, so I'm far from an expert, but I'll just say this...

1. The best "farm" is a neighborhood where you already have or have had several listings. This gives you credibility. Otherwise, you're

simply another pretty face on a postcard.

2. If you're going to invest the money in geographic farming, you must commit to more than one mailing. As your name becomes more familiar within your farm, your chances of anyone caring about you will increase.

3. Do open houses in the neighborhood, even if you have to do them for other agents. Also, preview, preview, preview so that you are the neighborhood expert, not just the best neighborhood mailer!

For Sale by Owners (FSBOs)

I never spent much effort prospecting to FSBOs. It's not that they are bad prospects; they can be wonderful clients, but I was just too introverted to track down strangers and ask for business. Contrary to popular belief, FSBOs are not usually hostile to real estate agents in general, but they very well may be hostile to those agents who treat them as if they're stupid for trying to sell their home their own. I would be hostile too! But if you're respectful and straightforward with them, you may very well get their business if they don't sell their home themselves. Or you may not. Many FSBOs have a friend in the business to whom they have already promised their listing after they try it on their own.

I'm not going to give you a step-by-step "program" for getting FSBO listings; just use your own judgment. How would you like to be approached if you were trying to sell your home on your own? Respectfully? Honestly? Enthusiastically? So do that. Call up the FSBO, tell them you're a real estate agent and that you would love to meet with them to discuss the possibility of your earning the honor of marketing their home if they ever consider listing it with a real estate agent. Promise not to hassle them or take up too much of their time; try to leave any salesy tendencies out of the conversation. Just be real.

Expired Listings

I prospected for expired listings for a period of around six months. I wrote a nice letter, followed up by a postcard campaign of four postcards, mailed every three days, followed by another letter. I added the seller to my SOI and included them in any general mailings I did. I got exactly one listing as a result of my efforts, and that listing expired again with me because the sellers weren't motivated. So, do I recommend prospecting to expired listings? Maybe, maybe not. Maybe you'll have more luck; I have heard many success stories from more charismatic agents who made more of an effort to actually speak to or even meet the sellers, instead of depending on a mailing campaign. It's not my style to bother people, so I never attempted to personalize my approach beyond my postcards.

Newspaper Advertising and Real Estate Magazines
These get a big NO from me. But if your office pays for them, go ahead and take advantage. Just don't use your own valuable marketing dollars on general print advertising. It doesn't work, and as fewer and fewer agents advertise this way, the rates just get higher. There are far more productive ways to spend your money—lunch dates, housewarming parties, even web marketing.

***

I'll leave you with one more bonus strategy. When you have plenty of business, go look for more. I know you'll be feeling overwhelmed, but that's the best time to prospect. You'll be glowing, with enthusiasm oozing out of every pore. Your attitude will be irresistible, and the universe will respond with even more business for you. Nothing generates additional business like being too busy to handle more.

Just don't whine about how busy you are, either to yourself or to anyone else. It's irritating and self-defeating. Practice saying, "Business is unbelievable—I never thought I'd enjoy real estate so much!"

BE the Person Your Boyfriend Wouldn't Dream of Cheating On (yes, it's real estate-related)
A long time ago, in my early 20's, I was dating an equally young lad from Ireland. He was planning a "holiday" (as they say in Ireland) back home for three weeks. As an insecure young lass, I was terribly worried that he would meet back up with his high school sweetheart and, OMG, CHEAT on me.

So, I did what every other immature young woman with a boyfriend does...I whined, I pouted, I threatened, and I begged him not to cheat on me while he was gone. Every day for a month, I "reminded" him that he had to be good while away. Ugh. I'm embarrassed just thinking about it.

Then one day, my slightly more mature roommate said the magic words to me: "Jennifer, you need to BE the person your boyfriend wouldn't dream of cheating on."

Wow. WHAT A CONCEPT.

Okay, I promised this would relate to real estate, so let's rewrite my little story.

A long time ago, in my ~~early~~ late 20's, I was ~~dating~~ starting up a real estate career in ~~an equally young lad from Ireland~~ Denver Colorado and was trying to drum up business for myself ~~He was planning a "holiday" (as they say in Ireland) back home for three weeks~~. As an insecure ~~young lass~~ new real estate agent, I was terribly worried that ~~he~~ my friends would ~~meet back up with his high school sweethearts~~ refer their business to someone else and, OMG, CHEAT on me.

So, I did what every other ~~immature young woman~~ new real estate agent ~~with a boyfriend~~ does...I whined, I pouted, I threatened, I begged ~~him~~ my friends not to cheat on me ~~while he was gone~~ when they had a house to buy or sell.

On the first Monday of every ~~Every day for a~~ month, I "reminded" ~~him~~ them that they ~~he had to be good while away~~ should remember how much I love referrals and how hurt I would be if they cheated*. Ugh. I'm embarrassed just thinking about it.

Then one day, my slightly more mature ~~roommate~~ inner voice said the magic words to me: "Jennifer, you need to BE the ~~person~~ agent your ~~boyfriend~~ friends wouldn't dream of cheating on."

Wow. WHAT A CONCEPT.

You can whine, pout, threaten, beg or just "remind," to get what you want. OR you can simply BE such a terrific ~~girlfriend~~ real estate agent that your ~~boyfriend~~ friends wouldn't dream of going anywhere else.

*I'm stretching the truth here for dramatic effect. I actually never did implement these referral-begging tactics in my career, but it makes the story much better to say I did...

*You can only have fun helping other people
have fun if you're having fun doing it.*

Unknown

Chapter Five

Playing the Numbers Game
(or not, as the case may be)

Ah, the Numbers Game of Prospecting. Is there a topic more exciting to traditional sales trainers than the sacred Numbers Game? You know how it goes—If you make enough cold calls or send out enough postcards or knock on enough doors, odds are that you'll eventually find someone who has a need for you. During your journey, you'll encounter loads of rejection—that is, lots of people will tell you NO. But it's all part of the fun because you know there's a YES somewhere in your future. Sales trainers even claim that you'll start to enjoy each NO because you know you're one step closer to a YES. Sounds delightful, doesn't it?

Market research firms even have some solid numbers for you to work by. They say if you make 100 cold calls, you'll generate 5.3 leads. If you send out 100 advertising mailers, you'll be rewarded with 2.2 inquiries. Now, don't get too excited yet; all you've gotten so far from your efforts are leads, not clients. Someone has expressed an interest, but they certainly haven't yet opened their checkbook.

There's nothing really wrong with the traditional numbers game as a prospecting strategy, other than the obvious (it sounds like a ghastly way to spend your time to me), as long as you understand the numbers and accept them. Oh, and as long as you have deep pockets (for advertising) and a deep sense of self-worth to deal with the 94.7 rejections you'll encounter on your way to those 5.3 golden yeses.

The truth seems to be that if you play the traditional numbers game correctly, you will see results from it – but you gotta play and play and play and play. That is, you can't give up after trying it a few times. This can get expensive, frustrating and, to my way of thinking, maddening. I just don't see the joy in bombarding your target audience enough times that eventually someone bites. But maybe I shouldn't give my opinion; after all, as they say, don't knock it till you've tried it... and I can say that I honestly have not tried it.

But that's not to say that you can't play a Numbers Game. I did, but I played according to My Rules – and I played it quite well. So let's talk about my Numbers Game, from an SOI perspective – that is, playing it with the people you already know.

The Numbers Game of SOI

Instead of sending out 100 postcards to 100 random strangers, let's say you sit down at your computer and send out 10 personal emails to your friends. No sales pitches or infomercials; just a casual catch-up: "Was just thinking about you, how's the puppy/kids/new apartment/new job going? Things are great here, keeping busy, let's have coffee" type of thing.

How many people do you think will respond to your email? If your email is truly personal and not a thinly veiled plea for business or referrals, probably pretty close to 10, or 100%, don't you think? Maybe one or two of your friends is on vacation or otherwise occupied, so let's say 8 respond, for a rate of return for your effort of 80%.

Will you get any immediate leads from your ten emails? You might. There's a good chance you will, actually. But if you stay in friendly touch with these eight people (follow through on your suggestion to go have coffee!), I can guarantee that sooner or later you will. From all of them? No. But all it takes is one or two to jump on your band wagon for you to see some business headed your way.

But for analytical types, here's the cool thing: If you send out a mailing and touch 100 strangers, you're hoping that one of those 100 has a need for your product or service and will give you a shot at their business. But I don't think anyone who mass-mails is expecting that any of those 100 will become a referral source for them, at least not simply from a postcard campaign. In other words, you don't send out those postcards hoping to generate referrals from the people who receive them; you're just after their business if they have any to give. Which of course, most won't. It's not as if the person who received your fancy postcard is going to sing your praises at their next social function. "Hey! You need a real estate agent? Last week, I got the coolest Broncos' football schedule postcard! You really need to call this lady!"

Uh, no, not gonna happen.

Conversely, those ten friends who received your catching-up email are certainly potential referral sources for you. Even if none of those ten are in the market for your stuff this week or next, think about how many other people those ten friends know? If all ten know just 20 other people, you've just exposed yourself to 210 people who might have a need you could fill, AND you'll be personally referred to them!

So, let's assume that you accept the premise that you can win the Numbers Game when you play it with your friends, but what about strangers? Are you destined to cold-call, door-knock, advertise and mass-mail to attract their attention? Nope.

Here's the thing. We self-employed people who have to generate a steady stream of business for ourselves tend to look at prospecting as a volume proposition. What I mean by that is that we try to touch as many people as we can with our sales pitch, in the most efficient manner possible. Even when we SOI, many of our efforts are directed to our SOI in total – not on an individual basis. And that philosophy has its place, to be sure.

In a real estate business, each closed sale has the potential to pay your mortgage, your car payment and maybe even your food bill for the month. In other words, we get big paychecks when we perform. As a real estate agent, you're not in the same business as, say, someone who sells real estate books for a living who must reach a large audience in order generate enough income to live on. Selling real estate is not a volume business – you don't have to sell 40,000 houses in a year to make a decent living; for many agents, simply selling ten or twenty would pay the bills quite nicely. Or maybe 40 or 50. In any case, that's only a few dozen people in the whole town who have to hire you.

Each new client you gain gives you a little thrill, and every existing client you lose puts you into a funk, at least for 15 minutes or so. Your business comes in one warm body at a time. Therefore, doesn't it make sense to treat your potential new clients accordingly, that is, not like a number?

With me so far?

My point is that you can approach your prospecting efforts with a Quality over Quantity mindset. Good leads come in one at a time, not ten at a time. It's worth taking that extra time with each potential lead or lead-giver/gatekeeper to ensure that the person you're spending time with thinks highly of you and doesn't feel as if you feel he's just a number in your game.

Touching versus Impressing

Many relationship/SOI-based prospecting programs mention "touching" as many of your SOI as you can, as often as you can. I've heard rumors of a program that advises 33 Touches a year to ensure that your Sphere of Influence doesn't forget who you are. Truth be told, this struck me as rather odd, and certainly overkill.

First, I don't know many real estate agents who are organized and/or disciplined enough to actually stick to such a plan, although I have to assume most of these 33 Touches are handled by some sort of system (you'll read more about my feelings on "systems" later in this chapter).

But more importantly, I can't imagine that too many members of your Sphere of Influence really want to be "touched" 33 times in the next 365 days. If your 33 Touches are more personal than salesy (coffee dates, personal phone calls, personal emails, etc.), that's probably more attention than anyone wants. If your 33 Touches are more salesy than personal (newsletters, postcards, drip campaigns), then you've likely actually harmed your relationships by positioning yourself primarily as a salesperson.

The argument for a 33 Touching campaign is that in order to make an impression on someone, you have to have been in their face, one way or the other, on a regular basis to be memorable.

I disagree. With all my heart.

Why? Because there's a big distinction between "touching" and "impressing." I can pretty easily touch 100 people in a day with a mass email or a postal mailing. And that's fine – it has its place. But I can also make an effort to impress the people I run into during my day-to-day travels, whether it's business or personal. If you can combine the two concepts – a volume "touching" campaign with a concerted effort to make a good impression on people when you have the opportunity, your prospecting results will improve exponentially.

Of course, you probably can't personally impress 100 people a day, and that's kind of the point. But if you were to impress one person per day? That's 365 impressed people in a year. Two a week? Even one a week? It sounds pretty obvious. But again, I think we get so caught up mass-prospecting that we forget the Power of One, that is, if every person you know refers just one person to you in a year, you'll probably have a banner year. And the chances of that happening are a whole lot better if everyone you know thinks you're pretty darn cool... *instead of simply sort of knowing who you are.*

Maybe I should explain what I mean by "impress." You can probably guess that I don't mean "brag about myself" or "blow someone away with a fantastic elevator speech." No, by impress, I mean that the person you just interacted with walks away from the interaction feeling just a little bit (or a whole lot) better than he did before. He's not saying to himself, "Thank GOD I got away – I thought she'd never shut up." Or, "That's the last time I answer the phone when HE calls" or, "What a flake, I don't know how he gets any business." Earlier, we talked about how to present yourself as a Reasonably Competent Human Being to the people you know and the people you meet, but in general, I think we all intuitively know how to behave in a business or social setting... it's just that sometimes our sales training gets the better of us and we forget.

Let me give you a specific example of "impressing" someone from our world:

Let's say that a potential buyer stumbles into your office while you're on floor time, or calls off one of your For Sale signs. He tells you that he's not ready to buy a house just yet, but he wants to start looking so he can be ready when his lease is up in six months. Or, maybe he wants to wait six months to save up a bigger down payment. In any case, he's asking for your help, but is very clear that he won't be leading you to a paycheck any time soon.

Many agents would shoo him away because they'd consider him a waste of time. But what if you spent an hour or two with him, educating him on the process and the market; maybe even showing him some houses in neighborhoods you think might work for him. Then stay in touch, keep him updated on the market as his timeframe to buy gets closer, and offer to take him out any time he wants to go. He probably won't take you up on it, but make the offer.

Maybe he'll buy something from you in six months, maybe he won't. Maybe he'll buy in a year, maybe in two years, or maybe never. But I can guarantee that he'll never buy anything from you, or more importantly, never refer his friends to you if you don't take the time to impress him upfront. And spending a few hours with someone who has come to you looking for help is probably a better use of your time than any cold prospecting you might be doing instead.

And I'll tell ya what—if this guy has been talking to other agents and presenting them with the same situation, they have probably blown him off. Therefore if you give him the time of day, you'll look really good, compared to these other agents who aren't willing to "waste their time" with him!

Here's another example, outside of the real estate world. A few years ago I moved from one house to another. On the evening of moving day, I was sitting in my new house, curled up in my jammies, watching TV, a lovely glass of red wine in my hand. At 8:30, the phone rings. It's my old neighbor, frantic that he can't find his cat.

> **Words of Wisdom from the Trenches**
> *courtesy of Susan Haughton*
> *"This is such a bizarre concept...wasting an agent's time! 'Go away...I am too busy having the phone hung up in my ear.' 'Go away...I am too busy having doors slammed in my face.'"*

He's positive that the cat got locked in my old house while the movers were there and asked if I'd come over and let him look through the house.

Sheesh. Getting up off my couch, getting dressed and driving across town was pretty much the last thing I wanted to do. And, I knew the cat wasn't there, because I'd gone through the house room by room before I locked it up. I came this close to telling my neighbor that and then stopped myself. I realized how worried I'd be if my dog were missing and how dismayed I'd be if my neighbor refused to help me find her.

So, I pulled my lazy butt off the couch, changed from jammies into sweats and headed out. Sure enough, the cat was not in the house, but as I left, I handed my business card to the neighbor and asked him to call me when he found his pet. About an hour later, he called with the good news that Kitty had shown up, and offered profuse thank-you's for my willingness to help.

You think I made a good impression on him that evening?

Opportunities to impress other human beings on the planet are all around you, I swear. Start looking for them, and they'll appear. Make it a goal to impress at least one person per week; it might take you all of one hour to do.

JENNIFER'S BLOG: *Treat Every Buyer Like the Gold Mine He Might Be*

Imagine this scenario...you're sitting in your office and the receptionist forwards you a floor call from a potential buyer. The caller says something like this: "I'm lookin' fer a little piece of land on the outskirts of town to move my double-wide to. Just a nice little place fer me and the missus to retire on. Kin you hep me?"

Okay, so you're probably not overly excited about hep'ing this particular buyer, unless little pieces of land on the outskirts of town are your thing. You might be tempted to politely brush off this particular caller or, if you're in a particularly generous frame of mind, find someone a little hungrier than you are to refer him to (and get that juicy 25% referral!).

But what if he followed up by saying, "Oh, 'n my uncle will be movin' up this-a-away in a few months and he'll be looking fer a place to keep his collection of vintage Ferrari's—mebbe something with a view and a pool, with a nice pasture fer his thoroughbreds."

Hmmmmmm...Suddenly you might see Mr. Double-Wide in a whole new light, might you not?

Here's the thing. Everyone you encounter during the course of doing business has friends, family and mebbe even a rich uncle or two. Whether or not Mr. DW ever buys his little piece of heaven outside of town really isn't the point. Whether Rich Uncle DW ever shows up—or even exists—isn't the point, either.

What IS the point? That it won't hurt any of us to take that extra hour (maybe even two!) to make an effort to impress any warm body who voluntarily puts himself or herself in our presence. Even if he's not- yet- qualified. Even if she doesn't plan to buy or sell for 2 years. Even if they're looking for a little piece of land in the flood plain.

Every person who crosses your path is a potential gold mine of business for you, if you treat them respectfully and competently. Treat every buyer like he has a rich uncle waiting in the wings and you may be surprised how many of them do!

Antenna Up for Follow-Ups

Want an easy way to get your once-weekly impressing duty done? Every time you have a conversation with someone, make an effort to learn One Thing about them that you can follow up on in a week or so. And once you've identified that One Thing, WRITE IT DOWN somewhere to remind yourself to follow up, and DO IT.

For example, as I write this, a girlfriend of mine is flying home from a job interview in Hawaii. It's on my list to call her tonight and find out how it went. A few months ago, I went out for drinks with another girlfriend who had to cut our date short to run home and check on her brand new puppy. I emailed her the following week, asking for photos of the puppy. Another friend of mine is embroiled in an ugly legal matter, so I'll check in with her in a week or two to see how it's going.

Is that simple, or what?

But let me get back to something I said earlier in passing...Good leads come in One at a Time.

What do I mean by this? Well, for most of us, we'll gather our clients from a wide variety of sources. If you have 50 sales this year, you probably found those clients at least 20 different ways. Maybe you met one at an open house, one at a wedding, one at a funeral, one referral from your accountant, one referral from your husband, one from your website, one at the dog park, one from a past client...etc., etc., etc. I got a listing one summer because my lawn guy saw the RE/MAX signs in my back yard and asked if I'd be interested in selling his house.

But it's funny that if you have a mass-marketing mindset, these onesie opportunities just don't seem to happen as much, or perhaps you're just missing them on your radar. But when your antenna is up, even in your down time, potential business crosses your path all the time. It's up to you to recognize and capture it.

I used to be a moderator on a popular real estate agent forum. There was question that popped up once in a while, in various forms, that went something like this: "I read that most homebuyers are married. Where can I meet married people?" Or: "I think prospecting to divorcing people would be a great niche. Where can I meet couples getting divorced?"

My response was usually a mildly sarcastic "Go out and meet some people. Many of them will be married." No one else seemed to agree because the threads always continued with all sorts of advice about advertising to married folks. Questions about pursuing divorcing couples followed the same line of thought with suggestions to watch the public notices and make friends with divorce attorneys.

Similar questions were frequently posted as to how to meet builders, investors or first time home-buyers...My friends, good prospects are all around you! Go out and meet people, and many of them will be married or divorcing, some will have a family member who recently passed away, some will be home-builders, some will have just had a baby or gotten a new puppy...etc., etc., etc.!

There's no club where these people hang out or secret newspaper they all read. No, they're just like you and me – out there in the world hoping to run into someone who can solve their problems. The more often you're out there in the world with a smile on your face and your RCHB hat on your head, the more often you'll meet people whose problems you can solve.

So, what's the moral of the story here?

First... the numbers game of SOI has a far higher potential return than the numbers game of mass-marketing

Second...taking the time to be nice to people is never a waste of time

Third...Quality over Quantity is a better way to build a business than the other way around

And last... people who need your product or service are all around you. Just get out there and meet them!

Some More Compelling Numbers from the Numbers Game...

Not yet convinced? Here are a few more numbers for you to ponder...

If you attend one social event (wedding, housewarming party, Sunday BBQ) or neighborhood activity (street fair, festival, block party) per week, in a year, that's 52 opportunities you created for yourself to meet one (and probably more) people who might have a need for your services in the next six months.

Of course, it's also an opportunity to touch all the people those new friends of yours know who might have a need for your service.

If you go to lunch with one friend per week (and don't bore him or her to death with your sales pitch), in a year, that's 52 GREAT opportunities to touch everyone your friends know. And that "everyone" can number in the thousands.

If you add just one person per day to your SOI contact database, that's... holy cow! 365 new contacts in just a year.

If you spend one hour per month writing an interesting, non-salesy email newsletter to send to your SOI (including all the NEW friends you're meeting), that's 1,800 times in a year you're touching someone who knows your name and knows what you do for a living (assuming a contact database of 150 names).

Some more numbers in dollars and cents...

The Cost to:

Attend a social event you're invited to:	$0
Attend a neighborhood fair:	$0—$25
Go to lunch with a friend:	$25 per week, if you pay every time (and you don't have to)
Meet one new person per day	$0—?? depending on how you meet them
Once-a-month email to SOI:	$0-$35

If you were to do all these things, I promise your business will explode. And doesn't this stuff sound like MORE FUN than calling up 1,000 strangers or mailing out 1,000 postcards?

Don't Oversystematize Your Prospecting Efforts

We real estate agents LOVE our systems. If we can purchase a product that will help us streamline our prospecting efforts, we're all for it.

But...but...but...let me fly in the face of convention here and say...STOP! Stop with all the systems and programs and products!

Why? Because when pursuing business from the Very Important People Who Know You (that is, your Sphere of Influence or SOI), it's important to make them feel special. And no system, program or product is going to do that for you. You actually have to do it yourself.

I am often asked by my readers if I recommend putting past clients on a 5-year drip campaign that automatically sends out anniversary cards and seasonal postcards. My answer? NO!

Your SOI database (and especially you past client database) is precious to you. Every name on there has the potential to bring thousands of dollars to your business and deserves your respect and attention. Before I sent anything out to my SOI, I'd go through my list carefully to make sure it was up to date, with accurate information. This exercise also inspired me to personally "touch" those who I enjoyed getting to know with a more personal effort (phone call, personal email, whatever). I wanted to stay intimately in touch with the names in my database. If I had put my SOI on any sort of automatic drip campaign, I'd lose that intimacy and connection and would be just another real estate agent looking for business.

I once sent out a mass email to my SOI, offering to put interested parties on a list to receive a monthly market report created by a local economist. When the responses started coming in, I tried to figure out a "system" to track respondents and automatically send out the report every month. But then I caught myself...by systematizing this process, I'm throwing away a wonderful opportunity to connect with my SOI every single month when I personally email them the report. I mean, DUH! They are ASKING to hear from me; why waste the chance to toss in a short personal note each month that might make them smile? (And believe me, that personal note will have nothing to do with how much I love referrals! Ick.)

Another question I get from time to time is whether an agent should purchase a program that automatically sends out birthday cards to one's SOI. Sheesh. Is it really too hard to actually sign and mail a card to someone you care about? I mean, c'mon!!! Are we real estate agents so important and so busy that we can't take five minutes to write "Happy Birthday!" on a card, sign it personally, address the envelope and slap a stamp on it? Please say it isn't so!

One thing I love about the real estate business is that every little thing you do that goes above and beyond what you "have" to do can result in a huge financial payoff for you. Personal notes (that you actually write yourself), personal emails, and personal phone calls... this is where the money is!

The More Fun You Have Selling Real Estate...

> *It's more fun when you're not the only one having it.* **99**
> *Unknown*

Chapter Six

Our Buyers Aren't Liars!

How to Chase Away Your Perfectly Qualified, Perfectly Loyal Buyers

Want to start up a lively discussion? Next time you're hanging out with a group of real estate agents, bring up the topic of whether or not to require buyer pre-approval and/or a buyer agency agreement prior to showing a home.

Many agents proclaim that it's a waste of time to work with a buyer who does not have a pre-approval stamped to his forehead and/or hesitates to sign a buyer agency agreement upfront.

Me? I disagree with all my heart, and I have to ask...are real estate agents So Darn Busy with buyers and motivated sellers that they need to actively turn away those who show up at their doors looking

> **Words of Wisdom from the Trenches**
> *courtesy of Susan Haughton*
> *"It is astounding how many roadblocks agents put up in front of the prospects they burn up so much shoe leather to obtain."*

for help? Wow! As I've always said in these situations, "I LOVE a full pipeline! Send 'em my way! I'll take great care of them and probably sell them a house eventually...as well as to all their friends through the years. And I'll be happy to pay you a referral fee."

I have used the services of many real estate agents in my lifetime, and I promise you that if any of them had shown more interest upfront in my financial qualifications than in my housing needs, I'd have found someone else who showed me the respect I think I deserve. And I certainly would not be interested in obligating myself to anyone I barely know. Oooooh, I get bristly just thinking about it.

I submit that many agents are chasing away perfectly good buyers who are 100% sincere in their desire to purchase a house—and are likely perfectly well-qualified to do so. But with these disrespectful efforts to tie them down, all they're accomplishing is sending them elsewhere, fulfilling the prophecy that buyers are liars and confirming the belief that stronger "rules" are needed in the future.

I believe that this approach simply irritates buyers, so they look elsewhere for more respectful assistance. I have to wonder if spending time with a buyer without a hint of obligation or pressure might be a much better use of time than fussing so much over whether or not they're worthy of a little time.

Relationships take time. There's no way you can know upfront if a buyer will buy, regardless of the pieces of paper they bring with them or are willing to sign. If an agent can't afford the $20 in gas or the two hours of time it might take to create some trust and rapport, then by all means, that agent will probably do better referring these potential clients out. And please don't forget: We get serious paychecks when someone buys. Our paychecks more than offset the risk of a little gas money and time.

My friends, most buyers are not liars...Most people have better things to do than waste our precious time. Their time is precious, too. They simply want to be treated kindly, and with RESPECT.

I never enforced buyer agency agreements on my buyers. And as far as I can recall, I never regretted it. Sure, I lost buyers to other agents, but in every single case, it was a good decision for the buyer, either because we weren't clicking or because they found an agent who better met their needs for one reason or another. Once I lost a buyer because she changed her search parameters and realized that she could probably do better with someone more familiar with her new desired location. It hurt my feelings and made me mad for about 15 minutes, but within 20 minutes I realized she was right. Even if I'd had a buyer agency agreement with her, I'd have never enforced it.

That said, I do remember back in the days of a Seller's Market in the late 1990's (when every breathing agent had 20 buyers to work with and nothing to sell), I felt that a buyer agency agreement made some sense. Those who were willing to commit to their buyer agent might get first dibs on hot new listings, or be the one the agent chooses to spend his Saturday with.

Whether or not you require new buyers to commit to you exclusively is a business decision on your part. There are plenty of arguments both for and against, and your broker or state license law may have a say in the matter as well. Just promise me that you'll approach the conversation respectfully, always considering how your words and actions will be perceived by that Very Important Person sitting on the other side of the desk.

Turning Over the Reins to Your Buyers

Let me put your mind at ease about something.

Do your buyers seem to be doing most of the legwork finding the houses they want to look at? Do they email you every day with their list of houses they want to see? And do you feel a little guilty with every emailed list? I did. Wasn't that MY job—to peruse the MLS, searching for Just the Right Home for them? But they beat me to it, and between you and me, I was happy to let them, guilt and all.

And you know what? They're happy to do it! Buyers have always wanted direct access to our precious MLS database, and now that they have it, they're tickled. When I bought my first house back in 1994, I remember actually ~~stealing~~ borrowing my agent's MLS book when she wasn't looking and poring through it for hours. I hated waiting for her daily phone call with the details of new listings and always wondered if she was screening out The Right One for me!

So don't fret about proving your worth to buyers by beating them to the MLS every day. Let them take control of that part of the buying process if they want to; there's plenty more value you bring to the table that they can't possibly do themselves.

That said, I must confess that I missed the intimacy I had with my MLS in the early days when I was solely responsible for choosing the properties my buyers saw. Before the days of a public MLS and automated email notifications, I was in my MLS several times a day searching for new listings, which, by default, kept my finger on the pulse of my local market.

Selecting the Right Homes to Show

In the event your buyer wants you to find The One for him or her, here are some tips:

It can be tougher than it sounds, especially with a new buyer. This is your one opportunity to make a great first impression; buyers subconsciously expect you to intuitively know what they're looking for, even if they don't. A great way to lose a new buyer is to show him homes he has absolutely no interest in. He may decide that you and he are not a good fit, or he may even lose his enthusiasm for buying a home at all. The next phone call you get is the one telling you he found a great rental house and signed a one-year lease.

So, you need to do your homework ahead of time, both with your new buyer and with the market. The first step, of course, is to find out what your buyer is looking for. A buyer's preferred neighborhood is probably the most important factor. If he's new to town or otherwise unfamiliar with your city, find out what kind of neighborhood he thinks he'd like—urban, suburban, rural, mountains, coastal? Any particular commuting distance? Does he like charming older homes near the city center or new contemporary homes near the shopping malls? Price range?

Next, move to your buyer's "must have" list. Number of bedrooms, baths, garage? Any special needs? Don't get too specific, though. Pushing buyers for too many details is counterproductive, believe it or not. If you keep pushing, he may start making things up to please you. Doesn't everyone want a garage and more than one bath? But he might not really care that much, and if you limit your search to his non-critical parameters, you'll miss a lot of great homes.

Are Buyers Really Liars?

Buyers can be hard to nail down and we've all heard about the "Buyers Are Liars" phenomenon. It's a phrase usually used in frustration, either when an agent loses a buyer or when he's at his wit's end showing homes that the buyer says work for her, but don't inspire her to make an offer. It simply means that buyers don't really know what they want, and often it's true.

Back in 2005, I went shopping for a second home in Alabama, I told my agent that my "must have's" were four bedrooms, a two-car garage and high-speed Internet access. What did I buy? A three-bedroom home with no garage and dial-up access only. But my agent was sharp enough to switch gears in the middle of our search when she saw that I was emotionally responding to homes in the country, even if they didn't have everything I claimed I had to have.

The other danger in asking for too many details is that your buyer will start telling you things like, "I really want a window over the kitchen sink," or, "I want an open floor plan with lots of light." Depending on your inventory, you may end up with nothing to show her if you rely strictly on her wish list. And if you show her homes that don't meet her stated requirements, she may think you weren't listening. You (and she) need to gauge her reactions to different styles of homes in person. Remember, buyers don't shop for homes every day and don't really know what they will respond to until they've seen it.

I always told my new buyers that our first trip out together would be fishing expedition, that we probably wouldn't find a house for them to buy that first day. That our goal was to get them to start developing opinions on neighborhood, style, vintage and features, and to test their tolerance for fix-up. I felt this subtly assured them that I was looking out for their best interests and that I wouldn't push them to make a decision until they were darn good and ready. Don't worry, it won't slow down their home-buying decision process; if they find a house they like on the first trip out they'll buy it regardless of what you told them ahead of time.

To pick out the best homes to show on your first showing tour, go through your MLS and find around 20 homes that might work for this buyer, based on his location preferences and his Must-Have list. Unless you're absolutely sure that your buyer wants a fix-up home, narrow down your list to homes that appear to be in excellent condition. (See "Most Fix-Up Buyers Aren't," following this section.)

CAUTION!

Beware of showing a home that backs to a highway or has some other major location flaw—it will appear to your buyer that you don't know your market or don't care about his home as an investment. If he picks out such a home from an Internet search or by driving around, then by all means show it to him, but don't pick it out yourself. Buyers assume we are familiar with every house in town, so when we show a house that is clearly a bad investment, a buyer will think we're stupid, uncaring or, worse, inexperienced.

Then go preview all of them. I promise you, you'll be glad you did. At least half of the homes you preview will have a fatal flaw (an unfixable "feature" of a home that makes it unappealing to the majority of buyers, e.g., proximity to a highway or an unusually small yard, making the home a bad investment). These are easily eliminated from your tour. You are looking for the best five to nine

> **Preview**
> *Looking at listed properties without a buyer. Agents preview for three reasons: 1) To prepare for an upcoming listing appointment, 2) To screen properties for a busy buyer or 3) To keep up on the market*

homes to show your buyer. Even in a buyer's market, don't be surprised if you can't find enough good homes to show! If this is the case, either find a few more truly wonderful homes that don't quite meet your buyer's criteria, or go ahead and show a few homes that have all the buyer's requirements but don't show as well.

I knew the Denver market, especially the central neighborhoods. Yet I still usually previewed before going out with a new buyer. However, if I was showing homes in the suburbs (definitely not my specialty), I always, always, always previewed. At the very least, I drove by all the homes— one, to make sure the location is acceptable and two, to make sure I could find them!

This last is an important point. Nothing is more unraveling than getting lost with a buyer in your car. Talk about putting your antiperspirant to work. Denver proper is laid out in a grid, and most streets are alphabetical (Ash, Birch, Cherry, Dexter), so getting around is a breeze. However, in the suburbs, you might find 67th Circle, 67th Drive, 67th Avenue, 67th Place, with lots of cul-de-sacs and dead-ends. My first year, I worked in the foothills west of Denver, which were a nightmare to navigate. Homes could be five tedious miles up winding, unmarked roads, some not even on my map. Previewing for buyers could take all day, but was worth every hairpin turn.

A GPS is not the answer. You need to be able to get from house to house smoothly and effortlessly, as if you know every thoroughfare and side street in town...without that nice Garmin lady interrupting your conversation every 30 seconds. Being able to talk with your buyers as you navigate will do wonders for your air of professionalism. And of course, becoming increasingly frazzled as you make u-turns and wrong turns will have the opposite effect!

You might think condos would be easier. After all, once you find the complex, you know you're in the right place. Actually, I found condos to be more difficult to show and even more important to preview. First, in a large complex, just finding the unit can be a challenge, and that's before you've hunted down the lockbox! Many condominiums and lofts are in secured buildings, so the lockbox is placed outside on the front railing. There might be 20 other lockboxes hanging there, too! Or, I've seen units where the door handle design isn't conducive to hanging a lockbox, so the lockbox is hiding in a nearby stairwell. High rise buildings might require you to check in with the front desk to pick up a key.

You'll be a basket-case after your day of showings if you aren't prepared. If you look the slightest bit flustered in front of your buyer, your credibility will take a huge hit, and you might even lose the buyer. Have I made you nervous? I hope so, because it's far better to let your nervousness force you to prepare than to be cocky and make a fool of yourself.

Most Fix-Up Buyers Aren't

I'd guess that throughout my career, 70% of my new buyer clients identified themselves as potential "fix-up buyers." They'd enthusiastically support the idea of replacing carpet, painting walls, redoing a kitchen. They wanted some of that good old sweat equity in their pocket, and it's always trendy to say you want to fix up a property, especially during boom years when everyone seems to be doing it profitably.

Don't believe them. What buyers intellectually know and what they emotionally respond to are two very different things. In my experience fewer than 10% of my buyer clients were truly open to fixing up a home.

So don't waste your time or damage your credibility. Unless your buyer is a contractor looking for a fix-n-flip, show only the nicest homes to your new buyer on your first trip out. Maybe throw in a dated (I said dated, not dumpy) home or two to test his tolerance, but otherwise, Pottery Barn homes only: well-decorated, great street appeal, nice-smelling—you get the point. The vast majority of buyers will not respond to grandma's house, regardless of what a great deal it is. They want to see Martha Stewart.

If you ignore this advice and show them homes they have no emotional response to, you will have irreparably damaged your credibility and taken their enthusiasm down a few notches. You might even lose the buyers after they stumble into a beautifully presented open house in their price range and wonder why you didn't show it to them. They will never remember telling you they wanted to "fix up" a home.

After your first showing date, if the buyer tells you he wants to look at homes that need more work, then by all means, comply with his wishes. But at first, you are much better off erring on the Pottery Barn side.

Let Your Buyer's Emotions Make the Decision, Not Yours

There is an interesting phenomenon in real estate sales that will give you fits until you recognize it. Here's a common scenario...

You are out previewing and you find The One for your difficult buyer. It's everything she ever wanted, at the right price, in the right neighborhood. You are so excited, you call her from the living room and gush over how you have finally found the house for her.

You insist she look at the home right away because you know it will sell quickly. You lead her in the door and—nothing. She is lukewarm. She may try to be polite because she sees how excited you are, but she finds fault with every room, the location, the yard. You are crushed and frustrated and consider firing her on the spot.

Scenario #2: You are working with a couple. You and the wife usually preview the properties together so that you only show the best ones to her husband 'cause he's so busy. You and the missus find The One. She's euphoric, delirious, can't wait to show it to her husband. She's already moving in. You catch on to the excitement, and you both call him from the house to tell him all about the wonderful home. You pass the cell phone back and forth between you, so you can share in the excitement of telling him all the details.

You show him the house as soon as he can get away from work. Thud. He doesn't like it at all. Even though it's everything he said he wanted, he just doesn't warm up to it. The wife and husband get into a terrible fight and decide not to buy a house at all. You're glad you're not going home with them, but you're incredibly discouraged at his reaction. "What a controlling jerk he is!" you say to yourself.

This happens all the time. The explanation is that buyers need to discover The One for themselves. It's human nature to resist being told what to do, and your strong reaction is essentially that—telling the buyers that they are going to buy this house.

Scenario #2 is caused primarily by jealousy. Yes, jealousy. The spouse who doesn't participate in the home search, even at his or her request (I'm not assuming that all husbands work and all wives shop for homes; I've seen it happen equally with both sexes) feels left out. He may feel that you are out having a good time with his wife while he's "stuck" at work. He may even worry that you and his wife are out flirting with men (if you're female), or flirting with each other (if you're male). These aren't rational reactions, but they're there—underneath the lackluster response to the dream home. It's his way of controlling the situation, even though he agreed to take a back-seat in the process. He may know darn good and well that his wife is going to make the final decision, but that doesn't mean he's 100% comfortable with it.

So, hopefully the solution to both scenarios is obvious. Control your emotions. In Scenario #1, calmly call your buyer and tell her you found an interesting home she should look at. Maybe come up with a few others to show at the same time. Don't rave about the home or pressure her to come see it right away.

In Scenario #2, you have two ways, used in conjunction, to head off this problem. First, insist that the husband accompany you and his wife on your first outing. This way he feels involved in the process and you can see how he responds to homes. After one showing tour, he will feel more in control and that he is "handing off" house hunting responsibilities to his wife instead of being shut out. Secondly, convince the wife to control her emotions when you do find a great house. She may not believe you when you explain how the husband might react to her excitement. If necessary, set up a few other homes to show him at the same time you show him The One. He needs to feel as if he had a choice and that his wife (and you) respect his opinion and his choice.

Another emotional decision that must be made by your buyer, not by you, is a comfort level with location. You may know that a neighborhood is in the process of "turning around" (although Fair Housing laws limit what you can say about this) and would make a great investment for your buyer. But if your buyer isn't as comfortable with that concept as you are, don't push! Give your opinion once and let him do his own research and soul-searching. You will lose if your buyer gives in to your pressure and purchases a home against his gut instinct. If he (or his neighbors) are burglarized, which can happen anywhere, it will be All Your Fault. As a real estate agent, you may always be thinking "investment" (and you should be), but this is not the typical priority of a buyer, especially a first-time buyer.

I once helped some adorable first-time buyers who should have bought a home in the suburbs but fancied themselves urban dwellers. Like many first time buyers, they desired a neighborhood they couldn't afford. However, their favored neighborhood had more affordable housing on its fringes, and they were willing to explore that option.

We found a great home in their price range. It was located in an up-and-coming neighborhood that offered almost guaranteed market appreciation as the neighborhood improved. I knew it was a great investment. They were clearly hesitant about the location, but unfortunately, I pushed and wouldn't take no for an answer. We put the home under contract, and my buyers pretended to be excited. I overlooked their discomfort and moved forward with scheduling the inspection.

When we arrived for the home inspection, the tenant greeted us at the door with a detailed description of a robbery in the home the previous night. A man had broken through the back door, come into her bedroom and taken her jewelry, along with some other items, before running out. The tenant was hysterical. My buyers were speechless. Thankfully, my good sense kicked in (better late than never) and, rather than try to convince them that this was probably an isolated event, I advised them to cancel the inspection right then. I assured them that we could easily terminate the contract under our inspection rights and resume our house hunt.

Which is what my buyers eventually did. I found them much less of a home in a much safer neighborhood, and they are still happily living there.

Please keep in mind that your commission, regardless of how badly you need it, is secondary to your buyers' wants and needs. Your job is to represent and protect their interests, not yours. You will win far more brownie points by risking your commission (buyers aren't stupid; they know how you are paid, or at least they should) than you will trying to sell them on a property or situation they are clearly uncomfortable with. The minute a buyer feels that you are placing more importance on your paycheck than on his needs, you have lost his trust. In a buyer's mind, it is not only market knowledge and contractual expertise that earns trust, it is the feeling that you are truly on his side.

In fact, the more you "risk your paycheck" in front of your buyers, the more they will trust you. I had an investor client who told everyone about "Jennifer's nose wrinkle." Apparently, I made a face whenever we walked into a home that I didn't think was a good buy for him. He told his friends that he knew right then that we might as well leave, because Jennifer wasn't going to let him buy that house. It was meant as a sincere compliment, and I took it as such. And his friends all called me when they needed real estate service.

When Your Buyer Wants to Purchase a "Fatally-Flawed" Property

A "fatally-flawed" property is one that has one or more unfixable defects the market will likely perceive as insurmountable. Examples of fatal flaws might include a location on a busy street or backing to an unappealing commercial property (gas station, liquor store, etc.), high tension power lines over the home, an unusually small lot or a shared yard, noticeable structural damage, a strong smell of cat urine or smoke, no basement, an ugly exterior...the list goes on and on.

Most buyers don't want an imperfect home, much less a fatally-flawed one. However, every once in a while, you will work with a buyer who is determined to live in a particular neighborhood that is way out of her price range. Or someone in a time crunch who must buy a home in the next two days. Or, in an out-of-control market, a buyer who will buy anything that hasn't sold out from under him, regardless of future resale issues. When the market cools and he goes to sell...he gets burned.

I once had a buyer who insisted on looking at homes on very busy streets in good neighborhoods because her top priority was square footage and, secondarily, location. By "location," she meant she wanted to live in a nice neighborhood but wasn't willing to pay the inflated prices of the homes on the more desirable streets. As a seasoned buyer agent, it was surprisingly hard for me to search for homes on busy streets; I was too accustomed to automatically screening them out for the majority of my buyers. It went against everything I believed in to assist a buyer in purchasing a home I knew would be difficult to sell later on. But she insisted.

It was kind of fun, actually. The homes we looked at were screaming deals if you didn't look out the front or back doors—large, beautiful, Victorian mansions at a fraction of the cost of smaller homes just a block away. Yes, traffic was whizzing by outside, but inside, the homes were lovely. My client purchased a home just two doors in from a busy commercial street. I believe she paid $180,000 for a 4-bedroom, 3-bath home with amazing architectural details and a new gourmet kitchen. The same home just one block away would have been over $300,000.

But most of your buyers won't intentionally set out to buy a fatally-flawed home. They'll fall in love with a feature of the home and try to convince themselves they can live with the fatal flaw. When they look to you for advice, you need to be honest with them. If you see a serious resale issue, be sure they are aware of it. You don't want to dampen their enthusiasm, especially if they truly can't afford the home of their dreams, but make sure you go down on record as stating that the home has a problem that may affect resale.

If you don't—if you act as if everything is hunky-dory—it will be All Your Fault later on when the buyer's friends and family are skeptical about their choice of home or when they go to sell and the market rejects their home due to the fatal flaw. They won't want to take the blame for a poor decision and will be happy to blame it on you. The best you can do in this situation is to negotiate the best deal you can for the home and make sure the buyers know that when they sell the home, they will need to remember why they got such a great price and be willing to price it accordingly at resale.

Out-of-town buyers who are under pressure to buy and aren't familiar with the nuances of your market are particularly susceptible to purchasing undesirable homes. They don't know that they can do better, and if they are from a more expensive market, they might think they're getting a great deal! I wouldn't be surprised if many fatally-flawed homes eventually sell to out-of-towners working with unsoulful buyer agents who see an easy commission.

If your buyer has vision, he might be able to turn a fatally-flawed home into a great investment. It all depends on the flaw. A location flaw? Never. But if the home needs structural repair, floor plan improvement or an exterior renovation, your buyer could really make a killing.

Don't be afraid to write lowball offers on a fatally-flawed home. It's possible you aren't the first buyer agent to make a low offer on the house, and your buyer might just be the one to wear down a stubborn seller.

"Special" Buyers

There are two categories of buyers who deserve their own "special" discussion, because both can be gold mines for you—or make you dread getting up in the morning. I guarantee that you will have lots of fun learning experiences when you work with these special folks—amateur investors and out-of-town buyers.

Amateur Investors

Every real estate market has what I call "Amateur Investors." These are relatively handy people who have a little cash and some spare time on their hands and have heard rumors of quick-n-easy money to be made renovating beautiful old Victorian homes. During the real estate boom in Denver, I worked almost exclusively with amateur investors, which was profitable, yet brain damaging, and just plain hard work.

One good investor client can make your year, or at least give you a great head start. A bad one will make you wish you had chosen a different profession. So, first, what is a 'good' investor?

A good investor takes the process seriously. When you call your investor with a hot property, he wants to look at it right away. He shows up with his laptop computer, ready to input cost estimates into his prepared spreadsheet. If the numbers look as if they might work, he wants to make an offer right away—not tomorrow, not next week after he's gotten bids from three different contractors. He's reasonable with his offer. Sure, he'll probably lowball, but he is sensitive to the needs of the seller, too. He'll try to make his offer as attractive as possible with regard to closing dates, inspection conditions and loan approvals.

If your offer is successfully negotiated, he'll get his inspections done quickly and won't get fussy over the minor issues. He understands that a home that is a good cosmetic fix-up project will probably have other maintenance issues, too.

A good investor is well-qualified financially. He's not going to try to do an FHA or low-downpayment loan that will get kicked back at the appraisal due to the poor condition of the home.

A good investor client will hire you to market the home for him when it's been renovated, and if he expects a discount in your listing fee, that's reasonable. I consider myself part of the team. If I can help make money for the investor by reducing my fee, he can afford to buy more properties and is more likely to be loyal to me.

Some investors are a little more trouble. They are...indecisive. They know the house is a good deal, but they just aren't ready to make an offer. However, they don't want you telling your other investor clients about it just yet. They make ridiculous offers with 90-day closings and three-week inspection periods. They freely admit to being bottom-feeders and are hoping that eventually they'll find sellers who are desperate enough to give away their homes. And, eventually, they do get their house. But not until you've wasted hours of time and gallons of gas, written dozens of unacceptable offers and generally embarrassed yourself in the real estate community (at least, that's what it feels like).

If you do ever put a home under contract with an investor like this, he will probably try to sell the home himself after renovation, mainly because he spent too much money and time renovating it and can't afford to pay you. Let him do it—he will likely need to overprice the home to break even and will be difficult to work with.

Something to keep in mind if you're working with a first time fix-n-flipper: first projects are rarely money-makers for the investor, and you need to tell him that. He won't believe you, but in the majority of cases, you will be the only one who walks away with a paycheck. Inexperienced renovators always underestimate the cost and time involved in the renovations and often forget to factor in the monthly cost of holding the property. They will be lucky to just break even, but hopefully they consider their first project as an educational experience.

Finding Good Projects for Your Amateur Investors
Homes advertised as "fix up's" are generally too awful for the average amateur investor. If you suspect your investor is more of a "paint and carpet" kind of guy, here are five smart ways to find him good projects.

1. Grandma's House
"Original owner" homes are some of the best projects. They are usually well maintained, but they just don't appeal to the Pottery Barn crowd. With relatively minor upgrades (exposing hardwood floors, using trendy paint colors, etc.) these homes can be flipped for a tidy profit.

2. "Sleepers"
If a home is in an excellent location, but hasn't sold in a reasonable amount of time, look for the reason. Perhaps there is a problem with the home that the market perceives as insurmountable. Examples might be awkward floor plans, strong smoke smells, lack of a second bathroom or an antiquated heating system. The home is probably not being marketed to investors, and the retail buyers who are looking at it aren't responding emotionally to the home, or are overwhelmed by the "insurmountable challenge."

3. Market Timing
Many, if not all, markets have a "selling season." It might be a four to six month period during the year when most of the annual market appreciation takes place. In Denver, we had what I called Spring Fever. Sometime between January and March, buyers would come out of hiding and listings started to sell quickly. During this Spring Fever, prices appreciated, and by June, there was a noticeable increase in the average sales price of homes.

The rush slowed down on the Fourth of July and the market was somewhat dead until Thanksgiving. The tail end of this slow period was a great time to buy a home to renovate. Sellers were nervous (thus motivated) and the market just felt lousy. An investor could work on his project during the first few months of the rush and be ready for market at the height of the selling season.

4. Poor Renovations
Sometimes your amateur investor can take advantage of another amateur investor's mistakes. Perhaps the home was renovated poorly and it shows. Or perhaps the investor selected drab colors and finishes and the home

simply doesn't evoke any emotion. Maybe there was one problem the investor decided not to address and should have. The seller may not have enough room to negotiate much, but every once in a while you'll find someone who is desperate to unload.

5. Newer Construction
Many homes built within the last 15 years are showing signs of wear. Most already feel dated, but they're still good, solid homes. You won't be worrying about sewer lines or ancient furnaces and shouldn't have to do a major overhaul on the home's floor plan to bring it up to today's standards. Most investors are not competing against you yet (they're hot after the charming older homes), and none of these homes have been updated. So, if you can get a good price on a ten-year-old home, perhaps talk your investor into renting it for a few more years (assuming an appreciating market), then go in and cherry it out. Add the granite counters (if that's still vogue), Ralph Lauren paint, get rid of the brass light fixtures and hardware, add six-panel wood doors. Make it a Pottery Barn home that young, hip buyers will fall in love with.

Just make darn sure that your finished price will be within the neighborhood's value, or just slightly above. In a tract home subdivision, it's nearly impossible to get an appraiser to appraise a home higher than the recent highest sale, regardless of the improvements your client has made. In other words, if the market value of similar homes without updating is $235,000, don't try to sell your client's home for $270,000 and expect it to appraise.

In distressed markets, many amateur investors want to purchase bank-owned and short-sale properties. While I do not have extensive experience with the distressed property market, my agent friends who do tell me that these properties are rarely the great deals they're made out to be. Or, if they are, they get bid up by competing investors to the point where they're only marginally profitable.

Bad Projects for Amateur Investors
Some new investors get so excited about the prospect of fixing and flipping that they get impatient waiting for the right project. They'll want to jump on any fix-up project that comes along, whether or not it's a good project for them. As an agent working with an investor, you might be impatient as well. After all, you're working your backside off for this guy, showing him properties, writing low offers and doing

market research, and you'd really like to see a paycheck somewhere on the horizon. So, you might be tempted to support his bad decision, just to get him off your docket.

However, realize that you'll probably have to sell the renovated home your investor buys, and if it's a dog, it's going to be a frustrating for both of you. Your investor will never remember that he was the one who got impatient and jumped on this crummy property; no, he'll blame you, especially as his project languishes on the market and the mortgage payments start eating away at his profit.

Here are some poor prospects for your investor:

1. A Fatally-Flawed Location
Don't ever let your investor take a chance on location. If the home has a locational fatal flaw, such as close proximity to a noisy highway or train tracks, or is on the same block as an apartment building, low-income housing or an auto repair shop, don't let him buy it. This is not to say that he shouldn't buy in a "marginal" neighborhood; as long as he doesn't over-improve the home, there are always buyers for renovated homes, in all price ranges, and not every investor can afford the "best" neighborhoods. But no matter how nicely your investor remodels the home, he can never overcome a location objection. It's just not worth the risk for either of you.

2. A Fatally-Flawed Floor Plan or Yard
Other than location, there are other fatal flaws that make a home a poor investment. A home with an awkward floor plan (if your investor can't or won't fix it) will still be awkward and difficult to sell no matter how nicely it is renovated. For example, a one-bedroom or otherwise un-family friendly home is always a tough sell. (Never advise an investor to eliminate bedrooms in the interest of creating larger rooms, unless there are plenty of bedrooms to spare!) A home with an obvious addition (or two or three) is risky, as is a home that feels choppy or maze-like.

3. Structural Damage
Unless your investor is willing to professionally address and correct structural issues in a home, stay clear. And by "address and correct," I don't mean "paint over." Sloping floors, crooked doorways or cracking plaster will cause buyers to go screaming for the door. Even in a 150-year-old Victorian, buyers will not usually overlook a structural problem.

Even if they do, their buyer agent (or their parents!) will talk them out of purchasing your investor's property. However, if your investor is willing to repair structural concerns, this can be a great niche for him, as many investors are not.

4. The Lovely Aroma of Cat Urine
Cat lovers, cover your eyes. The smell of cat urine is very difficult to remove, especially in older homes with cellars or crawl spaces. Unless your investor has experience removing cat smell and is certain he can remove it, you should advise against purchasing a home with any odor of cat. If he cannot remove the smell, the home will be tough to sell. Many people are allergic to cats, so besides the offensive odor, they will be concerned about the previous feline residents giving them the sniffles on a daily basis.

5. A Unique Home
In central Denver, for example, urban buyers love their Bungalows, Tudors and Victorians. They are suspicious of other styles, such as Art Deco, Contemporary or Southwest. You can argue all day about the architectural appeal of one style over another, but it won't change what the market wants. Most retail buyers are looking for something predictable, something that makes sense to them. Investors should stick to what they know will sell, not what they personally prefer.

6. A Dark Home
The vast majority of home buyers want a light, bright and cheerful home. If a home is dark because it does not allow much natural light, it's a risk, even if it feels dramatic or cozy. Of course, if your investor can fix the lighting issue (e.g., adding skylights or removing awnings), this might be a terrific sleeper investment project for him.

7. A Too-Small Kitchen
An otherwise fabulous home with a too-small kitchen will never sell. Unless your investor can expand the kitchen without sacrificing the utility of the surrounding rooms, don't assume the market will overlook this flaw. It won't.

The Benefits of Working with Investors
Working with investors is a fantastic learning experience. Here's what you'll get:

1. Practice honing your pricing skills

An investor needs to know what the market value for his renovated home will be. You may need to do multiple CMAs for him on short notice, which will sharpen your skills significantly. Do the best you can to give him an accurate range. If you haven't yet seen the quality of your investor's work, be conservative. He may tell you that he's a perfectionist, but until you know for sure, don't assume that he is.

2. Practice writing and presenting lowball offers

Investors want a deal, and that's okay. They're not looking for their dream home; they're looking for a profit. The less they pay for the house, the more profit. Duh. Try to get them to honor the seller's needs wherever they can to get the best price. Sometimes it's embarrassing to present a low offer to the seller's agent, but you'll get used to it, especially if you work with a lot of investors.

3. Intense familiarity with neighborhoods

Most investors focus on specific neighborhoods or property types, so you will find yourself becoming the local expert in their preferred neighborhoods. Not only are you on a constant lookout for underpriced homes in these neighborhoods, you are also always looking at the sold data to help them determine whether or not a project is viable.

4. Construction knowledge

When your investor speaks, listen. Encourage him to tell you his plans, his concerns, his considerations. When he is evaluating a home as a potential investment property, he'll give you a great education on home construction and profitable renovation.

5. Find properties for yourself

There's no law that says you have to turn over great investment properties you find to your investor. If, during the course of searching for properties for him, you find something you want—go for it! Just don't put yourself in the position of bidding against him.

One negative aspect of focusing heavily on investor business is that you lose out on the fun of real estate. Investors don't get tears in their eyes when they close on their first home. They don't worry about offending the seller. They don't refer you to all their friends, because they aren't emotional about you, and if you're doing a good job, they don't want to share you. When the real estate boom in Denver subsided and the investors faded away, I started working with retail buyers again. And utterly enjoyed it.

Considerations When Selling Fix-n-Flipped Properties
Many fix-n-flip investors will want to put their project on the market before the renovations are complete. Try to talk them out of this strategy; it will only cost them money and introduce a lot of unwanted hassles. The typical buyer for a fully renovated home doesn't have a lot of vision. She can't imagine the finished product; she just sees sawdust, drywall and empty Big Gulps. This same buyer may be more than willing to pay top dollar for this project once it's spiffed up and shiny, but before that point, she just won't get it. You don't want your investor's project getting stale on the market.

Another reason to avoid putting the project on the market prematurely is that if you are able to find a buyer, she'll want to change everything. She won't like your client's taste in cabinetry, flooring, light fixtures or appliances. First-time fix-n-flippers may be flattered by the attention and may agree to accommodate her requests. If they do, don't be surprised if the buyer changes her mind...frequently. She'll hang out at the job site and drive the contractors crazy. She'll object to workers smoking in "her" house. She might even decide that the floor plan could use improvement.

Then she'll start fussing about the completion date, which is going to be a moving target for an amateur investor (even an experienced one). She'll threaten to back out of the contract (after all her changes have been implemented!) because her lease is up, the lock on her loan is expiring or she found something ready NOW. I'm sure you can see how this could get ugly fast...for everyone. You are the professional; advise your fix-n-flipper of these risks as soon as you can. If he insists on marketing the project pre-completion, do it and hope for the best.

A Second "Special" Category of Buyer: Out-of-Town Buyers
Out-of-town buyers are great. Sometimes. They can also be a big headache. If they're for real (a big if) and in town to buy a house this weekend, you will sell them a house this weekend, if you're prepared.

You will work with many types of out-of-town buyers during your career. All deserve your respect and attention, but it will serve you well to discern which ones are For Real and which ones will probably poof on you. The best type of out-of-town buyer is, of course, the buyer who is definitely moving to your town in the near future. Let's call him the Type One Buyer. He should be a top priority for you. The second type (Type Two) is the Rent for Now "Buyer," who is definitely moving, but plans to rent for a while. If you manage rentals as well as home sales, this type may also be a top priority. If you don't manage rental properties, I'd probably call her a medium priority. The Lookie-Loo (Type Three) is thinking about moving to your town but is considering other locations as well. If she has definite plans to visit your town, she is also a medium priority. Last, we have the Investor (Type Four) who has heard about your booming real estate market and wants a piece of it. This type is a tough call. If you're a newer agent, you should probably work with Type Fours, for the experience if nothing else.

Type One—The Sure Thing

They have a job; they've sold their current home; they need to buy a house. Preferably from you. You must be prepared for these buyers! They're not messing around and they don't want to waste their time. Once they're in town, you won't have time to do much market research or previewing. Clear your calendar the week/weekend of their visit. Get help if you need it. Preview, preview, preview, preview. Preview everything that might interest them. Take good notes. Get a list from them of homes they've seen online that interest them. Preview those too.

Show only the best properties, but show as many as you can. These buyers need to look at houses until they drop. Ten to 15 homes in one day, if they're up for it. On the other hand, if they have a young child in tow, ask them how much time to allot.

Don't plan to show too many homes in one neighborhood. If they don't like the neighborhood, they won't want to see any more inventory there. During the process, they will (hopefully) zero in on a few choice areas, and you can plan your next day accordingly.

It's not uncommon for relocating buyers to completely revise their search criteria in the middle of their visit, so stay flexible. I once had out-of-town buyers who switched gears from Charming Old Denver to Suburban Tract Home Hell four times during their six-day visit. That was their right, but it was tough on me. Tract Home Hell was not my forte, and I had a terrible time getting around without the chance to preview. However, they knew that I was an urban specialist, and luckily I had proven myself competent and confident in the urban neighborhoods before we headed off to foreign lands together.

Brush up on your Fair Housing speech for when they ask you about the safety, desirability or investment potential of a neighborhood. Because they will. Be as helpful as you can without risking your license. Be prepared with website addresses for local crime statistics and public school demographics, since these are sensitive topics and can get you in trouble.

When they find the home they want to buy, they will want all kinds of market data from you to help them determine their offer price. Yes, your opinion will be welcomed, but you will need to be able to back it up with solid data. Regardless of the great rapport you've built with these buyers, they are still suspicious of you. They don't know the market at all and don't want to make a mistake.

They may very well want to make a lowball offer. Out-of-town buyers almost always do. If you strongly disagree due to the current state of the market in your area, express your opinion, calmly and professionally, and then shut up. If they insist, cheerfully write it up. Remember, they need to buy a house this weekend more than you need to sell a house this weekend, but if you get into an argument with them over the offer price, they may abandon you and call up one of the other agents they spoke with before choosing you.

Put yourself in their shoes. They're nervous. They don't want to make a mistake. If their offer is countered or rejected, they may be willing to pay full price, but they need to feel they gave it their best shot first. With your 100% support, they can more easily make the right decision for themselves.

If you successfully put a home under contract for these buyers, you can proceed as normal toward the closing. Well, sort of. The buyers may not be in town for the inspection or even the closing. You'll need to do a lot of hand holding, especially during the inspection period. You'll likely need to help them gather estimates for repairs, even meet contractors at the home.

Do a good job for these buyers and you'll be rewarded with many referrals. Think about it: What's the first question they'll be asked at their new job? "How did the move go?" If you were great, you'll get some good press.

Type Two—The Rent-for-Now Buyer

Again, if you work in property management as well as real estate sales, go headlong after this buyer/renter. If not, it still won't hurt you to spend some time with him. If he's owned a home before, he may reconsider his decision to rent once he sees the rental inventory. In any case, he won't want to rent forever and may be ready to buy within six months.

His first priority when he visits your town will be to secure housing, so let him explore his rental options. Be cheerfully available to him to answer his questions about what he's seeing. If he seems interested and for real, offer to take him on a little tour of neighborhoods you think he'd consider buying in. Show him some homes, if he asks. Your goal is to build rapport and get your business card in his hand so he'll call you in six months. Get his new address, put him in your SOI database and schedule some follow-up calls.

Type Three—The Lookie-Loo Buyer

Frankly, this buyer is probably a time-waster, but it won't kill you to spend some time with her. Build an email rapport with her; be cheerfully responsive to her dozens of questions about your city. If she actually makes a trip to your town, you'll need to spend a lot of time with her, just as you would with the Type One buyers. Don't make a half-a$$ed effort with her—if she falls in love with a home you show her, she just might escalate her plans and move next month. I've seen it happen! If she's definitely not in a position to move for several months or more, spend a day with her and play it by ear after that.

But stay in touch. She's probably an online shopper and will likely talk to other agents during her information-gathering period. Don't bother her with a buyer agency agreement or anything like that; just strive to be her best resource for information.

Type Four—The Investor

This buyer is a high-maintenance, high-risk prospect. However, if he pans out, he could be a gold mine.

Imagine yourself as this buyer. You hear a rumor that a certain area is anticipating double-digit appreciation for whatever reason. You have some money to invest and would like to buy some real estate in a growing market. You get all revved up one morning and start emailing brokers in your new favorite city.

You tell them that you're an investor and are interested in purchasing a home or two in their city. For investment. No, you've never been there, but you've heard it's hot. You'd like the agent to send you some listings of under-market properties for your review. If you like the look of the homes, you'll come visit—sometime.

Most experienced agents would ignore you. I probably would. A hot market is no secret; plenty of local investors (including real estate agents) are watching the market closely for "under-market properties." Great deals are not sitting around on the MLS waiting for an out-of-town investor to review at his leisure.

Whether or not to work with an out-of-town investor is a judgment call on your part. If the investor has no idea what he wants, no familiarity with your city and no firm plans to visit, I'd probably let him go or refer him. If your market is truly hot, you'll easily find plenty of local investors to go after.

On the other hand, if the out-of-town investor is familiar with your city, has some local connections (friends, family) and is planning to visit next month, go ahead and play along for a while. Some of my best clients and sources of referrals started out just this way.

"I Sell Real Estate Every Day...Sometimes I Even Get Paid For It!"
I used this mantra on two general occasions...

The first (to myself) was when I was feeling frustrated that my buyers weren't buying or my listings weren't selling—at least not fast enough to suit my impatient nature. It's not that I was mad at them—not at all, but when something gets on my to-do list, I want it done so I can enjoy that feeling of satisfaction upon accomplishing a task. Reminding myself that everything I did, every day, might be leading me to a paycheck eventually kept me sane.

But the more important "use" I had for my "I sell real estate every day" mantra was to put my buyers at ease when they started to feel that they're being too picky or too indecisive. Contrary to what you might believe, that's the LAST thing I wanted them to feel! I DID have all the time in the world for my buyers, and as long as I thought they were reasonably serious about being homeowners I was delighted to take my time with them—however much time that was. Every once in a while, I'd work with a buyer who seemed almost embarrassed if he hadn't selected a home within a few weeks, and I really, really, really didn't want him to stop contacting me out of this embarrassment!

“ Happy are those who get to talk.
Happier are those who get listened to. ”
Unknown

Chapter Seven

Rethinking the List(en)ing Presentation

You wanna know the top search term that brings new surfers to my website (www.SellwithSoul.com)? Okay, there are two. The first is "New agent announcement letter." The second is "Sample listing presentation."

I offer a free sample listing presentation on my website (http://www.sellwithsoul.com/vip_lounge.html). Seems to be a popular item. I'm rather proud of my listing presentation. There's nothing boiler-plate or corporate about it; it's direct and to-the-point, conversational and informative. I used it or a similar version for years.

But in the last few years of my career, I found myself rethinking the idea of a formal listing presentation. I experimented with not doing one and walked away from my listing appointments much more pleased with myself. But I wasn't 100% sure.

Then, I met with a real estate agent to discuss listing a property of mine out-of-state. She came to the house and asked me to show her around. She asked questions and actually listened to my (sometimes long-winded) answers. She took notes. As we toured, she casually mentioned other homes she'd seen or sold recently that were comparable to mine. Because she knew I was also in the biz, she respectfully asked for my thoughts on a marketing strategy. And listened.

After I was done showing her the house and grounds, she said she wanted to go back to the office and do her homework, now that she'd seen the property. She'd be ready to present her findings the next day, if that was okay with me. It was and she did and I hired her.

No presentation. No fancy graphs or charts. No bio, resume or testimonials. Just a subtly demonstrated knowledge of the marketplace, a sincere interest in my situation and a respectful acknowledgment of my intelligence and experience. Had she shown up with a 90-minute formal presentation of how wonderful she was, how awesome her company is and how dangerous it is to OVERPRICE, I'd have tuned her out within 5 minutes.

Did I know her marketing plan? Oops, no, not really. I suppose I could have asked, and maybe I should have. But her non-salespitchy "presentation" made me trust her.

Now, truth be told, this sort of quiet confidence takes a while to develop. I certainly didn't have it my first year or even my second; maybe not even by my third. Well, heck, there I was in my 13th year just realizing that I didn't need a fancy presentation!

I'm a big fan of proving your competence to prospects and clients, rather than just telling them about it. Tell someone how great you are, and they'll immediately start to look for reasons you aren't. That's just human nature. And, frankly, most of a listing presentation is a sales pitch where the agent tries to convince a seller that he's the best man for the job, based on his FABULOUS marketing plan and INCREDIBLE company support.

But what if, instead of your fancy listing presentation, you were to walk into a listing appointment with a sincere desire to help, a sincere interest in the seller's situation (instead of simply a sincere interest in your paycheck) and a dead-on understanding of the local real estate marketplace?

Hmmmmm...care about your seller and know your stuff...it might really be that simple.

That said, I do believe that the process of creating a formal presentation is good for the soul—it helps you to figure out what you offer and why you're special, and for the times when a seller seems to want something in writing, you have it ready to go. I have much of my presentation available on my website, so sellers can check me out ahead of time or after they've met me.

> **Words of Wisdom from the Trenches**
> *Courtesy of Susan Haughton*
> *"I never do a formal listing presentation; I take comps (information on comparable sales in the area) so it looks as if I at least came with something. I talk with the sellers about the market, about their home, about their goals. I don't even take the listing paperwork. I'm just there to have a conversation with them, and if we decide to proceed together, then I'll get the listing paperwork to them for their signatures. I like to think this approach conveys that I don't need props—I have knowledge, skill and confidence."*

Pricing It Right with a Persuasive CMA

Even if you don't do a formal listing presentation, you'll obviously need to determine what the right price is for the home you're considering (or being considered for the honor of) listing. But that's only half the battle. Even if you're convinced you know what the house will sell for, the other half is persuasively communicating your findings to a seller, especially if that seller won't be delighted with your analysis!

First, let me say that I don't believe that data, statistics, scripts or closing strategies are "persuasive" when talking with a potential seller. What is persuasive? Empathy, respect and confidence.

Confidence Envelopes You When You Care Enough to Make a Difference
by Meyer Leibovitch

If you are like I was at one time, you get nervous thinking about your appointment days before. For whatever reasons, the butterflies show up in your stomach, and you dread even knocking on their door. There was a time when I even would wish that appointments would cancel.

I began to wonder; what am I going to say that makes me stand out from the competition? All good agents had the same tools. I think that's what bothered me more than anything. On top of that, if I knew I was competing with agents that had better track records than I had, my nerves got worse.

At the time, I didn't know it, but my focus was completely in the wrong place. I was focused on how I could make myself look better in their eyes without genuinely focusing on them. I know a good presentation can make you look good, but if you're more concerned about getting the listing than you are with your client's needs, there is a disconnect and it was that disconnect that was making me nervous. I didn't consciously see the connection, but I know that I was more interested in impressing them than helping them.

It wasn't until I realized that I cared about my clients and wanted to really, genuinely help them, that I overcame my appointment fears. I was so wrapped up in what I was going to say about myself and my service to get them to like and choose me, that I wasn't really focusing on their needs.

"Confidence envelops you the moment you realize that you care enough to make a difference."

Before, my appointments would consist of immediately going through client's homes and making small talk or showing buyers listings on the computer. On listing appointments I would take notes and then I would get to the table, break out my canned presentation and answer any questions at the end. It did work sometimes. But it wasn't the best way for me to do business.

After an appointment with a pushy financial adviser, I had a paradigm shift. This adviser clearly didn't care about me or my family. I felt it, and I realized that was a terrible way to be. I put myself in my client's position, and it was easy to see what I had been missing. I had definitely wanted to be the best real estate agent out there, making the most money, even providing the best service, but the way I was getting there was all wrong. It couldn't have been any clearer; I was more interested in me than I was in my clients. For whatever reason, from that day on, my paradigm changed. My focus was on their needs, not how good I could look on the appointment.

For years now, my appointments consist much more of two-way conversation, with the client doing more than the lion's share of the talking. Instead of putting on a show about how good I am and how much I sell, to impress them, I listen to what's important to them. I make sure that all of their concerns are addressed personally. I find out what they know about the process and what they want to know. Sometimes I don't even open my book. If it's the clients that are doing the majority of the talking and I am doing the listening during my presentations, I know I am on the right track.

....

If a seller doesn't feel that you care more about selling his house than getting a paycheck, or even just getting a signed listing agreement, he's not going to trust you and probably won't believe you if you tell him something he doesn't want to hear—like—his house isn't worth what he thinks or "needs" it to be.

Instead, approach every listing interview as an opportunity to see if you can help, if you're the right (wo)man for the job. Don't look at it as an opportunity to sell yourself or persuade someone to hire you; rather, as an opportunity to have a conversation with someone who may or may not be a good fit for you. I took my role very seriously as someone a seller was considering trusting to manage a complicated process. If I truly didn't think I could sell the home or that our personalities didn't mesh well enough for me to be effective, I was happy to respectfully walk away. And this gave me tremendous personal power when talking with a seller about price. They felt that power and, I believe, were comforted by it. They saw me as an advisor, not a salesperson, so they were much more likely to trust me when I gave them my opinion of value.

I believe in creating a thorough CMA that includes every possible property the seller might be comparing his home to, even if the property isn't comparable. There's nothing like a seller asking you about a sale down the street that you don't know anything about to trash your confidence! I always had the details of any home that had sold within a one-block radius of my seller's property, within the last 18 months. I didn't necessarily include this detail in my CMA, but I had the information available. Time flies, so a seller may tell you his neighbor's house sold a few months ago, when in reality, it was over a year ago.

I also previewed like a madwoman before a listing interview. I wanted to know everything I could about the currently active listings, and again, I'd look at every house within a one-block radius, even if the house was completely different from the seller's property.

Always do your own CMAs. At one brief period in my career, I had an assistant, and, think-ing I was such a hot shot, I had her put together preliminary CMAs for me. I sent her out to preview the competition and to choose the comparable sales and run them through my CMA program. But I quickly figured out after my first few listing appointments

> **CMA**
> CMA traditionally stands for Competitive Market Analysis or Comparative Market Analysis, however, I recently heard a much better definition (courtesy of Broker Bryant Tutas (http://www.brokerbryant.com) "Compilation of Market Activity." A CMA is a report prepared by a real estate agent to determine the market value of a home.

using this strategy that it was a really bad idea. When I got in front of the seller, I had no familiarity with the data and had a tough time sounding like I knew what I was talking about —mainly because I didn't. That was when I realized that the process of preparing a CMA was as much for my benefit as it was for the seller's.

So, let's talk about how to present market data to a seller.

First, make sure your market analysis is well-organized, summarized and easy to understand. Some sellers will want every single detail; some won't, so be prepared to offer both—a summary of the data backed up with the details. The format of your CMA will be largely dependent on what's available to you through your MLS, but be sure you understand it backwards and forwards. Become as familiar as you can with the data, so that when you're going through it with the seller, it appears that you have the whole darn market memorized. You don't have to memorize it, of course, but the more conversational you can be while presenting the data, the more credibility you'll have. Be able to make comparisons among comparables and talk knowledgeably about each comparable's location compared to the seller's property. Stuff like that gives you confidence in yourself and helps the seller be confident in you. You can see a sample copy of my CMA in the Appendix

I don't ever remember being in the position of having to "buy" a listing. What I mean by that is talking with a seller who is pretty clearly going to hire the highest bidder. My sellers seemed to understand the realities of the market and truly wanted to know what it was going to take to sell their homes. Several times, my seller prospect even ridiculed the other agents they'd interviewed for clearly recommending a pie-in-the-sky price.

Was I just lucky to have had above-average-intelligence sellers? Maybe, but I believe that my taking an advisory instead of a sales approach brought me a lot of trust and credibility.

Do You Want the Listing?
So, Big Question. Do you want this listing? When making this decision, try to leave your ego out of it. You need to ask yourself some very honest questions and decide for yourself how you feel about the answers.

Here were some of the requirements I made of my sellers before I agreed to take a listing:

- Will the seller agree to vacate for showings?
- Allow short-notice showings?
- Maintain the home in showing condition?
- Stop smoking in the house?
- Consult with a home stager?
- Price reasonably from day one?

The answers to these questions will give you some insight into the seller's motivation and willingness to cooperate with your suggestions.

It's also important that you feel good about this listing you're getting ready to take.

Ask yourself:
- Am I excited about this listing? Why or why not?
- Would I show this listing to my buyers?
- Am I proud of this listing?
- Am I worried about selling this listing?
- Do I feel comfortable enough with these sellers to be up front and direct with them?
- Does the home have a good vibe?
- Do the sellers intimidate me?

If you come away with a pretty good feel about the answers to these questions, then you probably have a sellable listing. If you're going through the checklists, and you come away with, wow, this is really going to be a drag, you might want to be emotionally prepared to walk away from the listing.

Believe me, having listings you can't sell is no fun! There were agents in my market who apparently would take any listing they could get, at any price they could get it at, and I don't know how they slept at night. But their signs were everywhere, and that made me mad. Not because I was jealous, but because all their overpriced, unmarketable listings made our market look stagnant., even when it wasn't.

JENNIFER'S BLOG: *I Got the Listing by Being Soulful. YES, Nice Gals Do Win!*

I've been interviewing for a listing here in my 'hood for about a month. The seller really did her homework – she interviewed five agents, asked for recommendations, read our blogs, reviewed our public online marketing and, at least in my case and I assume for everyone else, contacted us several times after our interview with additional questions.

Okay, so I got the listing. Yay! Go, Me!

My new client was kind enough to outline for me why she chose me over the competition. Here's what she said:

Jennifer,

I wanted to let you know that after a somewhat grueling process of interviewing prospective agents, doing as much research ourselves as we could, playing with the numbers and just thinking about what we want to do, I think we have finally come to a decision about our house. It was much harder to make a decision than I'd expected — each agent was very different, with different pluses and minuses, and overall, they really all seemed quite excellent. But after weighing all the various factors, we've decided that we do, indeed, want to move forward with selling our home, and we want to work with you.

It's funny, because even though I say it was a difficult decision, and in many ways it was, in other ways I pretty much hoped all along that this would be where we'd end up, because I liked your philosophies and approach, and I feel confident in your abilities to be the kick-ass agent we're looking for :)

But I'd like to share with you a little list of the things that sold me on you, just in case it's useful feedback:

1) Your website and blog

2) You were one of the only agents who didn't in any way disparage other agent, companies, etc. I was amazed that several people did this, and it's kind of a turnoff. Your approach seemed very honest and straightforward and like you weren't trying so hard to sell yourself. You even said, "I'm sure anyone you go with, given the referrals you've received, will be excellent," and I liked that.

3) I like that you specialize in the cute charming old neighborhoods of Denver, allowing you to see and appreciate the charm of our beloved old home, and making me feel good about your ability to help us find the perfect replacement home that would really suit us. Also, your experience renovating old homes seemed like a plus in helping us avoid potential money-pits-in-cute-homes'-clothing;

4) I wanted to make sure we went with someone we'd actually enjoy spending time with, because I can imagine it can end up being quite a bit of time!

5) You just seemed pretty up front with us. This may again be partly due to your website and our subsequent casual email exchanges. But you also were the only one who came over and just chatted with us, found out more about what we're looking for, what we're thinking, etc., instead of sitting down and starting a formal sales pitch before we even had a chance to get to know each other at all.

6) You always responded to every call or email promptly. This seems so minor, but it's a big deal.

7) I looked at examples of listings every agent had either recently sold or currently has on the market, and I just really liked the marketing you do—the photos, the written narrative, what you choose to highlight, the Craigslist ads, etc — are all professional, quality, make the place sound great, and full of personality.

8) Of course it mainly also comes down to skills—you seemed to have the best combination of the factors mentioned above with the experience and skills to do a great job helping us get the most out of our home, sell it at the best price we can get for it, find a great new home, and navigate the whole complicated path through all the facets of those two transactions.

If you don't do it excellently, don't do it at all. Because if it's not excellent, it won't be profitable or fun, and if you're not in business for fun or profit, what the hell are you doing there?

Robert Townsend

Chapter Eight

The New 3P's of Getting Listings SOLD!

I n Chapter Seven, we talked about strategies for getting good listings, but here, we're going to talk about something far more important: getting those good listings SOLD.

In my opinion, there is far too much emphasis in our industry on getting more listings, with very little fanfare into how to sell the listings you have. In a boom market, perhaps this makes some sense. After all, in a strong seller's market, any listing with a pulse is guaranteed money in the bank. Or close enough, anyway.

But most of the time, there are going to be more homes for sale than buyers to buy them. Which means that some houses aren't going to sell. Which means that, not only has the agent of the non-selling home wasted his time, money and energy, but also that he has disappointed his hopeful seller client who entrusted the sale of her home to him.

Yet listing agents continue to market homes the way they always have— using the infamous 3P's. Know what they are? There are a few variations,

but the 3P's go something like this:
1. Put a Sign in the Yard
2. Put it in the MLS
3. Pray

Now we all laugh at this and smugly apply it to the Other Guy, but I tell ya—in my experience, this is how the vast majority of homes are marketed. And when the home doesn't sell using the agent's 32-Point marketing plan (which basically amounts to a fluffed-up version of the 3P's), the only solution the agent knows to offer is the 4th P—the Price Reduction.

When I was an active real estate agent, I was always on the lookout for other good agents in the Denver area to refer to when a client came along who wasn't a good fit for me for whatever reason. Whenever I met an agent I liked, I would do a little informal interview to determine if he or she were someone I'd want to include in my network.

JENNIFER'S BLOG: *"I'm the Best Listing Agent I Know." Are you?*

"I'm the Best Listing Agent I Know." Arrogant, eh?

Not really. It's not as if I said "I'm the prettiest girl I know" or "I'm the smartest girl I know." It's more along the lines of "I'm the hardest worker I know." It's a choice.

I choose to be a terrific listing agent. It's not a God-given skill or something I was lucky enough to be born with. It's a choice.

I choose to spend time (and gas money) properly pricing my properties. I choose to have relationships with exceptional home stagers and responsive home improvement contractors. I choose to be respectfully upfront with my sellers as to what they need to do to help me get their homes sold. I choose to own a great camera with a wide-angle lens. I choose to write killer MLS descriptions and ensure that they are accurate. I choose to work for a company that offers a 7-day/week showing service and to pursue feedback from all showing agents. I choose to frequently update my seller on the competing market activity. I choose to build and maintain rapport with my sellers so that they trust me when I offer advice and recommendations. I choose to keep my brochure boxes full. I choose to be prepared for and attend my appraisals. I CHOOSE TO CARE MORE ABOUT THE CLIENTS I HAVE TODAY THAN THE CLIENTS I HOPE TO HAVE TOMORROW.

I'm a heckuva listing agent. Are you?

I would ask these agents some rather specific questions about how they handled their businesses and how they treated their clients. Overall, I was usually pretty impressed, but there's one area that I was shall we say, less so. The agents usually had a great handle on working with buyers; they understood short sales, and had decent systems in place to keep themselves organized and efficient so they can provide great customer service. But when we talked about their listing strategies, I rarely met one who seemed to be confident in their listing abilities. When I asked the question: "How do you get your listings sold?" the response I most often got was a deer-in-headlights stare and a pretty weak stumbling response about pricing right.

Honestly, I felt kind of sorry for them because they almost seemed to feel helpless when it came to getting their listings sold. And that must be a terrible feeling—to feel powerless over such an important aspect of your business.

But you know what? We AREN'T helpless. We aren't powerless when it comes to selling houses. Even in difficult markets, we have far more power and control over whether our listings sell than we give ourselves credit for. Sure, it may take a lot more work than it does in a strong market, and contrary to popular belief, involves more than simply pricing it right, but imagine what it would do to the public perception of our industry and of the local real estate market if houses were to sell quickly, even in difficult markets?

We have the power to make that happen.

So, that's what this chapter is about: how to SELL those listings you work so hard to get, so that you actually see a paycheck for your efforts and, of course, get yourself a delighted seller who will be happy to refer business to you for years to come. Because... it doesn't matter if you're the best FSBO converter on the planet—or have an expired campaign to die for—if you can't sell those listings you're so good at getting, then what's the point?

The New 3P's

Let's talk about the New 3P's. They're a little more work than the old 3P's, but far more effective and, frankly, a lot more fun, because, not only will your listings be more likely to sell, but you'll get to use your creativity to get the job done.

Here are the New 3P's:
1. Prepare the Relationship
2. Prepare the Product
3. Put the Product on the Market

Which of these three P's do you think is the most important?

Which do you think is the least important?

Okay, I'll get back to that in a minute.

But first, WHY should you care if your listings sell? After all, even if your listing is a dog, isn't it cool to have your sign in a yard, so you can generate calls from buyers?

Other than the obvious benefit of getting a paycheck, why else might you want your listings to sell?

- Better Sleep—I don't know about you, but when I had a bunch of listings that weren't selling, I worried All night long. Every night. I hated that.
- Referrals and Repeat Business—As we'll discuss in a bit, it's pretty darn easy to disappoint a seller, and that seller will be talking to everyone he knows about his disappointment. That's not good for business at all. But if you perform for your seller, especially in a tough market, he'll sing your praises all over town (and call on you the next time he needs real estate services).
- Improved Market Perception—Can you imagine what it would do for the morale of your local market if SOLD signs started popping up on a regular basis?
- It's Our Duty—Sellers hire us to sell their homes, not to try to sell their homes. If you've ever had your own home on the market with another agent, you know how frustrating it is if your agent doesn't seem to care much about getting your house sold. I've gone through that before, and I felt deeply disappointed—almost hurt—that my agent didn't seem to be taking his duty as my listing agent seriously.
- Ego, Pride and Confidence—Hey, I'm an ego-maniac. But while I can admit I enjoy seeing my name on a sign in a yard, I'm way more enamored with that sign when it has a SOLD rider on top of it.

So, back to the question of which "P" is the most important. While they're all critical, of course, I believe that the second P (Preparing the Product) is #1. Followed by the first P (Preparing the Relationship), followed by the third (Putting it on the Market).

Does that surprise you?

Whether or not your listing is going to sell is determined before the sign ever goes into the yard, starting with your first meeting with a seller prospect. Once that property is on the market, our incredibly efficient systems take over, and the market will determine whether or not your product is sellable. If the market deems your product—that is, your listing—to be unsellable, then nothing you do will change that, with a few exceptions we'll discuss later.

So let's get to the First P, Preparing the Relationship.

P1—Preparing the Relationship

When I speak of the "relationship," I'm referring to your relationship with your potential seller. You desperately need that seller's trust and affection, but unfortunately the way our Get-a-Listing system is set up, it's very easy to create an adversarial relationship off the bat. After all, in that very first encounter with someone who will hopefully be your PARTNER in the home-sale adventure, you'll very likely be talking about two potentially confrontational topics: your listing fee and the market value of the seller's home.

But first, why is it so important to have a good relationship with a seller?

Because you're going to be giving your seller advice that he really needs to listen to, and if he's feeling a little hostile toward you or feeling that you're not 100% on his team, he may very well not listen or believe you. I know from personal experience with my own properties that if I'm mad at my listing agent, I might sabotage her efforts just to express my displeasure. Dumb? Childish? Oh yeah, but hey, I can admit that if I feel disrespected or ignored, I'll fight back.

Your seller needs to know that you care just as deeply about selling his house as he does. He needs to know that you are not condemning or belittling his situation. If your seller feels that you're there in his home to truly help him, over and above your desires for a paycheck or a signed listing agreement, he'll be your partner and he'll do what you ask.

So, how do you build this rapport? It starts with your very first meeting, even before the seller hires you. Unfortunately, the way we go after listings puts us in an adversarial position with someone we'll then have to work closely with. Think about it: first, we meet the sellers, tour their home, ooh and ahh over the wallpaper and the new granite countertops and pet the dog... then we sit them down and lecture them for an hour about market value and the value of our services. Then, if we get the listing, we're suddenly on the same team again with the common goal of getting the house sold. Can you see where this period in between can really damage the relationship?

Be Upfront With Your Commission

Talking about your fee is uncomfortable for everyone, so let's just get it out of the way. Stop making your seller prospects wonder what you're going to charge them. Have you ever sat through a sales pitch for a product you already wanted to buy, and the salesperson refused to give you the cost of it until the very end, after he's proudly gone through his dog and pony show? Aren't you sitting there nervous and on edge waiting for the punch line? It's a sales tactic, and it has no business in our conversations with a potential seller. It creates a wall between the two parties because it becomes clear that you're trying to sell the person something, rather than simply being there as a professional advisor to see if you can help.

Let me digress on this topic for a moment and then I'll get back to the commission negotiation question.

When you meet with a seller, don't think of the meeting as an opportunity to sell him on you. Look at it as a consultation to see if you can help. Maybe you can and maybe you can't; that's why you're there—to determine if it's a relationship worth pursuing for both of you. Go into the meeting emotionally prepared to turn down the listing, not because the seller is stupid or irresponsible or unrealistic, but because you simply may not be the right man for the job. If you and the seller are a good fit, well then, yes, you have a fee for your service, and that's fair. But don't look at a listing appointment as an opportunity to sell. It's a mutual interview where you both decide if you should work together.

Okay, back to your commission. Be upfront with it. Get it out of the way as early as you can. I actually had my commission posted on my website for all the world to see. If a potential seller asked me what I charged, I either answered the question directly or referred him to my website. Done.

If he wanted to argue with me about my fee, I'm was fine with that, and I didn't get up on a high horse and act offended or defensive. It's a reasonable question, and I treated it respectfully.

So, get the commission conversation out of the way as soon as you can. Then you and the seller can both calm down and relax. Try this strategy a few times and see if your relationship with the potential sellers starts off on a better foot. (We'll talk more about commission negotiation in Chapter Ten.)

The Market Value of the Home

The second potentially confrontational conversation is about the market value of the home. Unfortunately, if a seller is upside down in his mortgage, it's not likely there's anything you can say to make him feel better about it. But you can help him to see the true market value of the home without being condescending, patronizing or disrespectful. Besides the fact that being condescending, patronizing or disrespectful is rude, it also creates a wall between you and your seller, thus damaging the rapport you need in order to get this house sold.

So, how do you reach agreement on market value with an unhappy seller? Or for that matter, even a happy one?

Here's how I did it.

First, I always prepared a very detailed CMA. Some sellers wanted the gory details; others just wanted me to summarize it, but I always hadthe details available. Depending on the seller's personality, I'd either go through the CMA line by line, or I wouldn't, but regardless of my presentation, **I DID NOT provide any analysis of my data** during this initial conversation. Oh, I probably knew what the price range ought to be, but I didn't tell them that upfront. I didn't even include an analysis page in my CMA.

Why? Well, I wanted the sellers to review the data at their leisure and reach their own conclusion without being told what that conclusion ought to be by some smarty-pants real estate agent. Chances are that their initial expectation for pricing is going to be too high, so if I jumped right in and delivered the bad news, I'm the enemy. I'm someone they need to protect themselves from, almost. Then, I have to spend the rest of our time justifying my recommendation and convincing them, against their will, that I'm right.

But, here's what happens when you don't jump right in with your price: The sellers will ASK you for your opinion of market value, and they might even ask you what they need to do to get top dollar. Once they've asked, you're now perceived as the expert. They'll listen to you. They might even believe you. Sure, they're disappointed, but they aren't angry.

Also, when you give the sellers time to review your data, they'll very often reach the right conclusion, or at least be within shouting distance of it. You know how when you get bad news, you immediately panic and freak and cry and scream? And then, an hour later you calm down, accept reality and start figuring out how to deal with the problem. A few years ago, my computer crashed. At first, I was panic-stricken. I called Gateway, and the only option they offered was to send in the computer and wait a week to get it back. I was freaked out, but within an hour, I calmed down and started figuring out how to cope with this unexpected bad news.

Our sellers do the same thing, if given the time, space and respect they need.

This works like a charm. The seller feels he's a part of the process and that you respect his decision-making abilities.

If your seller IS upside down or in another distressed situation, it should go without saying that you don't belittle or lecture him or imply with your expression that you aren't sympathetic. Pretend that this seller is your mother or your grandmother—how would you want a real estate agent to treat your Mom or Grandma? With respect? With empathy? Or with a barely-disguised contempt for her poor judgment or inexperience with the home-selling process?

JENNIFER'S BLOG: *Houses Aren't Pet Rocks! No Amount of Marketing Can Sell a Stupid Product*

I remember interviewing for my second listing back in 1997. The seller asked me this question: "Jennifer, I assume our house will sell quickly because it's so cute (it was), but if it doesn't sell right away, what will you do?"

Hmmmmmmmmm. Heck, I dunno. I was a green bean agent; I'd only had one other listing in my career and didn't have a clue. I came up with something that probably sounded like this: "I'll do a broker open house; I'll do mid-week open houses; I'll distribute color brochures throughout the neighborhood and post an ad on the nearby college's bulletin board."

Lucky for me, the house did sell quickly, so I didn't have to implement my admittedly weak Plan B.

But it's now 12 years later and I still don't have a good answer to the question: "What will you do in 30 days if my house hasn't sold?"

However, with 12 years of experience under my belt, I KNOW that there ISN'T a great answer to the question! Especially if the seller is expecting me to reach into some magic bag of tricks and pull out a secret marketing strategy that I reserve only for my non-selling listings!

Here's the thing. Even if I HAD a magic bag of secret marketing tricks, why would I hold out using them until after the listing is stale? Wouldn't it make more sense to hit the market with all guns blazing?

But the truth is, I don't have a magic bag of tricks (and neither do you).

NO AMOUNT OF MARKETING CAN SELL AN UNSELLABLE HOME.

You can do broker opens every day of the week, distribute enough color brochures to kill a small forest and refresh your Craigslist ad every 21 days for the next five years and your listing will not sell if it's not properly priced, properly prepared and properly presented!

NO AMOUNT OF MARKETING CAN SELL AN UNSELLABLE HOME!

Our job as professional real estate agents is to know what it's going to take to get a house sold. We need to know how to price the home to sell; how to prepare our sellers for the reality of Being on the Market and how to help them prepare the home to evoke the most positive emotional reaction from the greatest number of potential buyers (and their agents). It needs to look good, smell good and photograph well. It needs to be easy to show without the distraction of barking dogs or a work-at-home owner. If there's an obstacle to sale, we need to recognize it and have the courage to be frank with our sellers about it (and help 'em fix it).

That's how you sell your listing. By working with your sellers to create a marketable product, not to throw time and money at advertising after the sign goes in the yard. Frankly, the MLS is an incredibly efficient system to sell houses and there's nothing we can do individually to out-market that MLS.

So, that's the first "P"—Preparing the Relationship. If you do this properly, the next "P" will go a lot smoother—Preparing the Product.

P2—Preparing the Product

Contrary to popular belief, the trick to selling a house is not in creative or aggressive marketing. Yes, marketing plays a part, but the truth is, the vast majority of the marketing agents do for their listings is mostly to market themselves. As we'll discuss here in a bit, a well-priced and well-presented listing will truly sell itself without a lot of effort on your part. Conversely, a poorly-priced and presented listing won't sell, no matter how many marketing dollars you throw at it.

Pricing

Stay tuned for Chapter Nine, which goes into deeper detail on pricing strategies and quandaries, but for our purposes now, let me just say that it's our job as professional real estate agents to know what the right price for a home is and be able to demonstrate that price to a seller without antagonizing him.

Especially when you are in a buyer's market, your price must beat the market, not just match it. If your listing is "fairly" priced compared to the competition, it probably won't sell unless there's something really special about it. If there IS something really special about it—like a fabulous mountain view or an extra-large lot or an unexpected gourmet kitchen—you still need to be priced in line with the less-fabulous competition, which your seller will likely see as underpriced. Your listing needs to be priced so that a buyer and his agent walk into the home and wonder if the listing agent (that would be you) blew it on the price. Your price needs to inspire the "wow" reaction, not just an "it's nice" reaction.

When pricing a home, be willing to talk to your gut about the right price. Unless you work in a tract home market, pricing is far more an art than a science. Yes, you need to take the objective parameters into consideration—the bedrooms, baths, square footage, etc.—but at least half of the Right Price will come from your experience with buyers and your gut reaction to the home.

I once trained a newer agent in my office, and had her help me get a listing ready for market. I sent her out with the assignment to do a market analysis on the subject property, and I did my own at the same time. We compared notes, and her suggested price for the house was $295,000.

Mine was $260,000. Why the difference?

Well, she showed me how she'd done her analysis, and it was 100% data. Facts, figures, numbers and averages. It was actually a pretty decent technical analysis, and I was impressed. But it was wrong.

Why was it wrong? Well, she didn't take into account a couple of issues which dramatically affect the market value of this home.

First, it was one house in from a very busy street. From the front porch and from the back yard, traffic noise was seriously apparent. It wasn't ON the busy corner, but was definitely affected by traffic.

Second, it only had one bathroom in a price range where two bathrooms were expected. The other otherwise comparable homes all had two baths, so my trainee adjusted for the lack of a bath by deducting $3,000 or so. But the reality is that the lack of that second bath is worth far more than that, because many buyers won't even consider a one-bathroom home—actually, they won't even know it's there because they'll screen it out during their search.

On paper, the houses she used as comparables were comparable. But she didn't have enough experience with buyers to know to adjust for features that will certainly be objections to buyers who look at the house.

To contrast, I looked at the exact same comparables she did and I adjusted for the gut reaction deficiencies. I asked myself, "At what price would I be excited about this listing?" and "At what price do I think I can sell this house?" I worked with buyers on a regular basis, so I could trust my gut reaction price, often much more than I trusted the objective facts and figures price.

There is no formula for properly pricing a house. Your experience really needs to factor in to come up with the right price. We know what buyers respond to, and sometimes that's the number of bedrooms and bathrooms. But most often, as we know, it's not. So trust your gut, or rather, ask your gut when you're pricing a house if you're in the right ballpark.

When you approach a listing interview as an opportunity to see if you can help—to see if you're the right man for the job and not as an

JENNIFER'S BLOG: *Two Types of Seller's Regret – Which Would You Prefer?*

Y'know, it's tough being a listing agent. No matter how good of a job you do, the margin for error is huge. If you sell the house too fast... you blew it on the price and "cost your seller money." If the house takes too long to sell... well, we all know what happens then. We didn't live up to our promises, and we disappointed our seller.

I just had a listing go under contract with multiple offers. Fortunately (for me), a good friend of mine had the same thing happen to him just a few days earlier and (unfortunately for him), his seller wasn't prepared. She blasted him for under-pricing her home and told him, rather snottily, that she had no intention of making any repairs at inspection.

So, Miss Smarty Pants me, I had warned my sellers up-front about what I call "Seller's Regret."

Here's the thing. In today's market, almost every seller will experience Seller's Regret. But it's their choice (sort of) which type of Seller's Regret they'll experience.

Type 1: "Darn! We underpriced our home! We should have priced it higher! That lousy real estate agent – she cost us money!"

Type 2: "Blimey. I wish we'd listened to our agent upfront. We should have made the repairs, staged it right away and priced it lower. Now, five months later, our listing is stale, we've paid $9,000 of our interest-only mortgage and are fair game for low-ball offers, if we get any at all. Let's look into renting it out."

If your seller is lucky enough to experience Type 1, he may never know the pain and angst of Type 2, and he may always wonder if he should have/ could have priced it higher.

But I find that when my sellers understand upfront what might happen, they're much less likely to "blame" me when it does!

opportunity to sell yourself or persuade someone to hire you—it gives you tremendous personal power when talking to a seller about price. The seller feels that power and, I believe, is comforted by it. They see you as an advisor, not a salesperson, so they are much more likely to trust you when you give them your opinion of value.

Okay, we talked about price, and price is critical. However, there are two other factors that can dramatically affect the market value of a home, and both are within total control of the seller. These factors are condition and accessibility. Let's hit condition first.

The Importance of the First Impression

When a listed property shows poorly, I blame the listing agent. Sure, it's technically the seller's fault if his home is dirty or not well-maintained or cluttered or whatever, but it's part of our job to make sure a seller understands just how critical condition is to the market value and the sales potential of his home. If we don't make him understand this, we have no one to blame but ourselves when an otherwise marketable listing doesn't sell.

Because our listing clients don't do this every day, they may truly not understand how important it is that their home makes a good first impression. They may not understand that if it's dirty, or if there are a lot of deferred maintenance items how much this will turn a buyer off. They almost certainly won't realize that a carpet or paint allowance will never overcome the disappointment a buyer feels when he walks into a house that needs new flooring or paint.

Several years ago, I met with a potential seller to discuss putting his tenant-occupied rental house on the market. The house was a mess. It smelled like renters; it looked like renters; it showed very poorly. Well, what the seller wanted to do was to display pictures of what the home looked like when he lived there, when it was well-decorated and smelled nice.

Well, I understand that, I really do. But the problem is, when a buyer walks in the door, she forms an impression. If that impression is that the home is dirty, that it smells, or that it's not well-kept, that house is toast. There's no way to overcome that first impression. She's not going to walk over the dining room table and look at the pictures of it and exclaim, "Isn't this lovely? I now like the house." No, she walks into the house, doesn't like it, and no pretty pictures are going to overcome that.

As long as you understand and believe in the importance of that first impression, then you will be able to convince a seller respectfully that the first impression is very important.

How to do this? Well, frankly, I cheated. I let my home stager do it. I had a fabulous stager who had the most amazing people skills, but she wasn't afraid to tell sellers what they needed to do. She didn't apologize for her recommendations, and by the end of her visit, the sellers were falling all over each other to do what she asked. I've seen her in action, and it's beautiful. She acts as if the sellers are perfectly willing to do everything she recommends, and that confidence both in herself and in the sellers works.

But what if you don't have a home stager?

Again, your belief and confidence in your own experience and expertise is key. If you can confidently, sweetly and gently tell your seller that his home needs to be as close to model condition as possible in order to get top dollar—or perhaps to even sell—he'll listen.

However, here's the REAL trick to getting your sellers to get their home in model condition.

Help them. No, you don't have to paint and clean, although probably most of us have at one time or another. I've watered lawns, painted bedrooms, mopped floors and even laid tile. But no, that's not what I'm talking about.

I'm talking about having the human resources available to help your seller get his house ready. If you can do that, you're golden. If you can offer up your handyman, house-cleaner and painter, the seller really has no excuse not to get his house ready.

I once listed my out-of-town rental property with a top agent in the area. Prior to putting the house on the market, my agent met me there and gave me a big laundry list of items she recommended I correct. Unfortunately, I was going back home in two days and didn't have time to coordinate all the repairs, and besides, I didn't know any local contractors. So, I didn't do them. My agent didn't offer to help, either; she just shrugged her shoulders and told me not to worry about it—maybe buyers would overlook the issues. Well, they didn't, and guess what? The house didn't sell. Of course, I was disappointed, but keep in mind that the real estate agent didn't get paid either. Had she offered to help me coordinate the repairs or even given me a list of reliable contractors to call, chances are would have gotten most of the work done.

The thing is, most homeowners don't have time to do the repairs themselves, and they don't know who to call. They also assume that having someone else make repairs will be expensive, and if they open up the yellow pages and start calling, they're probably right. But if you have reliable and reasonably priced contractors in your pocket, you'll be the hero.

My secret weapon was Bob. He once met me at my new listing and went through the house with the seller, identifying all the repairs that needed to be made prior to marketing the house. I'm sure my seller was expecting an estimate in the many thousands of dollars, so you can imagine her delight when his total bid came in under $2,000. Oh, and he could get it done in a week. And the repairs he made literally brought her tens of thousands of dollars, all for the cost of of one mortgage payment

Believe me, I was the hero that day — I now had myself a marketable listing.

So what if you show up at your listing appointment and the house is dirty, smelly and the lawn isn't mowed? The sellers apologize for the condition and promise you that it'll be cleaned up and ready to go by the time you go on the market. Don't take it as gospel. Because if they're willing to have you come look at their home when it's a disaster, chances are, they're willing to let buyers look at it that way as well.

What I did in this situation was to tell the seller I would give them a ballpark price in the current condition, then when were get ready to go on the market, if they'd done all these things, we would reprice and re-evaluate. Don't give them a price as if it's going to show like a model home, because you just don't know.

Unseen is Unsold—Accessibility

Your seller needs to know what to expect once his home goes on the market – the good, the bad and the ugly. He needs to understand how showings work: who will call him to let him know about a showing, who will show up at his door (especially if it won't be you!), how long they might stay, what they will be looking for and looking at. He needs to know that buyers will open his closet doors, look under his bathroom sink and even use his toilet. If he has any valuables, it's best if they're put away. Don't try to scare him, just deliver this information calmly, without any accompanying horror stories.

He needs to know what a preview is and why agents do previews. He needs to know that we, as listing agents, have very little control over who looks at a home, although we can certainly assure him that all buyers will be accompanied by a licensed agent. We are not in a position to screen buyers for financial qualification or "seriousness;" many buyers who look at his home may not be ready to buy for six months or more!

"Dear Jennifer: Should I try to enforce a 'pre-qualified buyers only' requirement on my listings? If so, how?"

JAH's ANSWER: Every once in a while I'll hear an agent say that he (or she) restricts showings on his listings only to buyers who are already pre-qualified for the purchase price. His rationale is that it's inappropriate to inconvenience a seller by allowing showings to buyers who in all likelihood cannot, or will not, purchase the property.

I disagree. I think it's simply a matter of setting appropriate expectations with a seller. In all my years, I never had a seller ask me to screen buyer showings; probably because I warned them upfront I have no control over who looks at their home. Some will be real buyers, some will be agents previewing the competition for their upcoming listing and some will be buyers out for the first time who won't buy for six months.

"However," I continue, "any activity is good activity, even if it doesn't result in a sale, because the home has been exposed to one more (actually probably two or three more, counting the agent and buyers) and exposure is always a good thing. We should do everything we can to encourage showings, rather than look for ways to trim them down. I'd much rather risk your being a bit inconvenienced by lookie-loo's than miss a previously lukewarm buyer who suddenly turns into a red-hot one."

My sellers ALWAYS said, "Of course! We want as many people as possible to look at our home!"

As a wise (wo)man once said..."Unseen is Unsold!"

Don't promise your seller anything you can't deliver...and you never know, sometimes those lookie-loo's turn into real buyers when they see the right property.

Why the Seller Must SCRAM for Showings

If you only have one conversation with your seller about improving the marketability of his home, have this one. Be sure he knows and understands that he needs to leave his home during showings. It's so important. Buyers need to be able to explore his home on their own, without worrying about annoying or offending the seller who is hovering nearby.

If a buyer has to whisper commentary to her agent or make polite conversation with the owner of the home, she's not going to feel at home. She's going to feel as if she's invading someone else's space and won't be able to get comfortable. If she's not comfortable, she won't fall in love.

Being at home is hard on the seller, too. He feels invaded but wants to do his part to sell his home to every buyer who comes over. He talks too much, hovers too much, offers too much helpful information and generally annoys the buyer and her agent. He's dying to know what the buyer thinks of his home and if that buyer appears noncommittal, his feelings get hurt.

I have sold many of my own homes, and even knowing the above, I still can't help myself. I talk to buyers and their agents; I point out special features; I follow them around. Even if I manage to restrain myself and stay out of the way, I'm still listening as hard as I can for any useful or interesting commentary about my home. If I can't practice what I preach, I know my sellers won't be able to either. So, for that reason alone, it's best that the seller vacate the home during showings.

What about the seller who works from home? The best you can offer is that he leave the house immediately when a buyer arrives. He should not return until the buyer leaves. He must make every effort to be polite and friendly when the buyer arrives at his door and to refrain from appearing inconvenienced or frankly, anything but joyful at the buyer's presence. He should grab his keys and head out the door with as little interaction with the buyer as possible.

Seller-Imposed Showing Restrictions

Living in a home that is on the market is inconvenient. If you've never done it, imagine how intrusive it would be to have strangers coming to tour your home, sometimes with less than an hour's notice. Strangers who are free to open cabinet doors, explore your closets or use your toilet. They might show up early, late or not at all. Sometimes you don't get the message that you have a showing, and you are surprised stepping out of the shower by a buyer agent and his client. You have to make your bed every morning, clean up your kitchen every time you use it, make sure the toothpaste spit is cleaned out of your sink! And this can go on for weeks or even months.

It's no wonder that sellers ask us if they can request notice for showings or impose limitations on the times their home can be shown. For heaven's sake, they still have lives to lead, children to feed, showers to take and, yes, they need their personal time so they can do whatever naughty things they like. And unfortunately, it's up to us to tell them the cold, hard facts of "being on the market."

The harder it is to show a property, the fewer showings we will have. The fewer showings we have, the longer the home will sit on the market. The longer it sits on the market, the lower the eventual sales price will be. A one-hour showing notice requirement probably won't affect the number of showings; a 24-hour notice requirement most definitely will.

If a seller imposes showing limitations, such as "no showings between 1p.m and 4p.m. for baby's naptime," we will miss showings. Will the home sell? Hope so. But missing showings does nothing to improve the marketing time and sales price of a home and will likely adversely affect both. I'm not saying it's fair, I'm not saying it's fun, it's just the way it is. And your seller needs to know this so that he can make the decision for himself and his family.

Remember that most sellers don't understand the process of working with a buyer. They don't realize that a buyer agent schedules time with the buyer to go look at houses, say from 1p.m. to 3p.m. on Tuesday. They'll want to look at as many homes as they can during those two hours. If early afternoon is not convenient for your seller and he turns down the showing requested by this buyer agent, it's likely the buyer will never see the seller's home.

How many times have you been asked, when setting showings for a buyer, if you can "come tomorrow morning instead." Well, no, I won't be with my buyer tomorrow morning, I'll be with her today! So, that listing gets put aside and probably forgotten about, especially in a buyer's market.

Your seller isn't trying to be difficult (usually); he just doesn't understand.

It's your job to make sure he does. Remember, our sellers don't do this every day. They don't know what to expect. They don't know what their role is in the process. And if we don't tell them, they're probably not going to know, and they're going to make up their own rules. They're going to think that it's helpful for them to be there to help show the property to prospective buyers. They might be angry when they find out you don't attend all showings. They may be surprised the first time they get one-hour notice for a showing.

If a seller is not prepared for the realities of being on the market, we're going to have a very unhappy seller, who, believe me, is telling everyone he knows how unhappy he is.

(See the Appendix for my "What to Expect" brochure for sellers to help them understand what they could expect from the process and from me, and what I expected from them.)

P3—Putting it on the Market

If you've done P1 and P2 properly, the third P—Putting it on the Market—will pretty much take care of itself, with a few exceptions that I'll get to in a sec. With our MLS systems and showing services and lockboxes and automatic Internet coverage, our system is brilliantly designed to efficiently sell houses. Truly, if a real buyer is looking for a house, he knows where to go, either directly to a real estate agent or to one of the better known Internet sites. If your product—that is—your listing is well-priced and well-presented, a real buyer will find it using the systems our industry has put in place.

That said, I believe that the primary audience for your listings is the real estate agent community, not the unattached buyers out there. Most serious buyers have an agent, and those buyer agents have tremendous power over which properties their buyers see.

How do you reach the real estate agent community?

With pricing, accessibility, an accurate and appealing MLS description and great interior photos. Would you agree?

I spent probably 70% of my marketing efforts on the real estate community and 30% on buyers. And I will say that the 30% I spent marketing to buyers was mostly to keep my seller happy. Most buyers are going to come through the agents, and it's our job to make that listing appealing to the agents.

So, if you've done the first two P's, and you have a marketable product that has a great MLS description and photos and is easy to show, **what else should you do to market it?**

In Denver, frankly, there wasn't much else I needed to do. Oh, I DID do other things, but as I mentioned, they were mostly to keep my seller happy, or perhaps to attract some unattached buyers my way. Yes, I did open houses; I did color brochures; I did virtual tours. I used Postlets and Craigslist, and I put the listing on my own website. But I didn't do broker opens, eflyers or enhanced REALTOR.com listings. I didn't do newspaper ads. However, if any of these marketing avenues are truly beneficial in your market, by all means do them. I worked in a resort community for a year and there was a need for advertising beyond the MLS. *Just don't depend on an aggressive marketing campaign to sell a product that isn't sellable.*

So, what if you believe your listing IS sellable, but it's not selling? Well, this happens to all of us, but I'll state for the record that I don't believe every listing is sellable. There are some properties for which there is truly not a buyer on the planet at this time, and there's nothing we can do to manufacture one. I had a listing once in a sweet little suburban neighborhood where there hadn't been a sale for over a year. Plenty of listings, but not one sale. I listed the house at a great price and had there been a buyer, the house would have been the first one to sell. But there wasn't, and it didn't. Eight months later there still hadn't been any sales in that neighborhood.

But what if that's not the case? What if houses in your listing's neighborhood are selling, just not yours? What if you are getting showings and inquiries, but no offers?

What's the first thing you should look at?

All together now... PRICE?

Nope.

When I have a listing that's not selling, the first thing I look at is NOT the price. Why?

Well, lots of reasons.

First, I'm pretty proud of my pricing expertise, and if I put a price on a property, unless the market has declined, I'm pretty sure I'm in the ballpark. And the thing is, buyers are well aware that they can "make an offer," so a minimal price reduction—say, $229,000 to $224,000 probably isn't going to make much of an impression on the market. In order for a price reduction to be meaningful, it's going to have to take that listing into a different pricing tier, thus introducing it to a whole new set of buyers who weren't looking at it before. And, depending on the price range of the property, that might mean a price reduction of $20,000 or more.

Now, think about what we could do with that $20,000—seriously. I'll get back to that in a few minutes.

Another reason I don't like the concept of automatically resorting to the solution of reducing the price is that it's really not what a seller wants to hear, and in that mindset, he's likely to question my professionalism and commitment. Let's face it, a price reduction is an awfully easy solution to offer and often abused by the real estate community. We all know agents who "buy" listings at a too-high price and then, as part of their game plan, beat up the seller later for a price reduction. And this isn't a secret to the general public—a lot of sellers are aware this happens, too. So, when your first and only solution is a price reduction, I believe it can really damage your credibility, especially if you recommended or agreed to the price in the first place.

But the main reason I'm opposed to looking at the price as the solution is because it's rarely the best solution for the seller.

When you have a listing that isn't selling, play detective to see if you can figure out what the problem is. This is where you earn money—and I say that with enthusiasm! It's a wonderful feeling to figure out a solution to problem and then watch the problem go away. Makes you feel really smart.

So, what might the problem be? It may be price, but it very well may not be. Spend some time really focusing on that listing that isn't selling.

Determine if there are potentially buyers and if so, why aren't they buying?

The solution might be very simple:

- It might be that your MLS listing is inaccurate or dull. Take a close look and jazz it up if you think it might help. Make sure your photos are in season.
- Check on the lockbox and make sure that the key is still working in the lock, or even that there's still a key IN the box. I can't tell you how many times I haven't been able to look at a house because there was a problem with the key or the lockbox.
- Schedule a surprise preview of your listing so you can see how well the sellers are keeping up the property. Sometimes they are, sometimes they aren't. Preview the house, or show it to a buyer, and don't tell the sellers that it's you who is coming.
- Evaluate the recent sales to see if there's some trend as to the houses that are selling, versus yours. Maybe all the houses that are selling are ranches and yours is a two-story, or vice versa. You can't necessarily fix this, but it might enlighten you as to what's going on. At least then you can look smart in front of your sellers!
- Look at your showing activity to see if your sellers are declining showings.

It might just be one or two of these simple items. However, the problem might be a little more complicated, but that doesn't mean it can't be solved outside of a price reduction.

Solve the Problem Instead of Reducing the Price

It's tough to price aggressively enough to encourage a buyer to overlook a structural problem, unpleasant smell or a lack of light, because you're dealing with a buyer's emotions with these issues, not his intellect. And as you know, the buying decision is almost always an emotional one.

Other issues, such as the lack of a second bathroom or garage, will keep buyers away from the home all together, because the home doesn't meet the parameters they gave their real estate agent. ("I need at least two bathrooms and a garage.") So again, price is not necessarily the best answer, especially if the buyer can have his wish list in his price range.

It's often much cheaper to Solve the Problem than to price for the issue that is keeping the home from selling.

Let me give you an example. Here was the description of a home for sale in old Denver:

"Lovely Victorian home, totally renovated. Gleaming hardwood floors, high ceilings, claw-foot tub, crown molding, new kitchen and baths, open and airy. New deck off the master suite, two-car garage, private yard with garden."

This home was listed with another agent and originally priced at $299,900, which seemed to be a reasonable price for the home, and it was a strong market. However, it didn't sell. And it didn't sell. And didn't sell some more. The price came down, down, down. After six months on the market, it was all the way down to $235,000.

I interviewed for the listing after it expired. When I met the seller at the home for my listing interview, the problem with the home was oh-so-obvious. The floors on both levels sloped dramatically. Almost nauseatingly. The average buyer would walk in, see the SCARY STRUCTURAL DAMAGE and go screaming out the door.

I called in my structural contractor to assess the situation. Turned out that the structural concerns could be safely repaired for around $15,000. If the seller agreed to the make the repairs, I told him I would be happy to market the home at $300,000. If he refused or was unable to make the repairs, I told him I would respectfully decline the opportunity to list his home.

He made the repairs. We put the house back on the market and sold it quickly for nearly full price.

The only solution his previous agent offered was to play the Reduce the Price game, trying to find a buyer willing to deal with a structural concern. Not many of those out there, I promise you. Buyers may deal with ugly carpet, smoke smells or bad landscaping but will rarely take on a foundation problem. You see, structural problems are nearly insurmountable in real estate. You almost can't price a home low enough to offset a buyer's concern that they're buying a money pit.

Here's another one:
I again took over a listing from another agent after a year of unsuccessful marketing. It was an exceptionally well-renovated five-bedroom home

on beautiful lot in a trendy Denver neighborhood. The first agent had also played the Reduce the Price game, and now the price appeared excellent. The sticking point wasn't readily apparent to me until I had been marketing the home myself for a month or so. The feedback coming in was that the kitchen was too small. Too small? In Denver? Older homes in Denver are not really expected to have generous eat-in kitchens, however, this was an unusually family-friendly home and was attracting young families in droves, since five bedrooms are hard to find in central Denver. Everyone who looked at the house loved it, but lost enthusiasm as they were mentally moving into the tiny kitchen.

I called in one of my independent contractors and got a bid to remove a wall in the kitchen and expand into the living room. It wasn't too expensive to do—around $7,000 and my seller was willing. Desperate is more like it. Fairy-tale ending...we sold the house immediately.

One more, just for fun:
My listing—a charming 1925 Bungalow in a popular neighborhood. Horrible kitchen, just horrible. A bad 1950's re-do with a vintage built-in oven that didn't work, a terrible layout, the refrigerator sticking way out into the room. When my seller and I discussed this potential problem, I gently suggested that we look into re-doing the kitchen. He got a look of horror in his eyes, and before he could say a word, I said "THAT'S the feeling buyers are going to have when they see this kitchen. We need to fix the problem for them." We were able to do a decent kitchen for around $5,000 (it was a small kitchen!), and the home sold without a hitch.

Obviously, these solutions were pricey, and not all sellers will be able to take them on. But more will than you might think, so it's worth having the conversation especially if you have the human resources to help them get it done. If the seller chooses not to address the problem, then you can resort to a price reduction, knowing you did your best! We'll talk more about this in the next chapter.

Don't be a listing agent who only contacts her sellers when she wants a price reduction. Do be a listing agent who solves her clients' problems. It's much more fun!

Under-promise and Over-deliver

Surprisingly, I see a lot of homes languish on the market because they are "over"-marketed. What do I mean by that? I mean that the MLS listing promises an attractive feature that, in reality, doesn't quite live up to its billing. The purpose of the over-promise is to, of course, encourage showings, hoping that if enough buyers walk through the door, one of them will buy the house. Duh.

Problem is... when buyers walk into a home and feel a sense of disappointment (instead of a sense of pleasant surprise), they emotionally detach from the home. Even if it's perfect for them in other ways.

Here's an example: I took a buyer to see a house that advertised a garage. The truth of the matter was that the garage was nothing more than a dilapidated metal shed in the back yard that might have been large enough to hold a small car. My buyer preferred a garage, but it wasn't on her "must have" list. However, her disappointment over the condition of the advertised garage soured her on the house overall, and we moved on.

I believe the listing agent would have been better advised to leave the garage off the listing and let buyers be pleasantly surprised by the nice big shed in the back yard.

If your listing has an awkward addition that isn't terribly useful, consider eliminating the square footage from your listing. When buyers and their agents look at the square footage figure in a listing, they make certain assumptions about the home's general layout and usability. When a significant portion of that square footage is tucked away and not part of the main home, the buyer will be disappointed in the functionality of the home and reject it.

It may be better to attract ONLY buyers who can live with the home's floor plan, buyers who will be delighted to have the "bonus" square footage, rather than buyers who actually need larger bedrooms, a formal dining room or whatever. Yes, this strategy will probably reduce the number of showings, but it will ensure that the buyers who do show up are more pre-disposed to like the home.

I once listed a home with a very nice enclosed sunroom off the kitchen. Including the sunroom, the home was around 1,100 square feet. However, the feedback we received was consistently along the lines of,

"The bedrooms are too small" and "The kitchen isn't big enough."

We realized that the buyers were anticipating a 1,100 square foot home, which implied certain dimensions of bedrooms and other living areas. But without the sunroom, the home was only 869 square feet which delivers a very different size of rooms! So we reduced the advertised square footage to 869, thus attracting buyers with lower expectations of room dimensions, yet who were pleasantly surprised by the "bonus" sunroom they weren't expecting!

Open Houses

Do you think open houses are a waste of time? The verdict is divided on this—some agents swear by them, others refuse to even consider doing them.

Well, I'm going to do my best to encourage you to do an open house for each and every one of your listings—at least once.

So...here we go—Jennifer's Four Reasons You Must Hold at Least One Open House for Your Listings:

Reason #1: It makes your seller happy.
Don't discount the power of a happy seller. And don't let the Old Fogies tell you it's possible to convince a seller that open houses are a waste of time. If you don't do at least one open house for your seller, he will doubt your commitment to the sale of his home. Oh, sure, he may agree with you to your face that open houses aren't necessary and that they only benefit the agent, blah, blah, blah, but when his house hasn't sold and he's getting nervous, he will remember that you haven't done an open house yet.

If I had a house on the market and my agent hadn't done an open house, he better not come asking me for a price reduction unless/until he does! Why? Because I'm pretty sure I'd feel he hadn't yet done his part to sell the house. Reasonable? Maybe, maybe not, but if I, as an experienced real estate agent feel this way, you better believe your sellers do, too.

Did you catch that? I think it would take some nerve to ask your seller to reduce his price if YOU haven't done the most visible, most expected form of real estate marketing there is—the open house. If your seller feels you're shirking open house duty, he might not be nearly as open to your suggestions as to what HE needs to do to help get the house sold.

A happy seller is a cooperative seller. And an uncooperative seller is a nightmare. You pick.

Reason #2: You can gather feedback from the public to share with your seller. I once held an open house for a new listing and it was fairly active— we had maybe 20 visitors in a three-hour period. It was a beautiful day, people seemed cheerful and chatty and the feedback was flowing. At the end of the day, I had a page and a half of scribbled down comments for my seller. Most of them were positive, a few mildly critical, but how long would it have taken me to get that much feedback from showing agents? Uh, like forever?

While my seller certainly appreciated the mass feedback, it is also incredibly helpful to me as the listing agent, to see firsthand what features really jumped out at the visitors. Every single one of them commented on the "great light and all the windows," and almost everyone complimented the oversized kitchen. Do you think this might help me in my marketing efforts?

I think spending three hours getting a concentrated dose of feedback from the general public is a great use of your time and a valuable service for your seller.

Reason #3: You'll become more familiar with your listing
How much do you really know about your listing? Chances are that you took a little tour with your seller on the day of your listing presentation and probably another one when you took your photos and measured the rooms. But you've probably never spent much quality time in the home by yourself, just absorbing the features or even the challenges the property offers.

When I did open houses, I'd check everything out, admittedly, often out of boredom. Yeah, I opened doors and drawers, wandered in and out of bathrooms, flipped switches to see what they did. And in the process, I discovered things I hadn't noticed before, especially if I'd always been accompanied by my seller on previous visits.

Okay, so this probably isn't a ginormous deal, but I do believe that by spending some quality time in listing without the distraction of rapport-building or just chattering with the seller, you'll be a better listing agent.

Reason #4: You might sell the house.
Yeah I know, fat chance, right? But it really shouldn't be discounted as a valid reason to hold the darn thing open for a few hours one Sunday.

« If it ain't fun, don't do it. »
Jack Canfield

Chapter Nine

Pricing Difficult Properties

(excerpted with revisions from my ebook The Art of Pricing)

I n *Sell with Soul*, I discussed some basic pricing strategies and approaches including the CMA Approach ("Five Steps to the Right Price") and the benefits and pitfalls of under-pricing. Let's dig a little deeper here.

Pricing Flawed Properties

Very few homes are perfect. Most buyers want perfect homes. Hmmmmmm.

Part of your job as a real estate agent is to be able to recognize property flaws and either offer solutions to the seller or understand how to price for the flaw(s), and, of course, how to tactfully communicate all this to a seller who may love his home just as it is or who doesn't have the time and/or the money to make the needed improvements.

Flaws can be either:
- Unfixable ("fatal"), or
- Fixable

Let's talk about fatal flaws first.

Fatally-Flawed Properties

As I mentioned in Chapter Five, a "fatally-flawed" property is one that has one or more unfixable defects that the market will likely perceive as insurmountable. Examples of fatal flaws might include a location on a busy street, a home that backs up to an unappealing commercial property (gas station, liquor store, etc.), high-tension power lines overhead, an unusually small lot or a shared yard, a lack of basement or an ugly exterior.

If your seller prospect's home has an obvious fatal flaw, you may want to consider declining the listing for the following reasons:
- There are very few buyers for a fatally-flawed home
- You'll do a lot of work and may never get paid
- Your seller prospect probably thinks his home is great
- Even if your seller acknowledges the flaw, he'll still blame you for the lack of activity
- The home will be expensive to market
- It may never sell
- If it does sell, the price will likely be unsatisfactory to the seller, and it will be all your fault

Fatal flaws can be either locational or property-specific.

Locational Fatal Flaws

Location, location, location. Heard that before? Sure you have! Home buyers want a great location. They may compromise on the number of bathrooms or the size of the garage, but they've been well-trained to want only the best address. Overcoming a bad location in real estate is tough, and the only answer is PRICE.

Here's an example: In Denver, there is a city-wide stretch of real estate I call the "Colfax Corridor." Colfax Avenue is a main thoroughfare that runs east-west through Denver, and there is nothing trendy about it. Colfax is where you find (depending on the part of town) liquor stores, car dealerships, drug dealers, strip clubs, cheap motels, McDonald's, etc. However, Colfax also runs through some rather desirable neighborhoods like Park Hill, Mayfair, East Montclair and Sloan's Lake.

A home one block north or one block of south of Colfax can be difficult to sell. The address is a dead giveaway—anything with a 1400 or 1500 address number is almost certainly within one block of Colfax.

Knowledgeable buyer agents often avoid showing homes on the 1400 and 1500 blocks because they know their buyers will be uncomfortable living that close to Colfax.

Other locational challenges may include:
- Homes on busy residential or commercial streets
- Homes on bus routes
- Homes that are subject to highway or train-track noise
- Homes in a flood zone
- Homes near apartment buildings or low-income housing
- Homes underneath high-tension power lines

Can you think of any locational flaws in your market?

Pricing for Locational Flaws
Locationally-challenged homes may be relatively easy to price, because there are probably other active and sold listings nearby with the same fatal flaw.

The First Step
Do a market analysis for the subject property using only similarly-challenged comparables. In other words, find other homes on the same street or block, or similar streets or blocks. For example, for Colfax Corridor homes, you would search for comparables sales with address numbers in the 1400's and 1500's.

If you are pricing a home on a busy residential street, search for comparable homes on that particular street, as well as other nearby busy streets. If you are pricing a home affected by highway noise, look at a map and find all the streets nearby that also are similarly affected by the highway, and then look for comparables on those blocks. If a home is affected by high-tension power lines, other homes in that neighborhood will be too.

These similarly-flawed comparables are your first line of attack. Technically, you should be able to determine the market value from this first CMA. However, it might not be enough ammunition for your seller prospect.

Let's take a moment and talk about that right now.

Chances are that your seller prospect has no idea he has a locational fatal flaw. Sellers rarely acknowledge that backing up to a restaurant or being a block from a highway might be a problem. When you mention it, he might argue vehemently to try to convince you that this "obstacle" is actually a benefit...and might even be worth extra!

If the home suffers from extreme highway noise and dirt, the seller claims that buyers will be willing to pay extra for the "easy highway access." A half block from Colfax? No problem, buyers will love the fact that they can walk to the...gas station. The home backs to a brightly lit grocery store? How convenient (and safe)!

Even if the seller doesn't claim that his fatal flaw is a benefit, he may still insist that buyers will overlook it (and you, as the listing agent, will surely help them). So, if they have high-tension power lines over their house that crackle and spark when it rains, you should point out to buyers that studies have shown no harmful effects from the electrical exposure. If there is low-income housing down the street, buyers will be proud to claim they don't suffer from "Nimby'ism" (Not in My Back Yard). If the home is on a busy street, you should ensure that buyers and their agents know how great the neighbors are.

If you take a fatally-flawed listing, it's now your problem, not the seller's. It will be your responsibility to educate the home-buying public out there as to why the locational fatal flaw is a non-issue or even a benefit. When the feedback starts coming in—and it's predictably that the home is "too close to the highway" or "too noisy" or "too close to the power lines"—the seller will get frustrated...with you, because your marketing isn't convincing buyers otherwise.

Step Two
So, step two of pricing a locationally-challenged home involves preparing a CMA for the home "as if" it didn't have the location flaw, as if it were one block over or two blocks to the north. You do this so that you are prepared when your seller prospect argues that "the home up the street just sold for much more than THAT!" You need to know what data the seller is referring to. If you are prepared, you won't be caught off-guard, which will do wonders for your confidence and air of expertise.

Step Three
After you've done both CMAs, try to determine the difference in value between the locationally-challenged homes and the homes without

the challenge. It won't be crystal clear, but you should be able to see some sort of relationship. For example, in Denver, homes in the Colfax Corridor can be priced up to $60,000 less than homes just a block or two farther from Colfax. This indicates that a price differential of $5,000 isn't going to cut it. Probably not even $10,000 or $20,000. Location-sensitive buyers (and most are) will pay $50,000 more for the exact same home that doesn't have a location issue. (The figures above assume a market with prices ranging from $250,000 to $450,000. Smaller or larger differentials will exist in lower- or higher-priced markets.)

Step Four
Next, take a look at the entry-level homes in the neighborhood. In other words, what is the cheapest home a buyer could buy in the subject property's neighborhood?

Do a quick market analysis using the cheapest homes (regardless of size) and comparing the features of your seller prospect's home to these homes. For example, if a buyer could buy into the neighborhood for $220,000, which gets him a small two-bedroom, one-bath home with no garage, and your prospect is a three-bedroom, two-bath home with a two-car garage, adjust the price accordingly, compared to these entry-level homes.

The reason for this fourth step is to determine the minimum amount buyers have to pay to live in that neighborhood. Most buyers buy location first. Once they're in love with a certain neighborhood or two, they will adjust their expectations to what they can afford. If your locationally challenged home competes favorably with the less-desirable entry-level homes in the same neighborhood, these buyers might just beat down the door and overlook the inferior location. In other words, if your listing is in the same general price range as much lesser homes, you'll be attracting the buyer who never thought she could afford such a nice home, and she'll be thrilled to sign on the dotted line. This strategy might even generate a bidding war, which we'll discuss shortly.

Step Five (when applicable)
If the seller purchased his home within the last three years, the MLS data from the time of his purchase may be available to you for review. He probably got a "discount" when he bought; a quick review of the sold comparables from the time period of his purchase should reveal that he did.

If so, you can gently remind him of this by saying, "It appears that you paid $150,000 for your home in 2014. As I recall, most homes in the area were selling over $200,000 at that time, so it looks to me as if the price you paid took the location into account."

Of note...
Please understand that a locational challenge does not mean a run-of-the-mill, "marginal" neighborhood. There are buyers in every price range, so the fact that a neighborhood is on the low end of the spectrum doesn't make it fatally-flawed.

However, if the reason the neighborhood is "cheap" is due to something external to the neighborhood (such as environmental contamination or proximity to a highway or airport), AND the buyer could look elsewhere and find more suitable housing in the same price range, that might constitute a fatal flaw.

Property-Specific Fatal Flaws
While location is the most common fatal flaw, there are plenty of others to deal with. If there is an issue with the home or lot itself, pricing will be more difficult than it is with a locational flaw. Because such a home is probably "unique," you won't be able to find solid comparables. In other words, there probably aren't three or four similar homes nearby with a similar challenge out there that have recently sold. So you're going to have to work a little harder than usual to determine the price. You'll really have to do your homework, both for yourself and to convince the seller.

Some examples of property-specific fatal flaws include:
- A steep driveway
- An atypical exterior
- A home that doesn't appear to fit in the neighborhood
- A too-close neighbor
- A shared yard or too-small lot
- Unfixable parking issues
- No basement in an area where basements are expected

But before you spend a lot of time pricing the home, ask yourself if the flaw is truly fatal or if it could it be fixed. For example, a structural problem can usually be safely repaired. It might be expensive to repair, but it can be done. Strong smoke smells can be removed by replacing carpet and window coverings, refinishing wood floors and trim and painting the walls. Even awkward floor plans can usually be improved by removing walls, building in dormers or expanding into attics or basements. Ugly exteriors can be beautified with the addition of a porch, a new exterior surface (stucco, new siding, paint) or professional landscaping.

Don't assume that your seller will be unwilling to take on a major project; even if he is resistant, you might plant a seed that will result in a sellable listing for you. And you'll look like the hero. When you truly try to solve your prospect's problem instead of just beating him over the head with price, he will appreciate your integrity and creativity, even if he can't or won't follow your advice.

If the problem truly is fatal (i.e. not fixable) or the seller is not in a position to fix it, then proceed with pricing the fatally-flawed home.

The steps in pricing a property-specific fatally-flawed home are similar to pricing a home with a fatally-flawed location.

Step One
The first step is to see if you can find any other properties that are truly comparable—that is, they have a similar challenge. For example, if most homes in the subject neighborhood have basements and your prospect's home does not, search for other homes without basements. Or if your prospect's home is ugly, search through the MLS photos of all the somewhat comparable homes to see if you can find some other ugly houses. If it is on an unusually small lot, search for other homes on small lots.

Ideally, you want to price your fatally-flawed listing against other fatally-flawed comparables, rather than simply deducting for the flaw. You want to see what the market is willing to pay for an inferior property.

If you can find enough similarly-challenged properties, do a CMA using the data from these homes. Once you've done this and have a market value in mind (or if you couldn't find any good comparables), move on to Step Two.

Step Two
Do a market analysis on the home as if it didn't have the flaw. For example, if it has no basement, compare it to similar homes with basements and deduct for the basement square footage as appropriate. If it's ugly, compare it to similar homes that aren't ugly.

Keep in mind that your seller prospect chose this home and, therefore, probably doesn't agree with you that he has a problem. If his home has no basement, he probably doesn't like basements and, therefore, believes that the lack of one is a bonus. Or, he thinks his ugly house is dreamy. So you'll need to know what his assumption of the price will probably be. It will likely be higher than yours.

Step Three
Next, as above, try to determine what the price differential should be to attract a buyer to the fatally-flawed home. If your second "as-if" CMA indicated a value of $310,000, for example, how much of a differential will you need to recommend to get buyers to overlook the fatal flaw? Be warned...the answer will be elusive and, therefore, difficult to explain to your seller.

To get to a number you feel comfortable with, try a few different things.
- Put on your buyer agent hat. If you had a buyer in the general price range of this home, what price would excite you enough to show it, even knowing about the challenge?
- What price would excite a buyer to make an offer, even though it's clear resale will probably be an issue down the road?
- What price would make this listing compete favorably with the competition?
- If you were to get the listing, what price would inspire you to call all your investors and tell them about it?

Communicating the News
If you're asking yourself how on earth you'll ever convince a seller that his home is worth $50,000 less than he thought, or that he should price his home to compete with "dumps" (in his opinion), that's a good question. Maybe you'll be able to pull it off, maybe you won't. A lot depends on the seller himself...how motivated he is to sell, how much trust he has in you and the real estate community in general, and whether or not someone else has already given him a much higher number.

Getting your seller prospect to agree with your pricing recommendation won't be easy. If you are prepared and the seller is intelligent and reasonable, you have a fighting chance. You have the facts on your side, and your confidence will go a long way toward convincing the seller that you are correct, even if other agents are advising him differently.

This is where your commitment to yourself is so important. You don't want this fatally-flawed listing if you can't have it at your price. That attitude alone will protect you, and it will be clear to the seller. Don't be snotty or defensive about it, just factual and perhaps a little sympathetic. Even if the seller doesn't agree with you, he will respect your professionalism and might even be impressed that you are willing to cheerfully walk away from his business.

If your seller prospect tells you that another agent said he can get more for the home than you believe possible, don't let that sway your thinking. If you've done your homework, you can be confident in your recommendation. The vast majority of real estate agents don't do their homework; they just wing it with the attitude that they'll deal with an overpriced listing after the paperwork is signed. So, don't feel that the rest of the world knows something about real estate that you don't. It's simply not true.

On the rare occasions when a seller acknowledges that he has a "problem," here are a few strategies to help him get to the correct decision.

- Discuss (don't promise) the possibility of a bidding war. Explain to the seller prospect that if you price the home aggressively, the market may notice and quickly bid up the price to a more appealing number. This is one of the best strategies for selling a difficult home—to price it way under market and generate a frenzy. Other agents and their buyers might even suspect that you (the agent) blew it—that you grossly underpriced the home, and oh boy, they better hurry and make an offer before someone else does! You can't guarantee a bidding war, of course; it just depends on how the market perceives the value of the home.

- If your seller prospect is sophisticated, you might try explaining that due to the marketing challenge her home presents, it needs to sell quickly before the listing gets stale. If a fatally-flawed home is on the market too long, buyers will shy away from it, simply because they know other buyers have. The reason a fatally-flawed listing hasn't sold is probably obvious, and very few buyers want to buy a home that so many other buyers have rejected. Reasonable sellers will understand this philosophy.

If your seller agrees to your pricing recommendation, take a moment to celebrate! You may sell this listing quickly, depending on the market and the extent of the flaw. You will probably see tons of action on the home (since on paper, it will look like a screaming deal). Prepare your seller for lots of activity. If the seller doesn't see things your way, that's okay. But you truly don't want the listing if she doesn't agree with you. Let the hungrier agents have it. It will be a good learning experience for them!

Fixable Flaws
Next, let's talk about fixable flaws.

We touched on Fixable Flaws in Chapter Eight in "Solve the Problem Instead of Reducing the Price." However, what if your seller can't or won't fix a flaw that you know will impede the sale of his home?

The first thing you must consider is whether or not you believe you can sell the home if the flaw is not fixed. I know your heart's in the right place when you agree to list a home that probably won't sell, but I beg you, just this once, to leave your heart out of it.

Fixable flaws that go unfixed will most often be perceived as fatal flaws by most buyers. But even if the buyer intellectually knows he can fix the problem, he probably doesn't want to, and if he's a retail buyer, he won't become emotionally attached to the home anyway.

So, assuming you decide you do want the listing, what are your options to maximize your chances of selling it?

Obviously, price is going to factor into the equation, perhaps big time. But let's touch on some other factors first that might offset the need for a dramatic pricing adjustment.

Maximize the First Impression
I don't believe that repair or decorating allowances are all that effective, especially considering that the lender won't allow such allowances over and above what can be applied toward closing costs, and many times, the buyer has already negotiated those into the deal. So, I'll just say this: allowances are best reserved for items that do not directly affect the buyer's emotional response to the home. No allowance can overcome an emotionally negative first impression, but might perhaps be effective to overcome more practical objections, such as an older furnace, dated appliances or landscaping.

Force the Issue (that is, disclose it in the MLS)

A counterintuitive approach to successfully marketing a substandard house is to be upfront, perhaps even obnoxiously so, about the home's deficiencies in your MLS description. For example, you might write: "Yep, this home is right next to the highway, so if that's a concern for your buyer, just pass this one by. But if your buyer is looking for more house than he can afford, with great access to transportation, put this house on your list."

Or: "Tenant-occupied and all that that implies. Tough to show and shows messy, and I guarantee the tenants will be there watching your every move, but it's priced to be worth the trouble."

Photos

Your MLS listing should always include interior photos, even if the house isn't terribly photogenic. Here's the thing—listings without interior photos, regardless of how well-deserved the lack of photos may be, are skipped over by agents and buyers during their online searches. Go ahead and post those photos, even though the home shows poorly. Just do your best to capture the best features of the home without misleading your audience as to its true condition.

Open your Checkbook

Of course, you can always pitch in and contribute toward the seller's efforts to get his home ready for market, either with your own manpower or your checkbook. I've done it, more than once, and in many instances it's been worth it to me (that is, I sold the house and got a paycheck). Would I have sold the home otherwise? Who knows? But if the needed repair or improvement is minor enough that you can afford it and you believe that it will make a difference in the marketability of the home, it's worth considering.

Staging

I'm religiously fanatical about home staging. Every one of my sellers in my last year hired my home stager upon my recommendation, and every last one of them felt it was money well-spent. However, I never recommend staging for a home that is poorly maintained or needs repairs. It creates a dissonance in the buyer's mind—the house looks pretty on the surface, but she can feel something isn't quite right. If she does contract on the home based on the pretty picture, the deal will almost certainly fall apart at inspection when all the deficiencies are pointed out to her.

That said, it is acceptable to stage a home that is dated but otherwise clean and in good repair. Just because the kitchen is vintage 1955 or the bathroom hasn't been updated in 30 years doesn't rule out the effectiveness of staging. Grandma's house that is clean and in decent shape can be an excellent candidate for a little stager-created Pottery Barn flair!

And again, this might be something you're willing to pay for, with an agreement of reimbursement from the seller at closing.

Price
Which leads us to the price. How do you price a home that doesn't show as well as its competition? Well, the first line of attack is to find active listings and sold comparables that also show(ed) poorly, and price accordingly. This is by far the most accurate pricing strategy in this situation.

It's far more difficult (not to mention inaccurate) to price against better-showing and/or maintained homes and adjust for the work needed. Besides the fact that the buyer for the two different types of properties is not the same person, you also have to factor in not only the raw cost of the needed improvements, but also the enhanced appeal and wider audience for the fixed-up property. Enhanced appeal + wider audience = more money... but how much more? That's a tough one.

At the end of the day, it's always your decision to choose to take a listing or politely decline. If you decide against it, don't worry; someone will take it, and they might even sell it. But I encourage you to ask your gut, and then trust what it tells you. You'll get far more enjoyment out of your real estate career if you follow your instincts!

> **‟** *The I'm-going-to-win-no-matter-how-I-have-to-do-it attitude just doesn't seem to fit. For me, a contest isn't a success unless it was fun, whether or not I win.* **”**
> *Margo Godfrey Oberg*

Chapter Ten

Getting What You Want—The Art of Negotiation and Persuasion

Negotiation

I used to be afraid of the word "negotiate." I considered it, paradoxically, to be both beneath me and also over my head. My vision of a master negotiator was someone who was expertly manipulative, who had the attitude of one of my first clients: "It's not a good negotiation until both sides feel some pain." I pictured a cheesy salesperson in an expensive suit making his opponent feel inadequate and inexperienced so that she eventually gives in against her will.

I wanted no part of that!

On the other hand, I was also intimidated by the concept of becoming a good negotiator. I read books on the Art of Persuasion and Negotiation and found the methods to be interesting but not terribly practical. When I'm having a conversation with someone, I simply can't intentionally steer the conversation in the direction I want it to go using rehearsed scripts. And, frankly, being a girl, it's important to me that there is a mutual trust in any conversation I have—y'know, that whole feminine relationship-building thing.

So, for years, the idea of being a great negotiator wasn't something I was interested in becoming.

But you know what? Somehow I became one without even trying. No, not by listening to subliminal sleep tapes, reading books or taking an expensive weekend course, but rather by trusting my own common sense and understanding of human nature.

In this chapter, we're going to talk about all sorts of negotiations, including some situations that may not exactly qualify as negotiations, but use the same skills and philosophies. I'll tell you this upfront—it all comes down to a few things:

1. Respecting and acknowledging the intelligence of the guy on the other side of the table
2. Looking for a win/win wherever possible
3. Striving to see the situation from all perspectives and acting accordingly

Commission Negotiation

In Chapter Eight, I discussed a very simple method for getting the listing commission out of the way when talking with a seller prospect so you can move on to less adversarial topics. Remember what I advised? Just tell 'em what you charge, upfront, without fanfare or sales pitch.

Later, in Chapter Twelve, you'll read my thoughts on the pros and cons of discounting your commission as a business model.

Here, we're going to cover some concepts and strategies for determining your own personal fee structure and communicating it to a seller in a way that is persuasive, yet respectful.

I once co-hosted a teleseminar workshop with four other experienced agents who shared their strategies for getting seller buy-in on their fee structure and compensation philosophy. One of the prerequisites for my guests was that they were not to describe any tactic that belittled or disrespected the seller or any technique that was centered on essentially whining about how little we end up with at the end of the day. No, I instructed my guests to present strategies that made the seller feel he was getting a fair price for the service provided, without feeling beat up, bullied or condescended to.

It was a great workshop, and we got tremendous feedback from the audience. What was particularly valuable was that among the four speakers, there were four different approaches, suited to four different personality types. Here is a summary of the different approaches presented:

Tupper Briggs (http://www.tuppersteam.com): Tupper Briggs is a top producing agent in the Evergreen, Colorado market. As of this writing, he's with RE/MAX and is one of the go to agents if you're looking for someone to refer to in the foothills outside of Denver. Tupper's approach to commission negotiation is based on his solid track record and prowess in his market area. He can objectively demonstrate, using up-to-the-minute data directly gathered from the MLS, that his listings sell faster and for more money than the "average" agent in Evergreen. If a seller balks at his fee, he can easily show the seller how his marketing package nets the seller more money, even if his fee is higher than the competition's.

Admittedly, this approach is only useful if you have the stats and reputation to back up your claims, along with the quiet confidence that being the market leader gives you. But it's certainly something to shoot for!

Jackie Leavenworth (http://www.coachjackie.com): Jackie is The Real Estate Whisperer, and if you haven't "met" her, you should. She and I have a somewhat similar approach to the art of selling real estate, so if you like me, you'll like her. Jackie's approach to commission negotiation left the audience in stunned silence. It was simple, logical and oh-so implementable.

First, Jackie describes her commission as a "success fee," which she says usually inspires the seller to ask her to explain. Neato! The perfect opportunity to remind a seller that we don't get paid until we perform, in case they forgot.

In the event that a seller asks Jackie if she will reduce her fee, Jackie has several responses, depending on the situation and personality of the seller.

Response #1: "No, but thank you for asking! Do you have any other questions I can answer for you?" When said with a warm smile, this response is amazingly effective, without being patronizing. Try it yourself and see how it feels.

Response #2: "No, but thank you for asking. I used to reduce my fee, but found that it didn't work for me." When the seller asks why, she explains that what sellers want most is an agent with integrity and charging one person less than another would jeopardize her integrity.

Response #3: "No, but thank you for asking. This is exactly when you should be testing my negotiation skills!" She explains to the sellers that, because their home is probably their most significant asset, they want to hire an agent (whether Jackie or someone else) who is a strong, confident negotiator.

If you're interested in Jackie's full dialogues for commission negotiation and other situations, check out her "Negotiations: The Games People Play" CD at her website (www.coachjackie.com).

Scott Nordby (http://www.iregroup.com): Scott is the broker/owner of Innovative Real Estate Group in Denver.

Scott's approach is to begin the conversation by asking the seller what are the three most important things to her when hiring a real estate agent. Depending on the seller's response, Scott then digs deeper into what she expects from her agent with regard to communication, marketing or whatever her hot-buttons are. If one of her hot-buttons is commission, Scott asks her what she believes a reasonable fee might be. According to Scott, the seller almost always responds with the number Scott is looking for, but if she doesn't, he gently explains that his fee is x% and why he's worth it. And the kicker is (for all of these strategies, actually), that he believes with all his heart that he IS worth that fee and is willing to risk losing business to protect it.

Loretta Hughes (http://www.exitrealtyfusion.com): Loretta is a broker/owner of an Exit Realty franchise in Regina, Saskatchewan. Loretta definitely Sells with Soul and teaches her agents to do the same. I always enjoy chatting with her about her latest successes!

Loretta's approach is to raise the total commission payable so that the buyer agent co-op is far above what most other agents are offering, thus encouraging showings. She demonstrates to the sellers if they net a higher price using this strategy (which is likely due to the increased activity), the higher commission they're paying is offset—that is—the sellers end up with a higher net proceeds. Loretta does not participate in the higher commission—she gives all of it (over and above her own normal listing fee) to the buyer agent.

One beautiful side benefit of this strategy is that the seller is far more interested in learning about how the higher buyer agent co-op approach works that he often completely forgets to attempt to negotiate Loretta's side of the commission!

Other Commission Considerations

Offering Sellers a Menu of Services

Have you ever heard the commission-negotiation-avoidance strategy of creating a menu of packages for a seller to choose among? For example (all figures are illustrative only), you might offer a 4% package that includes minimal services; a 5% package that has a moderate level of service and a 6% package that includes a kitchen-sink level of service.

Sounds good, doesn't it? After all, it demonstrates to the seller what you actually do to sell a house and probably reduces the likelihood of his asking for a discount. If he wants to pay less, he gets less. His choice.

I think this is a lousy idea. Why?

Oh, let me count the ways...

You want to sell the house don't you? Yes? Well, then why are you asking your seller how to market it? As the expert in selling houses, you know what needs to be done, and you, as a professional, should do those things.

You should also know what doesn't sell houses in your market. And you shouldn't be offering and charging for those services if you (as a professional real estate agent) know they aren't effective.

When I got a new listing, I really wanted to sell the darn thing, and I spent a lot of time and energy figuring out what we needed to do to make that happen. By "we," I mean me and my seller. I didn't market every house exactly the same, nor did I advise every seller to do the same things. It was part of my service to analyze each situation individually and proceed accordingly. Some listings benefit from open houses, some don't. Some (most) homes need staging, some don't. Some listings will benefit from newspaper ads, most won't. It's my job to know these things.

Besides, you want to provide exceptional service to all your clients, don't you? Don't you want their future business and referrals? By purposely limiting your service (if it affects the marketability of the home), you may be blowing your reputation and credibility with this client and potential source of future business. And of course, you may also be blowing your chances of getting a paycheck if your seller doesn't pick the right package and the house doesn't sell.

Be a professional real estate agent and do what it takes to sell your listings. That's your job.

JENNIFER'S BLOG: *Sex, Lies and the Assumptive Close*

I've been watching Sex, Lies and Videotape on DVD this week. Remember this movie? No? Well, it was made in 1989, so probably many of you missed it due to your crazy elementary school schedule. Anyway, earlier this week I promised to help out the more introverted among us with some tips for "smoothly closing" our clients when it's the right thing to do, and lo and behold...right there on my movie screen is a perfect example of a Soulful Assumptive Close! So, I'll start there.

In the movie, Graham (James Spader) asks Cynthia (Laura San Giacomo) to let him videotape her. I'll spare you the details, but let's just say that she's intrigued yet a little unsure. She wants to do it, that's clear, but she's uncomfortable coming right out and saying so.

Cynthia asks a series of delaying tactic questions ("How long will it take?" "Do I sit or stand?" "Will anyone else ever see this tape?"). Graham quietly answers her questions and at the same time, casually picks up his video camera, loads a tape and sets up the tripod. He sits down in an easy chair and gestures for her to relax on the sofa. He turns the camera on and begins asking questions. She can either answer them, thus agreeing to be videotaped, or refuse to answer, thus declining to be videotaped. The power was always in her hands; Graham just made it easy for her to say yes.

Fade Out

The Assumptive Close is defined as "acting as if the prospect has already made the decision." What you're supposed to do is to move the conversation toward the next steps without waiting for permission or a specific request to do so. Typical examples of the Assumptive Close in real estate include:

"Would you like to ask for the refrigerator in your offer?"

"Would this Friday be good to go on the market?"
"Let's meet back at the office in an hour to review the comparables."

When done respectfully and with the right intentions, the Assumptive Close will be welcomed by your buyer, seller or prospect. They'll be relieved you took control and will enthusiastically follow your direction. They'll happily go where you lead and love you for it.

And of course, they still have the power to say no or halt the process, and certainly you should respect their wishes if they do so.

Give it a try. The Assumptive Close should come naturally with a little practice. Try using it in other areas of your life if you're uncomfortable experimenting with your clients. When it works, it's a beautiful thing!

The Art of Persuasion

For some reason, the real estate industry seems to think that the best way to persuade someone to come over to your side of the argument is to prove to them that you're right and they're wrong. There are whole courses that teach agents how to "Overcome Objections" with ridiculous, condescending, patronizing scripts designed to prove your brilliance at the expense of your ~~opponent's~~ client's dignity.

But you know what? No one really wants, appreciates or believes someone else's opinion until, well, they want it.

How do you know they want it? They ask for it.

Have you ever noticed that your unsolicited advice to your friends, family, spouse or children is largely ignored or even resented? Irritating,

For example, here's a script I saw promoted as an "effective objection-buster" to a seller's concern about under-pricing his home:

"Mr./Ms. Seller, how long have you had your real estate license? Oh, you don't have a license? Well, I've been selling real estate since 1925 and have sold over 20,000 houses. Do you tell your accountant how to do your taxes? Do you instruct your veterinarian on how to treat your puppy? I didn't think so. You trust their knowledge and experience. I recommend we price your property here: _____. Sign here."

isn't it? I mean, you know what they're doing wrong, what they should be doing instead and exactly how to help them get there, and they just don't appreciate it?! Are we just surrounded by ingrates?

Ummm. Well. Truth be told, I don't much like being told what to do either, regardless of the good intention of the "tell-er". Any sentence that starts out with any semblance of words "you should" i likely to result in a bristly response from me. Probably from you, too...I can't say much appreciate any helpful advice on how my character or behavior could use some improving either. Might just spark an argument, in fact. Might? It definitely will.

So, if we stipulate that this is true in our personal lives, doesn't it make sense that it might also apply to our real estate careers?

I think it does. I think we can gain considerable credibility with our buyers and sellers by not offering them our advice and opinions off the bat. Let them tell their story. Then ask them lots of questions, and really listen to the answers; take notes. It's likely this will be the first time in a while that someone has actually shown such an interest in them, and believe me, they'll enjoy their moment in the spotlight!

But... but... but! Yeah, I know, didn't these people hire you for your brilliance? For your expert advice? Don't they want your opinions?

Well, maybe, but just because you're talking with them in a business environment doesn't negate the fact that they're human beings and probably don't care to be "advised" before they're ready to be.

The problem is that when you "advise" someone before they're ready, it will be perceived as "arguing." Yes, yes, I know. You consider it "sharing your expertise" or even "taking control of the situation." But for the sake of this chapter, let's call it what it is...arguing.

Say your buyer client changes her mind about where she wants to look for a home. She's dismayed by the prices in her preferred neighborhood and decides to look in a less desirable location so she can get more square footage. What do you do?

Or let's say that your seller wants to flat-out reject a low-ball offer on her home. What do you say?

How about the seller who accuses you of under-pricing his home when it sells on Day One? Do you defend yourself?

What about that buyer who falls in love with a townhouse, even though you know a single-family home would be a better investment?

How about when the parental units want to check out that house their darling child is considering buying?

Our clients are intelligent human beings, capable of making their own decisions. Okay, so maybe some might be more capable than others, but all deserve our respect and assumption that they have thought through their situation (after all, they have more at stake than we do) and reached a decision they feel works for them. That's the first step—to show our clients that we respect their intelligence and their right to make their own decisions. When you immediately "argue" with your client's point of view or decision, this sends the opposite message.

Now, I'm not saying that you shouldn't have an opinion or be allowed to voice one. But, if you don't want to be accused of being argumentative, you need to take a different approach from simply saying, "Are you sure you want to do that?" or "I really don't advise that" or "I don't think that's a good idea." Say something like that to me after I've given my personal situation some thought and y'know what? I'll dig in my heels and commit even stronger to my position.

You know what else? I think I'm a pretty smart cookie. I'll bet you think you're pretty smart, too. In fact, I'll bet most of the people on the planet have a healthy respect for their own intelligence. Argue with me, and guess what? I might think you aren't quite as smart as I thought you were. After all, you're arguing with me, and I think I'm right. What does that make you? Wrong...and kinda dumb. "Poor thing, you just don't get it," I think.

So, what's the solution? Ah, GLAD YOU ASKED. Because that's part of the solution. Wait for your clients to ask for your opinion or advice. Once they do, they'll actually listen to it. If they don't ask, they truly don't care, and any advice you give that is counter to their opinion will be discounted anyway. They're the boss, after all, and if they want to kill their deal, it's their choice. And it is their choice (not yours)!!!

If you show respect for your clients' positions and don't argue, they probably will, at some point, ask you for your thoughts. At that point, you can give your opinion respectfully, all the while keeping your paycheck out of the conversation or your thoughts.

So, let's take the scenarios presented above and see how we can respond without arguing:

Scenario #1: Your buyer wants to look for a home in a less desirable neighborhood so she can get more square footage. This is a no-brainer. Show her the houses. Let her do her own soul-searching. You can't predict the future anyway, so who knows? Maybe it'll turn out to be a great financial decision, maybe not, but there is no room for argument here. Last time I checked, adult human beings have the right to live where they want without getting permission from their real estate agent.

Scenario #2: Your seller is offended by a low-ball offer and wants to reject it outright. Obviously, we want the seller to counter any offer he receives, but first, we need to show support and be offended right along with him. He's probably expecting you to argue with him and is steeled for it, so by not arguing right off the bat, he'll relax. Once he does (if he doesn't, you might need to let him sleep on it and re-group the next day), you could offer to draft up an equally ridiculous counterproposal (full price, 21-day close, whatever) and see if he's open to that. Then maybe you can encourage him to give a little bit so the buyer doesn't feel like a total putz. But again, if he wants your advice, he'll ask for it. If he doesn't ask, he doesn't want it, won't listen to it and will just be annoyed by it.

Scenario #3: Your seller accuses you of under-pricing her home when it sells on Day One. Ouch. Okay, let's imagine what's happening in her life. She's telling all her friends that her house sold in 24 hours, and are they congratulating her? Nope. They're telling her that her idiot real estate agent under-priced the home. Yipes. Do you defend yourself? This is a tough one, because every bone in your body is screaming to do so. But be careful. Your seller is expecting you to be defensive, so don't be! Agree that the home might have been under-market. Congratulate her for having such a nice property and working so hard to get it ready for market. Leave YOUR efforts out of it. If you schmooze her, she'll return the favor. Argue with her, and she'll argue back. No fun.

Scenario #4: Your buyer decides to buy a townhouse, but you know that a single family home is a better investment. Another no-brainer. If she's concerned about investment, she'll let you know, and you can share your thoughts. But show her the respect she deserves, and let her make her own housing decision.

Scenario #5: How about our all-time favorite—when our buyer brings in dear old Dad to ask his advice on whether or not to buy that charming old house with the amazing woodwork? Ooooooh, this is a perfect time to not speak until spoken to! Offer advice that contradicts Dad's, and you're toast! Let Dad do his thing, and wait patiently for him to ask you what you think. Believe me, your buyer knows her Dad better than you do, so if he's being a pain in the a$$, your buyer recognizes it too.

We are in a business where egos and emotions are involved in almost every decision. Acknowledge it, work with it, use it to your advantage.

The Power of Reverse Psychology

Inquiring agents want to know..."What's the best way to convince a FSBO to hire an agent (preferably me)?" or "How do I persuade a prospect that I'm the best man/woman/child for the job?" Most of the advice provided involves beating clients and prospects over the head with a long list of "reasons" they "should" listen to you.

But think about it. When a sales-type comes at you with his practiced pitch full of "features and benefits," don't you tend to shift into defense mode, mentally arguing with him, point by point? After all, there's no way this salesperson is smarter or more informed than you are, so why is he standing right there telling you he is?

Brian Sullivan of Precise Selling (www.preciseselling.com) calls this behavior "Contrarian." He defines "Contrarian" as "somebody disposed to taking an opposite position: somebody who is prone to opposing policies, opinions or accepted wisdom." The reason for contrarianism is that we (human-types) love our OWN opinions far more than we love anyone else's. In order to connect with your contrarian customer or prospect, you need to let him make the statements of opinion (er, sorry, fact).

But enough pseudo-sales training from me; I know I'm no expert there. Here are some examples of reverse psychology in action from the world of real estate:

When competing for a listing...you say:

"Frankly, any competent real estate agent can sell a home that's well-priced and well-presented. When choosing an agent, just go with your gut feeling—who do you feel the most comfortable with and who seems to care the most getting your home sold?"

When talking with a FSBO...you say:
"I'm sure you'll be able to sell your home on your own. It's not rocket science, after all. But if you have any questions during the process, feel free to give me a call."

When working with a new buyer...you say:
"I have all the time in the world to help you find the perfect home. I want you to be thrilled with the home you purchase, and I'll be here for you no matter how long it takes."

When discussing market value with a seller...you say:
"If another agent thinks they can get you that price, I say, hire him! He may know something I don't about selling real estate in this market. I certainly don't want you to feel that you hired the wrong man for the job."

OR

"I'll tell you what. If you need that price to make selling worthwhile, let's wait a few months. Maybe the market will improve. I'll be happy to keep you updated on the neighborhood activity, and when it reaches that level, we'll hit the market right away!"

When you acknowledge the intelligence and competence of another human being, she will automatically think you're just a little bit smarter than she initially suspected. But lo and behold...she's still a Contrarian, so you may find that she begins to argue with you anyway! And that's what you want!

For example: "I have all the time in the world to help you find you a home..." Your buyer's response: "Oh, no, I want to find a home as quickly as possible!" (She said it, you didn't. It now becomes HER goal.)

OR: "If you need that price to make selling worthwhile, let's wait a few months..." Your seller prospect's response: "Oh, no, I need to sell right away! How can I do that?" (Now, suddenly, you're the expert. In HIS opinion.)

It might be different if we were doctors or attorneys or such. After all (lawyer jokes aside), the general public has a great deal of respect for these professions. But let's face it. We're real estate agents. We're perceived just slightly above car salespeople. We're paid on commission. We are not, as a general rule, the most believable group of people on the planet.

Try some reverse psychology next time you want something. Feel the power...

Please, Please Don't Bury My Deal Yet!!!
by Bryant Tutas (http://www.brokerbryant.com)

So, today I placed one of my listings pending. It took a week to get this deal negotiated. This deal is another example of how hanging in there and not giving up can have positive results. Now, this was not a huge deal; in fact, it's a vacant lot, and the final agreed price is only $41,000. But you know, that doesn't matter to me; it's the game, not the price, that I enjoy. I negotiate these deals just as hard as I would any other. After all, the last time I checked, $41,000 is a lot of money. My seller is happy to get it and can use the money.

Anyway, we have been going back and forth for a week with the buyer and their agent. The lot was listed at $49,000, and the Buyer's first offer was for $35,000. So, my seller decided to counter-offer at $45,000, since he really wants to sell the lot. Two days later, the other agent sends over another counter-offer of $37,500 and lets me know this is the best the buyer can do. He has no more money.

When real estate agents tell me that, I don't think I retain that information for more than about ten seconds. Rule number one in negotiating is never say, "this is our final or best offer." Always leave the door open for negotiations. Anyway, my seller counters back at $42,500. Miraculously, the buyer, who has no more money, counters at $40,000. My seller, feeling generous, counters again at $42,000.

Two days later, after not hearing back from the other agent, I decide to give her a call. She lets me know that the buyer is not willing to go any higher, so she decided the deal was dead. Now folks, I never let a deal die until I have tried everything I can to get an acceptance. So, I tell her I will let my seller know that the buyer's last offer stands. Of course, my seller has to counter one more time so he goes back at $41,000. Eureka!!!! The buyer accepts the offer and we are pending. NEXT!

The moral of this story is never ever give up on negotiations. Work it until it is either pending or dead and buried. You just never know. If I had not taken the initiative to call the other agent, this deal would not have happened. It may be a small deal, but my seller deserves no less than my full and complete attention towards getting this done for him. After all, $41,000 is a lot of money. Now he can afford to buy me a nice Christmas present. BTW, for anyone shopping for me, I wear JUMBO!!!

How to Convince a Buyer that NOW is a Great Time to Buy!

A common complaint around real estate offices is that buyers are sitting on the fence, unwilling to make a commitment to purchase a home. Prehaps they are concerned about the market, and don't want to buy a home that may plummet in value the day after closing.

So, how can you get your buyer off that fence and convince him now is a good time to buy?"

You can't, and you shouldn't.

It's just wrong to "convince" someone to make a huge decision like whether or not to purchase a home! Our buyers are adults and should be allowed to reach their own conclusions based on their personal circumstances, beliefs and tolerance for risk. That said, you can help them reach the right decision for themselves by being knowledgeable, supportive and non-pushy.

- Knowledgeable: Stay on top of market trends and data. Read those articles and reports that come across your desk or email regarding the local real estate market and economy (both the positive and the doom and gloom ones). Be prepared with facts and figures, in case your buyer asks for them (see below).

- Supportive: Did you ever notice that when someone argues with you, you tend to dig in your heels and hold even more firmly to your opinion? I know I do. You probably do, too. So, if your buyer declares that the timing isn't right for him to buy a house, acknowledge and respect his position. Don't argue with it! Have you heard the saying, "Those convinced against their will are of the same opinion still?"

- Non-pushy: Our buyers know that we're paid on commission. Therefore, if you appear to be pushing them to do something they've decided they don't want to do, you'll likely lose their trust and, subsequently their future business. Buyers expect their agent to be looking out for their best interests, so any indication to the contrary (i.e., the agent seems more concerned with a paycheck than with the buyer's needs) may seriously damage the relationship.

The Punch Line: Here's the cool part. If you are knowledgeable about your local market, supportive of your buyer's opinions and you don't push him, one of two things will probably happen.

First, once the buyer realizes you are on his team, he may actually ask you for your opinion on the matter, at which time you are free to give it (this is where having the above-mentioned market knowledge comes in handy). Once he asks for your advice, he'll be much more willing to listen to it than if you'd pushed it on him uninvited.

Or second, he may decide not to buy a home right now but will be back on your doorstep at a future date when he feels better about the market, the economy or his financial circumstances. And there's nothing wrong with a full pipeline!

Seven Bonus Negotiation Tips

Here are some additional random tips to help keep the balance of power tilted in favor of your buyer or seller.

1. When negotiations get hot and heavy...withdraw. Dead silence from your end. Let the other side wonder if they blew it with you. Overnight.
2. Never, ever call the buyer's agent and ask how the inspection went. Let him come to you. Just operate under the assumption that everything went fine. It is not your job to remind the buyer's agent to submit an inspection notice.

3. Never, ever call the buyer's agent on the loan approval deadline and ask if the buyer, indeed, has loan approval. Call the next day. Why? Because as the seller's agent, it is not your job to remind the buyer's agent to protect her client's earnest money deposit by asking for an

extension if the loan has not been approved.

4. When negotiating, try not to make the other side feel bullied or cornered. Build in a slight "putz" factor when you can to give the opposite team a way to accept without losing face. For example, if your buyer asks for a $2,000 credit for repairs and the seller counters with an unacceptable $1,000 credit, go back at $1,800 instead of standing firm at $2,000.

5. Always remember that the other side, whether buyer or seller, feels vulnerable as well, regardless of their stance during the negotiations.

6. You can always say NO. In fact, the other side probably fully expects you to. If they want to buy or sell, saying NO won't kill the deal. And sometimes, bending over backwards to make a deal go through can actually do more damage than simply saying NO.

7. Almost everyone likes to negotiate, regardless of any claims to the contrary. As a buyer agent, do not submit offers with the statement, "This is our highest and best—take it or leave it." It won't work. If you're the listing agent, always find something in an offer to counter. Both sides want and need to feel the thrill of a successful negotiation.

> *He who does not get fun and enjoyment out of every day...needs to reorganize his life*
>
> George Matthew Adams

Chapter Eleven

Real Estate Offers the ILLUSION of Controlling Your Time

Have you ever heard the term "Pop-Tart real estate agent?" It's usually used derogatively toward an agent who is willing to drop everything to race out the door and accommodate a client or a prospect on short notice. (Egads! What is the world coming to?).

Many agents congratulate themselves for breaking the Pop-Tart habit and enforcing rules and regulations on their clients and prospects so as not to be abused or mistreated by those pesky people who would like the services of their (or a) real estate agent.

Okay, so I'll agree that boundaries are appropriate, and it's wise to have a respectable level of control over one's calendar. But the extent to which many in our industry take this philosophy is... well... a bit ridiculous, in my opinion.

I can't tell you how many articles, blogs and advice columns I read where agents are sternly advised to guard their precious time and always be on the lookout for clients who are hell-bent on abusing their privileges as a client. And if the person hasn't yet formally hired you? You must do everything within your power to ensure that they will not waste even a minute of your time. After all, you have dozens of other qualified buyers and sellers lined up outside your door, don't you?

Here's what "they" say: "Would you expect your doctor or lawyer to drop everything when you call?" Uh, well, maybe. If I'm having a baby or a heart attack or got tossed in jail on suspicion of armed robbery, then yes, I probably would expect a prompt response from my doctor or lawyer. But that's a flawed analogy anyway. We are real estate agents, not doctors or attorneys. When it takes us seven to ten years of education before we can become licensed or we have to endure an internship or pass a bar exam, then talk to me. But for now, let's just accept that we are real estate agents, and frankly, we're a dime a dozen.

So what's my point?

Part of our appeal to our clients is that we are reasonably available to them. Even cheerfully so. Sure, there are times when we can't or will choose not to be available, but we need to accept it as a choice... a choice that may have consequences.

Many moons ago, when I was still in Corporate America, I remember a young woman in my office complaining that "it wasn't fair" that in order to reach the boardroom (i.e., be the CEO or president of the company), you had to be willing to work ungawdly hours and pretty much abandon your family. "It's too bad," she said, "that our culture requires such a sacrifice to reach the top."

Uh...HUH?

Even at my young age, with no notion of my future political leanings (I'm pretty conservative), I found this opinion bizarre. I mean, if there are people who are willing to work that hard and make the necessary sacrifices, then they will set the standard for what's expected to be The Boss.

I believe it's the same in our industry. As long as there are agents who are willing to work nights, weekends and holidays, that will be the standard. And there's nothing wrong with that.

So, let's say it's a holiday weekend. Being in real estate, you have real estate stuff going on. You need a lender on Friday afternoon. Who do you call?

Well, you probably know a lot of lenders. But a lot of the lenders don't work on the weekends. And a holiday weekend? Forgetaboutit. They're out playing or otherwise not answering their phones.

So you call a lender you know works seven days a week. He answers his phone, and he gets your new buyer —who, by the way, is slam-dunk perfect, approved up to $400,000. And we know this because your new favorite lender met with him on Saturday afternoon, on a holiday weekend.

As long as there are lenders who are willing to provide last-minute/holiday/weekend service, they will set the standard for what I expect from a lender. It's fine and dandy to set regular office hours and such, but then don't fuss when an impatient buyer (and his agent) choose to work with someone more flexible. It's a choice.

Is it wrong to take weekends off or spend Sundays with your family? Of course not! But it's a choice that not everyone chooses to make. And in this microwave world of instant gratification, I'm gonna choose the person I can reach...even on a holiday weekend.

My New Buyer Calls at 7:30 a.m. on Sunday Morning—Do I Jump? You Betcha!

One Friday morning, I got a referral from another agent. The buyers lived in the mountains outside of Denver and wanted to move to the city. That week? Nah, they had a house to sell first, so maybe sometime in the summer. That's cool—I like a full pipeline.

Around 2:00 that afternoon, the buyer calls me and wants to know if I can show her and her husband houses on Saturday. Yep, with a little re-arranging, I can do that. So, we did. Went well. Nice couple with two adorable little girls. Found a neighborhood they loved, so I promised to keep them updated on the market activity in there. They headed back up the hill to their mountain home.

7:30 Sunday morning, my cell phone rings. The buyers are so excited about what we saw yesterday that they want to make another road trip to Denver today to look at all the other houses for sale in the neighborhood, as well as the ones we saw on Saturday. Well, I had an open house at 1p.m., three offers to present at 4:30 and dinner plans that night, so if I was going to accommodate them, it would have to be that morning.

Did I rearrange my schedule for them? Oh, yeah. We're meeting at 11 a.m.. Are they going to buy a house today? Not a chance. Are they pre-approved? I'm not sure. I think so, but I haven't asked.

So, why was I willing to "waste my time?"

1. My past clients were an enormous source of business for me. Was it because I put them on a five-year drip campaign and hounded them for referrals? Uh, no. I think it had more to do with working my backside off for them and making their needs a priority over my paycheck. Even if (egads!) I'm inconvenienced.

2. The agent who referred them to me could also have been a sweet source of future business for me. She worked in a resort market just an hour away, so if I impressed her clients, in turn I'd impress her.

Here's the thing...meeting them as requested took maybe two hours out of my day. Big deal. I think that's a very good use of two hours that I'd otherwise probably be surfing online or even whining to myself that I wished I had a few more buyers. To me, taking advantage of the opportunity to impress someone who has the power to bless me with a $10,000 + paycheck is an excellent way to spend a Sunday morning.

I'm a Professional, and My Time Is Extremely Valuable
by Kim Brown

Oh yeah? Says who?

I see more posts than I can count making this statement (or something close to it) and the subsequent "atta boys" that follow in the comment thread make for a very well-attended pep rally.

(If you're one of the cheerleaders, you may want to quit reading now.)

I think it's time to stop waving the "I'm A Professional" flag in the face of every single potential client we meet. Furthermore, I think it's insulting to presume that our time is so much more valuable than theirs.

A few months ago, I sent an email out to some of the people in my SOI *asking them to describe what they thought were qualities of a GREAT real estate agent.*

The number one answer? TIME.

That tells me that they already value our time. Not only do they value it, they'd really like to share some of it, and they would like us to value their time as highly as we value our own. They want time to understand what's going on throughout a transaction, time to investigate their options, time to ask questions, time to talk about their needs, time to make a decision. Isn't it our job, as professionals, to share our expertise, experience, opinions and TIME with them?

Handing a first-time (or first-time-in-a-long-time) buyer a checklist of things they must do before you will spend any of your extremely valuable time with them isn't being professional. It's being dismissive.

Insisting that your time is too valuable to waste answering a few questions from someone who is not very familiar with the ins and outs of a real estate transaction isn't being professional. It's acting superior.

Assuming that because a buyer has not yet obtained a pre-approval from a lender, they are not a serious buyer isn't being professional. It's being shortsighted.

Sending clients away because they balk at jumping through all your pre-determined hoops isn't being professional. It's being inflexible.

If you are so busy that you truly don't have time to spend with another potential client, tell them so, and refer them to another agent who can spare the time. That's being professional, because...

If you're too busy to give your extremely valuable time to a client, then you are of little value to them.

All this said, there certainly is room in the calendar for some ME time, even if that ME time simply means sitting on the couch watching re-runs. Some months (heck, some years!) will be busier than others, and it's always your choice to forego a little business in the interest of a sanity break. But promise me you'll realize that it's a choice and that you are truly blessed to be busy enough and successful enough and in demand enough to be in the position to make that choice. Promise me you won't blame or resent your precious clients because they want and need your attention.

> **❝** *If it isn't any fun, why bother?* **❞**
> *Ben Howell Davis*

Chapter Twelve

Career Development and Quandaries

Screening Your Clients

You may find during your real estate career that there are certain types of people you don't want to work with. No, don't get worried. I'm not getting ready to advise you to throw your Fair Housing training out the window. I'm referring to personality types that you will realize are a bad fit for you. Relationships developed in the process of buying or selling homes can become rather intense, intimate and emotionally-charged. It stands to reason that every real estate agent is not a good fit for every buyer or seller.

I am extremely detail-oriented and responsive. Being an introvert, I am not schmoozy or chatty. If a buyer was looking for his real estate agent to be his new best friend, I was probably the wrong person for the job.

I am also a strong believer in fair negotiation. I did not beat up the other team just because we were on opposite sides of the closing table. I would not attempt to intimidate the other party's real estate agent or make ridiculous demands just to show off for an unreasonable client.

That's my style; it may be yours, it may not be. But when the personality fit is wrong, everyone suffers. If you're losing sleep over a client or getting a sick feeling in your stomach when their phone number pops up on your cell phone, you'll be amazed how much better you'll feel if you let 'em go.

NEXT!

In my corner of the world, I found that people from a certain affluent, liberally-minded town to the north tended to irritate me to the point I could not represent them properly. I found them to be unreasonably demanding, suspicious, untrusting and litigious. But that's just me. Perhaps you will have trouble with Missourians or New Yorkers or surfer dudes.

It took me a long time to figure out that not every real estate agent is a good fit for every client. Because my negotiating style tended to be more win/win than beat-'em-up, I was occasionally accused of being a soft negotiator by people who enjoyed more confrontation and animosity. In fact, I finally added a few hard-core tough-acting agents to my referral network! So, whenever I began to work with someone I suspected reveled in nasty negotiations, I either let them go or referred them to my nasty negotiating associate!

This leads me to my next topic...

When to Let a Buyer or Seller Go
This is truly an advanced skill. Even agents with 25 years of experience have trouble walking away from a troublesome client. Either you've invested dozens of your precious hours with them and want a payout on your investment, or you've spent lots of your precious dollars marketing their home and don't want to throw it all away.

Before I move on, let me say this: That tough client of yours is probably mean to everyone, not just you. He lives his life this way. His days are filled with confrontations, frustrations and general unhappiness. The entire world is a disappointment to him, and he's used to that feeling. It's really not personal. In fact, these people can become your biggest fans if you're lucky (and good). You might even think they hate you and would never send you a referral, but you could be wrong.

Some of my best referral sources were clients who terrified me at first;

who made me feel incompetent and even stupid. Consider this...if this type of person enthusiastically refers you to a friend of theirs, how much weight is that reference going to carry? A lot! Believe me, their friend knows how difficult they are to please, and if they're actually satisfied with your services, you must be something special.

Or...maybe not. But it does happen more than you think it would.

Letting Buyers Go

The most obvious reason to let a buyer go is if he isn't going to buy a house. You'll know soon enough if he's serious or not; some clues are his unwillingness to contact a mortgage broker, a general lack of excitement about the process OR even an overly enthusiastic response to every house you show him. You don't have to be rude about it; just don't make him a priority.

But there are other less obvious reasons to give up on a buyer. Perhaps you're feeling a breakdown of rapport between you. You notice that he argues with most of your comments or that he doesn't seem to trust you. Buyers who don't trust real estate agents or the process in general are lawsuits waiting to happen. If he doesn't laugh at your jokes or seems to take offense at your sense of humor, you might be in for a painful ride. If it's bad enough, he will probably fire you eventually anyway, after some (real or imagined) minor misstep you make.

Sometimes a buyer will fire you. Ooooooh, it's painful, but also a relief. You don't get fired by buyers you love; it's the ones who are making your life hell. Don't argue with him unless there is a true misunderstanding— maybe not even then. Mourn the loss for an hour or so, move on. Not every real estate agent is a good fit for every buyer. Let him torture someone else for a while.

Letting Sellers Go

From a technical perspective, it's harder to let a seller go, because your sign is in his yard, and most listing contracts don't really address the situation of broker termination. It's not as if you can just stop calling your seller or ignore his calls and hope he goes away. So, you may have to wait until your listing expires if you don't want to outright fire your seller.

Again, the most obvious reason to let a seller go is a lack of motivation. Perhaps he is refusing showings or otherwise impeding the possibility of sale. Maybe you've been under contract twice and he's refused to make reasonable inspection repairs. Maybe his price is too high and he's unwilling to reduce it.

But what about the motivated, yet terribly unpleasant, seller? She doesn't respect you, doesn't follow your recommendations, yet continuously complains that you aren't getting her house sold.

The last seller I wanted to fire knew more about selling real estate than all the agents in Denver combined. When I first listed the home, I gave her some suggestions on improvements she could make and explained why they were important. She discounted my suggestions, because I was Wrong. I told her that she needed to leave the house for showings and let the buyers discover the home without her presence. She disagreed. Her home was in a transitional neighborhood that did not command the prices of nearby neighborhoods, but she was sure that buyers would overlook the inferior location. If they didn't, I should call every real estate agent who showed it and convince them otherwise. Yeah, right.

I warned her that her listing price was probably too high, but that I was willing to try it for a little while, just in case. After a month, I reminded her of this conversation, but she wasn't interested in a price reduction. After all, she needed that price to make it worth selling.

I re-shot the exterior picture of her home four times because the lighting was never quite right. She didn't like the combination I used for my lockbox, so I had to change it. I reprinted her home brochures several times, every time she thought of a different approach.

Toward the end of our listing agreement, she requested a brainstorming session with me. She said she had some marketing ideas that she wanted to discuss. Previously, such sessions with her had been pointless, time-consuming and draining. I agreed to meet with her but sent her an email ahead of time detailing my frustrations. I listed all the suggestions I had made over the listing period and her across-the-board objections to them. I explained that her home was being marketed properly and aggressively, and that if she refused to consider my professional recommendations, I didn't see any point in expensive additional marketing. Blah, blah, blah. God, it felt good.

Not surprisingly, she did not like my email. She rejected my opinion that her reluctance to follow my recommendations was the primary reason her house hadn't sold. This exchange pretty much marked the end of our relationship. Her listing expired, and neither of us discussed renewal.

Energy Vampires

An energy vampire is a person who feeds off the energy of another, draining the host of their life force. An energy vampire is exhausting to be around and inspires a desperate need to flee from their presence.

You will run into energy vampires often, especially when listing houses. If, during the course of a listing presentation, you start to feel you're in the presence of an energy vampire, you're better off quitting while you're ahead. Finish up your appointment and don't pursue the business.

I once met with a young couple, their brand new baby and their overly needy cocker spaniel. Picture a small, somewhat smelly house, screaming baby, whining dog, TV blasting. The man and wife were both talking at the same time, going off in tangents that were unrelated to the market value of their home. They were arguing with each other, fussing with the baby and yelling at the dog. Dinner was cooking, and the ceiling fan was blowing my papers off the table. Just writing this makes my heart beat a little faster with the memory. It was chaotic, and just plain unpleasant. My face hurt with the effort of keeping a smile on my face. I wanted out of that house. When I finally got away, I went straight home and to bed. I honestly couldn't function the rest of the day; my energy was that zapped.

Another seller I worked with had severe ADD. He would call me and talk nonstop for half an hour about the most inane topics. He'd jump around from subject to subject, barely pausing to take a breath. He'd be telling me the saga of replacing his water heater and then jump to a story about renting his condo to a star basketball player who didn't show up to sign the lease, then to a discussion of the curtains in his basement. My participation was not needed, but these conversations were exhausting.

Don't take these listings. You aren't the only one who will feel the energy-zapping power of a vampire. Your life will be miserable, and the house probably won't sell anyway.

Discount Brokerage—Can It Work For You?

Up until the mortgage crisis hit in 2007, many real estate insiders (and outsiders) predicted that the discount brokerage model would take over the real estate world, much to the chagrin of the "traditional" real estate community, I might add! In line with that thinking, lots of discount firms popped up, with varying degrees of success. It became popular to bash the discount broker with all sorts of accusations of misleading the consumer by offering substandard service and de-professionalizing the industry by charging less than "normal." It seems I even saw continuing education-approved courses specifically teaching agents how to "combat" the discounters.

Whatever.

Last time I checked, we live in a capitalistic society, and each of us is entitled to create our own business model and succeed or fail based on the marketability of that model.

JENNIFER'S BLOG: Are You a Ritz? Or a LaQuinta? Or, Gawd Forbid...
a Hotel del Coronado?

I recently read an article written by a Faina Sechzer comparing the service one receives at the Ritz to the service one might receive from his or her real estate agent. I love analogies and this one was so dead-on—I can't say enough good things about it. If you missed it, take a minute to read it over. It's so good. http://activerain.com/blogsview/270720/Ten-reasons-real-estate

However, my own personal experience with luxury hotels is somewhat different. Several years ago, I went on a business trip with my future ex-husband. It was some fancy-schmantzy to-do for attorneys to get their continuing education credits in between golf games, I think. It was held at the Hotel Del Coronado in San Diego. The room rate was something like $400/night, although I'm sure we didn't pay that much.

Our room itself was decorated in 1970's hotel style, nothing special aside from the spectacular view of the Pacific Ocean. The hallways were dingy, and not everything in the room worked right. There was, of course, a gawd-awful expensive mini-bar and no free coffee in the lobby. A continental breakfast put you back $15 or so. Oh, and you had to PAY $20/day for the honor of parking your car in the lot. I somehow ran up $250 worth of phone calls, even though I used my calling card for every single one. The staff seemed, depending on the person and time of day, harried...or bored. Suffice to say that we were underwhelmed with the Hotel Del Coronado.

A few weeks later I stayed in a La Quinta Inn. What a difference! The room was clean and comfortable, and it had the nicest pillows I've ever slept on. The staff was friendly and accommodating. Parking was, of course, free. There was coffee in the lobby all day and a complimentary continental breakfast from 6 a.m. to 9 a.m. Cost? $49.99/night + tax.

So, what's my point? Well, contrary to Faina's experience at the Ritz, I felt ripped off by my Luxury Hotel & Resort experience. Conversely, I was tickled pink by the experience I had at the moderately-priced La Quinta.

Are you a Ritz? Or a La Quinta? Or, egads, a Hotel Del Coronado?

I've been both a Ritz and a La Quinta. I've charged "full price" and delivered way above and beyond expectations. I've also charged a less-than-full-price and delivered excellent value for the dollar spent.

There's plenty of room (and business) for both models, and whichever approach you take, your clients will be satisfied. Commit to one or the other, and go sell some houses!

Let me disclose that I am in full support of the discount brokerage concept. In the mid-2000's, I owned a discount brokerage that offered full service (above and beyond many full-fee companies) and was proud of my ability to provide terrific service for a lower-than-market fee. In my first year of business, I "saved" my clients over $115,000 in listing fees, compared to an (illustrative only) 6% commission. Of course, that meant that I sacrificed $115,000 off my income in listing fees! But, that was my choice, and I was proud of my ability to provide full service real estate at half the price.

And it worked, sort of. Yes, I got a lot of business, and yes, listing appointments were much easier (and quicker since we didn't have to battle for an hour over my fee). It was rewarding to offer great service and know that most of my seller clients felt that they received full value for the money paid.

However, along the way I encountered some unexpected challenges with my discount philosophy. I attracted difficult sellers. I had always gotten the vast majority of my business from friends and past clients, as well as referrals from friends and past clients, but some of the sellers I found myself working with were, in a word, cheap. They were stingy. They were (in my opinion), unreasonable. Some of them even embarrassed me with their stinginess, and it was hard for me to represent them.

Many of my clients were upside-down in their homes; they owed more on their home than it was worth. That's why they hired me—my low fee would help them retain a few pennies of their equity or at least reduce the damage. These sellers had to ask top dollar for their homes and weren't able to negotiate at all with buyers, which led to many crashed deals and frustration for everyone. (This was back in the days before most of us even knew what a short sale was!)

I was also surprised by the hostility of the other agents in town. Perhaps I should have expected it, but I guess I thought everyone had their own business to run and wouldn't worry about little old me and my discounted commission. Au contraire! One company was so worked up about me that I was the main topic of conversation at their weekly staff meeting —and I heard that they spent the entire meeting brainstorming how to shut me down! I was kind of flattered, actually.

Another issue that arises when you charge less than the "going rate" is that it's hard to get referred listing business. Think about it: if an agent is going to refer a client to someone to list their house, they're excited about getting a 20 percent referral fee...Well, 20 percent of a higher fee is a whole lot more than 20 percent of a lower fee! And of course, it was hard for me to pay out referral fees when my margin was so thin anyway.

Due to the massive amount of marketing that assaults us every day, our minds have become trained to make certain short-cuts when evaluating a potential offer. One of those short-cuts is: High Price = High Quality/ Low Cost = Low Quality. Most people will not take the time to actually analyze the offerings and benefits of a proposal—their minds will automatically make assumptions based on price. It can be hard to overcome that mindset, so no matter how good you are, people will place your value at whatever you charge. So, even though you're the world's best real estate agent, your sellers won't appreciate your low fee; they'll just assume that they got a fair price for your service.

I recently read a pricing philosophy that may have changed my outlook on discounting my service—any service. It goes something like this: If you charge half of what you are worth in order to generate a volume business, you are working twice as hard as you have to. Imagine what would happen if you charged a full-market rate...and promptly lost half your clients. You'd be making the same amount of money you were before, working half as hard. Hmmmmm. That makes a lot of sense to me, from a purely mercenary perspective.

A while back, I was watching some reality home show—Buy Me, I think it was. It was the story of a seller who had to sell her old farmhouse quickly. It had structural problems, a flooded basement, a falling-down garage; it was dirty, cluttered and in need of many other minor repairs. The comparables showed a value range of $220,000 to $250,000. The seller wanted to list for $295,000, as is.

The seller's real estate agent was a decent sort, and you could feel her angst. She didn't want this listing and was frustrated with her seller's attitude that buyers would overlook all the work needed. The seller said, "Well, we'll just need to disclose to buyers that the garage needs to be torn down and that the basement floods." Yeah, right. We'll just tell 'em that; that'll work fer sure.

Thankfully, the seller's parents stepped in and purchased the home from the seller. You could almost feel the real estate agent's sigh of relief.

So, how is this relevant to a discussion of a discount brokerage model?

Well, when you run a tight ship (which is necessary under a discount model), it's easy to turn down these listings. First, you don't have the margin to risk taking a listing you can't sell. It's simply not in your budget to spend money marketing properties that have little chance of ever bringing in a paycheck.

Second, because your potential paycheck on the listing isn't huge (in the above scenario, it would be $3,500, compared to $7,000 + if you charged a more typical listing fee), your greed doesn't kick in. You don't tell yourself, "Well, maybe I'll get lucky and sell it!" 'Cause even if you do get lucky (and you know you won't), the potential paycheck isn't worth the risk.

One of the attractions of a discount model used to be that you could attract a volume business without much marketing expense. A friend of mine worked at one of the better-known discounters and said the leads just poured into the office. She had minimal marketing expenses and claimed that her entire business was built from the leads she got from her office. Neato.

However, she eventually left the company, and once she was away from the discounter, she realized two important disadvantages of the model.

The first is that in a discounted commission model, there simply isn't enough pie to go around. Her company paid for lots of national advertising that brought in leads, and they wanted and deserved to get paid for it. That's fair. But since her commission was so low, her company needed to take a big chunk of that commission to pay their bills. Her net commission after split was hardly worth getting up in the morning for! In my humble opinion.

Second, the only way for a discount model to really work for an agent is if the prices of the agent's listings are in the upper ranges, rather than entry level. BUT who do you think all that expensive national marketing generates calls from? The upper-crust? Nope. The vast majority of her company-provided leads were in below-median price ranges. Most agents agree that sellers in upper price ranges are not nearly as concerned with a commission percentage as those in lower ranges. And besides, how comfortable is a $600,000 seller going to be with a "Discount Broker For Hire" For Sale sign in his yard?

My own discount company worked for me because, as the owner, I got 100% of every commission I brought in and my overhead was quite low.

So the moral of the story seems to be...if you want to be a discount broker (and there is nothing wrong with that) you may need to do it on your own. If you want the full support of an office (and are willing to pay for it), you will need to charge market rate. I don't think you can have it both ways.

Real Estate in Jammies?

Let's talk about your day-to-day work environment. As in...do you want to work from home or from a real estate office?

For some, the answer is obvious. The majority of real estate agents prefer the busyness and chaos of an office. They need the social interaction and would be unproductive at home. They claim that they can't work from home, because they'd be too distracted and wouldn't get anything done. If this sounds like you, you have your answer. Start sweet-talking your broker into giving you that corner office with a mountain view.

Those of you like me, naturally introverted, may find yourselves working primarily from home already. I did. Within one week of beginning my real estate career, I had a full office set up in my home and only went to my Coldwell Banker office a few times a week. I didn't do it intentionally; it just naturally happened.

It's important to honor your preference. Don't force yourself to go to the office if you're more comfortable and productive at home. Being an introvert all my life, I always felt a little guilty that I preferred my own company to the company of others. I forced myself into social situations that were disastrous for my peace of mind and productivity. For example, I joined a sorority in college (what was I thinking?), and when I noticed I wasn't fitting in, I decided to move into the sorority house for a semester. What a nightmare: no privacy, no personal space, no control over my environment. For an introvert, this is Bad. We need our privacy, space and control to function.

(FOR THOSE OF YOU WHO CAN'T RELATE TO WHAT I'M TALKING ABOUT, YOU CAN SKIP THE REST OF THIS SECTION!)

When you go to the office, do you feel as if you're productive, creative, ambitious? I found that when I forced myself to spend time in my real estate office, I could get my to-do list done but not much else. My creativity seemed stifled and my motivation low. I need my own space to pace, to talk to myself or to do a few sit-ups if the mood struck. Or even take a power nap.

When you spend time in the office, do you feel energized when you leave or drained? Do you enjoy the other agents in your office, or do they get on your nerves? When you walk in your door at night, do you stumble in, feeling as if you'd just put in a long day at the office? Or pleased with yourself and eager to go back tomorrow? One of the many benefits of a real estate career is the escape from the drudgery of a nine-to-five job. You should be feeling the euphoria of being your own boss and controlling your own destiny. Your work environment may very well be the key to finding the euphoria.

In retrospect, I realize that the ability to work from home changed my life. For the first time, I truly flourished and discovered a creative side to myself I'd never known existed. Being somewhat shy and a bit of a privacy freak, working in an office made me feel self-conscious and on display all the time. And it was so distracting! I need peace and quiet to focus. I need a sense of privacy to recharge my batteries. Surrounded by chatter, I feel myself getting anxious and frazzled. But that's just me.

If you're Just Like Me, give some serious consideration to setting up a true home office and not just a corner of the dining room for your computer desk. You'll need your own room, preferably away from any hustle and bustle of the living areas of your home—not just to ensure your peace and quiet, but so that your family doesn't feel as if they live in a real estate office.

In many of the homes I lived in during my career, my office was set up in a central location, and my husband deeply resented it. The phone rang constantly, and I was always working, right under his nose. He felt neglected and ignored—that my business was more important than he was and that his home was not a sanctuary from his own busy work day. Had my office been separate from the main living area, he could have enjoyed his own solitude and peace, but the way I set it up, he could not. It seemed to him that the whole house was my office and not our home.

So, if at all possible, find your own space that won't interfere with family life. Besides, you need to be able to escape from your office too! That's hard to do when your office is in the dining room.

Help! Help! I'm Drowning! Successfully Teaming Up

At some point in your career, if you haven't already, you might consider bringing on help...a full partner, a licensed assistant or an unlicensed assistant. I have done all three, with varying degrees of success. Some of my alliances crashed and burned; others were wildly successful, at least for a while. Partnerships are tough and while they offer significant benefits can also add much unneeded stress to an already stressful life as a real estate agent.

The primary reason people partner up in business is to get more business. By teaming up with another person, either as equals or in a boss/worker bee relationship, both parties hope that the partnership will create something bigger than the individual parts. In other words, if two people can earn $30,000 each working alone, they hope that by working together they can make $100,000 total.

Before Partnering...Search Your Soul

Why are you thinking about hiring or partnering? Is it because someone told you to? Or because you took a class that said you should? Were you approached by someone wanting a job or a partner?

Don't complicate your life by bringing on help for the wrong reasons. I promise you, bringing another warm body into your business world will not simplify your life. It might improve it but definitely won't simplify it. After several years of experimenting with assistants and partners, I finally decided that I would only take on as much business as I could handle myself, without help, and refer the rest. The stress of working with someone else simply wasn't worth it for me.

However, if you are truly overwhelmed and are pretty sure you need help, then let's talk about the right help for you.

First, make a list of the aspects of your job you enjoy doing. Truly enjoy. Do you like open houses? Do you like previewing homes? Showing buyers? Attending inspections? Negotiating inspections? Writing offers? Meeting with seller prospects? Cold calling? Warm calling? Going to lunch with your friends? Designing home brochures? Running errands? Filing? Making a daily to-do list? And checking it twice? Don't write down things that you wish you enjoyed, only those duties that you really like to do and are good at.

What aspects of your job do you dread? What stuff hardly ever gets done in a timely manner, if at all? Don't be ashamed of this list; be honest with yourself. And be detailed. Do you have a stack of closed files in the corner that needs to be organized and put away? An SOI database that hasn't been touched in six months? How about a computer that desperately needs to be backed up? Or maybe, like me, you dread open houses and buyer agent feedback calls? Or even working with buyers...or sellers?

If you are already detail-oriented and fairly well organized, it won't do you much good to hire a secretary-type. I made that mistake. I thought that by hiring an administrative assistant, I would get off my butt and get out of the office. What actually happened was that I continued to handle the administrative details myself and wondered why I hired help in the first place. If you're truly chomping at the bit to go prospect but the paperwork is holding you back, give it a try. But if you're using the paperwork as an excuse to stay in the office, having an assistant probably won't change that.

Conversely, if you like to chat with strangers and meet new people, don't hire someone to network for you. Do your own prospecting. No one else will do it nearly as well as you will.

The above applies not only to working with an assistant, but also to bringing on a partner. The best partnerships are where the members of the partnership specialize in different areas. If both partners do essentially the same job, sooner or later one or both will get resentful. One will be working harder (in his perception) and resent pulling the other along, and the other will resent being pushed to work harder than he wants to. If each partner has his or her individual responsibilities, directly linked to his or her skills and interests, the partnership has a great chance to thrive.

My partner and I had this kind of relationship. She enjoyed prospecting and talking to people, and I enjoyed handling the marketing and paperwork. She was in awe of my attention to detail (which was so easy for me), and I appreciated her willingness to get out there and drum up business. She saw networking as fun; I enjoyed pushing paper, and we each truly appreciated each other's contributions.

The moral of the story...when picking a partner or assistant, don't look for someone Just Like You; look for someone who complements (and compliments!) you.

So let's discuss the particulars.

Agent Hires Licensed Assistant
Hiring a licensed assistant is a logical step in a growing real estate career. It may not always be the right one, but it is logical. A licensed assistant can function anywhere from an overqualified in-box to a near partner. Your relationship with your licensed assistant will be unique—no one else on the real estate planet will have a working relationship exactly like yours—so I won't go into detail as to the what, when, where, why and how to's of working with your licensed assistant. You'll figure that out as you go along. In fact, you might stumble onto someone who isn't at all what you thought you were looking for but is so fabulous that you're willing to create a job just for her. So keep an open mind when you're on the hunt for help.

When looking for your licensed assistant, resist the urge to prowl the local real estate schools. A brand new licensee will be absolutely worthless to you. Not only will you have to train him in every single aspect of the job, you'll likely be training him to be your competition in a year or so. People don't go to real estate school to be licensed assistants—they go to real estate school to sell real estate. Any detour they take into licensed assistant-ing will only be temporary. His lack of experience is not your problem. You need help, now, and if you want to be a trainer or a mentor, you should get paid for it, not be asked to pay for that privilege!

Agent Hires Unlicensed Assistant
Frankly, I think every busy real estate agent could use an unlicensed assistant. I always had one, although I didn't call her my assistant—I actually called her my wife! She ran all my errands for me and took care of my "Fluffing and Flushing" duties in my vacant listings. As a real estate agent, you can spend hours and hours driving around doing menial errands that not only take up your time, but zap your energy. An errand boy or girl can free up an amazing amount of time.

Not that an unlicensed assistant is only good for running errands, oh no! But don't underestimate the value of having someone reliable to take care of the little things. So, if your business (or even your personal life) could use some non-licensed help, I think you'll truly enjoy the services of a personal assistant.

> *FLUFFING and FLUSHING*
> *Fluffing and Flushing is the act of checking on a vacant listing during the listing period to ensure that everything is as it should be.*

Agent Takes on a Partner
I'll bet that most real estate partnerships develop out of the need for vacation. One of the toughest things about being self-employed is finding someone reliable to watch your business so that you can get away. Long weekends, even a half-day ski trip, can be disastrous to your business if Murphy the Lawmaker rears his ugly head.

Vacation coverage is a prime benefit to having a partner. It's blissful, actually, especially if you've been selling real estate a long time. Your first vacation when you truly don't have to worry about business? You'll wonder why you didn't get a partner before.

One year, the market in Denver was slooooow. Deadly. Nuthin' happening. So, my partner and I decided to vacation instead of fret. Starting the first week in August, I went to Mexico...over Labor Day, she went to New Hampshire. In mid-September, I went to Alabama. The first of October, she took a cruise. Two weeks later, she visited her parents. Two weeks after that, I went back to Alabama. We were almost giddy about the whole thing. While I was gone, she handled the little business we had, and vice versa. It was nice for both of us: The one left minding the store was kept busy enough, even though it was slow; the one on vacation was...well...on vacation. And both of us had more time off to look forward to.

Anyway, I digress. Other than the obvious benefit of having the perfect vacation buddy, working with a partner offers other advantages, as well. If you and your partner have different temperaments, you can more easily handle a wider variety of personality types. One client might be an engineering type and respond better to the more straight-forward partner. Another might be looking for her new best friend. Perhaps one partner inadvertently upsets a client; the other can usually step in and take over. Unfortunately for us introverted-types, most of your clients will prefer the more warm and fuzzy partner, but you already knew that. Just capitalize on your strengths; I promise you, your extroverted partner is plenty jealous of you, too.

One thing I loved about having a partner was the fact that I got paid sometimes for doing nothing. At least it kind of felt that way. She would have a closing that I wasn't really involved in, and I got half—the same for her, of course. We shared all our expenses, too, so it felt as if everything was half price.

One word of advice for new partners...it may be tempting to be joined at the hip for your client's benefit, but don't do it. My partner and I were gung-ho about presenting the benefits of our "team" to the marketplace, so we both attended every listing presentation, thinking it would make the client feel important. Well, maybe it did, but the overall impression was that of chaos. Two people making a listing presentation is one too many.

We found the same phenomenon working with buyers. When we had to switch off, due to vacations or other scheduling conflicts, the buyer almost always got annoyed. Where we thought we were providing excellent service, the buyer felt as if they were being handed off to an assistant, even though the "assistant" was a full partner.

If the above benefits don't sound life-changing, that's because they aren't. You don't need a partner, in all likelihood. You'll probably continue to do just fine on your own. And of course, there are risks to taking on a partner. Even under the best of circumstances, problems will arise: control issues, financial issues, business decisions and, eventually, the dissolution of your partnership.

In all the excitement of forming your union, don't ignore the fact that your partnership will dissolve someday. If you're (very) lucky, it will be amicable and 100% mutual. In all likelihood, it won't be. And it will probably catch one of you off guard. It will be emotional and disruptive— not the best atmosphere and mindset to be making decisions and negotiating the distribution of assets. This needs to be discussed in the beginning, if not in gory detail, at least in spirit.

I have learned over the years that I am a good Chief and I am a good Indian. I am not a good partner. I am happy to be the boss and to take all the responsibility; I am also happy to be told what to do and have no responsibility. However, I am not happy sharing the power and the responsibility. Think about this for yourself. If it would drive you crazy to have to check in with someone every time you want to make a change, you may not be partner material.

Leaving the Business

Burn Out
Many agents go through the seven-year blahs. It can happen at any time but around seven years in the business seems typical. If they've been successful, they're probably tired. A successful career in real estate can be exhausting and overwhelming. They may also be a bit spoiled. They've made a lot of money and have forgotten what it's like to live paycheck-to-paycheck. They may even think a structured schedule...as in M-F 9-5... sounds pretty good! Taking a cut in pay seems like a fair trade-off for a less stressful lifestyle. Let someone else make the decisions and take the responsibility!

Did you ever notice that as you got better at being a real estate agent, the job seemed to get harder? It's as if the degree of difficulty of each transaction increased in direct relation to your ability to handle it. The problems are more complicated and the personalities more difficult. Many agents thrive on the ever-increasing challenges and feel a real sense of empowerment that they can successfully negotiate the intricacies of a difficult real estate transaction. I once had a streak of 29 closings that didn't fall apart, even though many of them tried to. It was quite a powerful feeling to have that kind of control over my income. At that point in my career, I was on Cloud 9.

But other times, things don't go quite as smoothly. Every client you have is a pain in the backside. No one seems to be satisfied with your service and you feel as if you can't give away your listings. Your high-maintenance client calls five times a day, sometimes at 10 p.m. She asks you the same questions you've already answered twice. Your million dollar buyer has vanished into thin air. You hate your job.

It happens. I experienced my first serious burn out in 1999. I remember how helpless I felt—nothing I did seemed to result in anything positive. The final straw was when I showed up for the closing of an extremely difficult transaction...at the wrong title company. By the time I realized I was in the wrong place and got myself where I needed to be, the closing was almost over. My buyer client (and his father, ouch) were even more annoyed with me than they had been the day before (it was an ugly deal). I went home and "quit." I got on the phone, called another agent in my office who was hungry for business and turned over my prospects to her, just like that. I took three months off and went to work for my husband part-time.

When I returned to the business three months later, I was recharged and revitalized. My business soon rocketed to a new level, and I enjoyed selling real estate again. So, if you're feeling the twinges of burn out, don't be afraid to take a break. It might be the best business move you've ever made.

Taking It Down a Notch
Another option for a burned-out agent is to transition to a support role for another agent. You will be a hot commodity! I've done it twice, and I had my pick of successful brokers to work for.

As an experienced agent, you already know everything you need to know to help your new boss, starting on Day One. He won't have to train you to use contract software, to set showings, to order title work, to use the MLS or to talk to clients and prospects on the phone. You can hit the ground running with him, which is an enormous advantage you have over a new agent who is just entering the field.

And chances are you have a great Sphere of Influence to bring with you! If your new boss is smart, he'll be salivating over it and is already dreaming up ways to work with you to bring in new business from your friends and past clients.

But let's talk about how being a licensed assistant is different from being a licensed salesperson.

It's quite different actually. You and your broker are a complementary team, not two peas in a pod. If he needed a sales partner, he'd get one. No, he needs an assistant— someone to assist him, someone to be his in-box, to be his...secretary. Okay, maybe your job will be a little more glamorous than taking dictation and doing the filing, but maybe not. You need to be at peace with the idea that you are now a worker-bee. You are an in-box. You will do the things he doesn't want to do. You may not want to do them either, but it's not really your choice anymore.

Before I continue, I should state the obvious. To be an effective licensed assistant, you need to have a healthy respect for organization. No, I said that wrong. You need to be organized. If you were/are a natural salesperson who can't be bothered with the details, a position as a licensed assistant probably isn't for you. I once hired my bubbly, outgoing, charismatic girlfriend to be my assistant because she needed a job. She was enthusiastic about doing my paperwork and filing, my data entry and mailings. She even said to me, "I'll do whatever it takes to make you successful!" Music to my ears, right?

Well, you can't change a leopard's spots, and you can't change a social butterfly into a detail fanatic. Her good intentions aside, she was worthless as my assistant. Besides, I'm pretty darn good myself at the details, so there was no real reason for me to hire someone else to attend to them for me. I finally got smart and put her on social duty, where she blossomed. She held open houses for me (yippee!), met sign-call buyers at my listings, delivered closing gifts and was the hostess at my broker open houses.

Anyway, remember that, as an assistant, it is no longer your business. Your input might be welcomed, but don't count on it. Top producing salespeople can be rather egocentric (I am, aren't you?) and have their own ways of doing things. You may not agree with the way your boss writes offers, negotiates inspections or promotes his business, but you have no say in the matter. And frankly, you might find that to be a relief. When you have no power, you have no real responsibility either. I found my first six months as a licensed assistant to be incredibly liberating. I just did what I was told and let my boss worry about putting and holding his deals together. I made very few decisions and, therefore, was very seldom wrong!

My point is that you need to respect his decisions, wrong as they may be (just kidding). You probably won't agree with a lot of them, simply because the nature of the self-employed is to be independent. You have your way of doing things, he has his. But when you are the assistant, he gets to make the rules.

Sharing Your Sphere of Influence

If you are planning to share your SOI with your new boss, this opens up a whole new world of opportunities and considerations. Your SOI is valuable—you worked hard to put it and keep it together, and you need to protect it as long as you can. Don't just hand it over, no matter how optimistic you are about your new working relationship. You need to maintain ownership and control of your SOI, unless someone is willing to pay you cash upfront for it...which isn't likely.

But that doesn't mean that you can be stingy and/or greedy with it, either. If you are no longer in the business of real estate sales, you need someone to happily take care of your past customers, thus generating referral fees for you. Yes, you can negotiate additional compensation for business you bring in, but you can't make your share so onerous that your new boss doesn't feel it's worth it to mess with your referrals. Remember how you felt when you had to pay a 35% referral fee on top of your office split for relocation business? It just doesn't seem worth the effort when there is plenty of other business out there with no referral fee obligations.

So have a frank discussion with your potential new boss about your SOI. If he's still "hungry; i.e., still in business-building mode, he'll probably be excited about the business you'll bring in from your SOI. If he's already a top producer, he might not. Ask him to be honest with you about it. Ask him what he thinks is fair. By the way, if you aren't comfortable having this discussion with a potential employer, the two of you might not be a good fit for each other. Just something to think about.

Marketing to your SOI is another consideration and another conversation to have. Will you take on the responsibility, financial and otherwise, of marketing to them? If you expect your new boss to pay for such marketing, you should probably be willing to take a lower percentage of the business he brings in from your SOI. It will be far more effective for any marketing that goes out to be in your name, especially if you intend to keep control of your SOI, and your new boss may not be willing to pay to promote you.

If your new boss is amenable, try to present your new relationship as a "partnership" when marketing to your SOI. It might be hard for you to announce to the world that you are now an assistant, and thus, perhaps difficult for you to generate enough enthusiasm to stay in touch with your SOI. But if you can say that you have entered a partnership with a successful broker, and explain how it will benefit your clients, you won't have any problem with your ego.

« For Every Way There's a Way of
Following that Way That's Fun. »
Unknown

In Conclusion... Are You in This Business for the Long Haul? (Or just another few months?)

We all look for a magic bullet, me included. While I know I'll have a mortgage payment due at this time next year, I'm far more concerned with the one due in 25 days, the one due in 55 days and the one due in 85 days.

But you know what? Next year will be here before you know it, and this year will be a distant memory. Where do you want to be next year? Do you intend to still be selling real estate? Or do you reckon you'll be doing something else by then?

If you really want to be selling some real estate in a year...in two years... and for many years after that—perhaps now would be a good time to start planning to do just that.

There are a gazillion things you can be doing today to ensure a happy next year—and then be tickled with yourself when next year rolls around and you are enjoying the fruits of your labor.

Okay, Jennifer, Miss Smarty Pants, what CAN I do today to ensure a Happy Next Year?

- Blog. Blogging is a long-term prospecting strategy. If you want to become a specialist in your market or in certain property types or certain client types, get blogging about them TODAY. In a year, you'll be glad you did.

- Nurture your personal relationships. Especially if you've approached the people you know as a salesperson first and as a friend second or third or fourth, you may have some repair work to do. Starting today, drop the sales pitch and start reconnecting with your social network as a real person...who cares about them...ho also happens to sell real estate.

- Take a little extra time with not-yet-ready-to-buy-or-sell prospects. Treat them respectfully and stay in touch. Never shuttle a potential future client out the door because they aren't leading you to a paycheck within 60 days. They could very well bring you a paycheck in 180 days.

- Become a Master of Your Market. The only way to really know and understand your local market is to be out in it. Take three hours a week to preview homes. Visit open houses two Sundays a month. Go to every Broker Open you're invited to. Read the neighborhood newspapers.

- Make your current clients your top priority (yep, ahead of your prospecting efforts). Go above and beyond for your sellers and buyers. Believe me, they'll notice, and they'll remember and will reward you for your efforts for years to come.

It's possible that NONE of the above activities will result in a sale in 30 days or even 60. But if you're in this for the long haul, I guarantee that in a year, you'll be thrilled with the results.

***

So, my friend, we've reached the end of this part of our journey together. If my ideas and philosophies have resonated with you, I'd love to know. Yes, even famous real estate gurus (HA!) need love, too! So, I'd truly appreciate your thoughts on The More Fun You Have Selling Real Estate... as well as any suggestions for additional topics of interest to you. Or, heck, just shoot me a note to say hello; I'd love to hear from you. Rumor has it I'm easy (to reach); just visit my website: www.sellwithsoul.com.

Go get 'em!

Jennifer Allan-Hagedorn

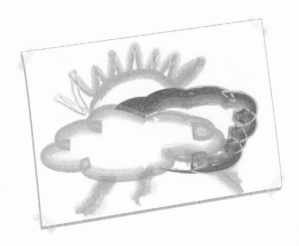

66 We could never learn to be brave and patient
if there were only joy in the world. 99
Helen Keller

Lessons from a Recession

T he original edition of this book was written in 2010, which, you may recall, was at the tail-end of a chaotic, discouraging time in our economic history. At the time of that writing, I decided to include a chapter on the Lessons I Learned from the recession, both as a real estate agent, and as an adult human being.

Thankfully, as of the writing of this version of FUN, the recession of 2007-2009 is a thing of the past. But I believe that the lessons learned by those of us who had the pleasure of struggling through a tough market are worth remembering, even though the tough market is behind us. I, for one, know that I will never be the same woman who blasé-ly committed to Club Level season tickets to the Broncos at $175 per ticket per game. I'll never again hire a $150/ hour graphic designer without closely checking references. I'll never contract for a $25,000 sunroom addition on my home if I can't pay cash for it. I'll never buy a brand new Miata on a whim because it's a beautiful summer day and I feel like showing off a bit for my new boyfriend.

Okay, I think you get the point. "I solemnly swear not to live above my means assuming that the market will always be on my side."

Following are some of my blogs written during these humbling, character-building, ego-deflating days. Please don't allow these admittedly melancholy words to dampen your enthusiasm; rather, allow them to inspire you to appreciate the good times!

Where'd My Money Tree Go?
originally posted: June 2008

Many moons ago, I had a Money Tree in my back yard. At least, it seemed as if I did. I was married to a successful lawyer; I had a thriving real estate career; I bought and sold houses for profit, and when I needed a little financial fix, I could tap into the equity of any one of several investment properties.

Life was good.

When we wanted to re-do our kitchen or add a bath...we did it. Season tickets (Club Level) at the new Bronco's stadium? No problem! Spur-of-the-moment trip to Mexico or San Francisco? Count us in!

I was spoiled.

Unfortunately, when you work on Monopoly Money commission, you get used to the idea of a Money Tree. Maybe THIS month wasn't a banner month, but next month probably will be, or at least the month after that. When you want something, you buy it. And yeah, it's fun.

Well...stuff happens. Divorces, sabbaticals, partnership disputes, subprime mortgage meltdowns...stuff happens.

It's taken some time, but I've finally realized that I do not have a Money Tree in my back yard, and even if I did, I will never live that old lifestyle again. Ever. If I can't afford it TODAY, after all my bills are paid, I can't have it. When you depend on the real estate market for your livelihood, you need some serious financial discipline and a nice little nest egg to fall back on. It's fun, actually, to take control of your finances instead of letting your finances control you. I now closely analyze every potential purchase and hiring decision. I'm not looking for someone to simply make my life easier; he or she better also earn their keep. Before I make a purchase, I ask myself if spending that money will make me $xxx happier or $xxx more efficient.

(For example, I have an old leather Franklin-Covey planner cover that my puppy-monster chewed on a few years ago. I considered buying a new one, but then asked myself, "Jennifer, will spending $65 on a new planner cover make you $65 happier?" The answer? "Heavens, no." Decision made.)

I Cannot Tell a Lie...It's Tougher Today...
originally posted: September 2008

About a year ago, my friend Loreena Yeo unintentionally challenged me. I had just written a series of blogs about a nice new real estate agent named Jake who went from the verge of failure to the heights of success, based on his effective Sphere of Influence campaign. On the second to last installment of the Jake story, Loreena asked the question: "Was Jake lucky? Did Jake begin his career during a boom time and, therefore, was able to experience success more easily than today's agent?"

Okay, so Loreena probably didn't mean it as a challenge, but I took it that way. Within a few months, I decided to return to the wonderful world of real estate sales after a two year write-my-book sabbatical to prove to...well...myself, if no one else...that the Selling Soulfully philosophies weren't just a bunch of nonsense that will work fine in a strong market... but not-so-fine in a difficult one.

So, in February of this year, I re-activated my license and started selling real estate again. Honestly, I didn't know what to expect, and yes, I was a little nervous. What if I failed? What if the methods and philosophies I've been preaching all this time were just a bunch of fluff and hooey in today's market? What if...egads...the only way to succeed in selling real estate was to aggressively prospect to strangers and pester your friends to death with your thinly-disguised sales pitches?

Thankfully, I have discovered that the methods I used to build my business back in the booming mid-90's work just dandily today. No need to spend a gazillion dollars marketing myself to strangers or to hassle my friends on a regular basis to "PLEASE SEND ME REFERRALS 'CAUSE I LOVE THEM." I have a steady stream of business that comes to me as a result of my SOI efforts and my commitment to Being Out There in the World with My Antenna Up and a bundle of market expertise in my back-pocket.

However, I will admit and acknowledge that, indeed, it IS harder today. Many trainers will give you a pep talk and convince you that if you aren't seeing the success of yesteryear, then you just aren't trying hard enough. That may be so, and I certainly won't stop anyone from working longer hours to get through these lean times, but what I want to say is this...

Whether you're a green-bean newbie or an experienced old fogie...if you're feeling discouraged by your YTD production or what's (not) in your pipeline...you are not alone. Even the most pompous, confident, arrogant top producers are feeling those feelings, I promise you. They may not admit it, and they may even tell you that they're having their best year ever, but that's probably a bunch of BS.

The good news is, as you've heard a hundred times, those who survive will likely thrive when this crisis passes. If you're new and have never experienced a strong or even stable market, you have something truly awesome to look forward to. For those of us who've been around a while, we can look forward to again enjoying that career we fell in love with.

There will be lots of agents who make it through to the next market. Hundreds of thousands of them, even. Is there any reason it won't be you?

What I Love About this Market...
originally posted: August 2008

Before I go any further, let me acknowledge that the Denver, Colorado, real estate market isn't that bad. We have qualified buyers and many of our sellers have enough equity to escape from their mortgages. If a home is well-priced and well-presented, it's likely to sell, perhaps even in a bidding war (got one of those going on right now).

However, it's certainly not anywhere near what it was in the mid-to-late 90's and some of the early 2000's. Where there might have been ten buyers up for grabs then, today there are maybe three. Amateur investors don't have $100k of "free money" in their personal homes to play with; even if they did, they may not be able to access it via those handy-dandy home equity loans of past. Fickle home- buyers who simply change their minds about the home they bought six months ago aren't able to unload it and still afford to pay their agent the way they used to be able to. The only fix-n-flippers left are the ones who do it very aggressively and professionally, and they typically don't need or want no stinkin' real estate agent.

In other words, there are simply fewer real estate commission dollars to go around. Whereas in years past I made $200k with no problem, today, I fight (and pray) for every dollar that finds its way to my bank account.

So, what on earth is there to love about this market? Bear with me as I get all confessional on y'all.

I was Very Spoiled during the majority of my real estate career. I was profitable my first year and doubled my income every year after that until I was consistently making...well...plenty. I remember wrinkling my nose at $2,000 paychecks. I remember being ripped off by a painter to the tune of $500 and not even bothering to protest. I remember arrogantly saying, "I don't get up in the morning for less than $1,000!"

Ahhhh, but I sing a different tune today. I got a royalty check yesterday for $424 and did a little happy dance. I'm still awaiting my state tax refund check of $488 and will smile when it (finally) arrives. My last closing resulted in a $1,677 paycheck, and I was tickled.

Not only have I rediscovered an appreciation for "smaller" paychecks, but I've also learned to maximize every opportunity for new business that presents itself to me. I check back in with people who called off my signs last week (and apparently no one else is doing this because I've converted 100% of them to clients!). I hang out at the office more and actually take floor calls or walk-ins. I'll show my listing way across town instead of simply referring the caller to a closer agent. I'll do open houses even if my seller isn't expecting me to.

In short, it appears that the current state of market has jolted me out of my complacency and given me back the enthusiasm and energy of a rookie. And I tell ya...when the good days return...I shall never take a paycheck for granted again. Maybe that's the lesson in all this!

The Realities of Today's
Less-than-Vibrant Real Estate Market
originally posted: December 2008

I've been thinking (and writing) a lot lately about the realities of today's real estate market. While I'd love to be all Rah-Rah and Positive and Enthusiastic and Optimistic, I just don't think such emotions are necessarily warranted in many parts of the country. I'm lucky to work in a market (Denver) where real estate IS moving. There ARE buyers; there ARE sellers, and there IS money to be made by the real estate community. In fact, I've even played in a few bidding war games the last several months for retail properties (that is, not underpriced REO's).

But that doesn't mean I'm not worried or stressed, and so is everyone else I know whose livelihood depends on real estate closings. And I can't even imagine what it must be like to work in markets like Detroit, Tampa or Phoenix. Or, for that matter, to be a brand new, green-bean rookie agent. Fact is, it's tough out there. Not impossible, but tough.

Don't get me wrong, I think this will pass, and that there will be a tremendous backlog of business unleashed upon the agents who are still around. The Good Old Days will very likely return to some degree— hopefully sooner than later. But the challenge is to still BE around six months, a year, two years from now, when those days are here again.

So, in my own self-interest, I've been examining some of my pet teachings to see if they still apply "as written" in this less-than-vibrant economy. I'm willing to make some changes to my business model in response to changing market conditions. But what changes exactly? Keep reading!

Today's Market Realities II -
Old Fogie Agents—Consider Living a Bit Less Large...
originally posted: December 2008

A h h h h h h h h h h...I remember when my average monthly income was $23,500...which meant some months were even higher. I remember two $50,000 months in a row. I remember the year I broke the $300,000 mark. I remember the year I burned out and half-heartedly worked only six months...and still brought in $179,000.

Sigh.

Trouble is, I got into the habit of spending those dollars, not frivolously, but spent them I did. If I wanted a new kitchen, I got it. A sweet little investment property that seemed like a good deal—I bought it. And yes, there was a bit of the princess in there—weekly massages, daily "maid" service and a cute little Caribbean blue Miata I just had to have.

Easy come...easy go.

And speaking of easy: it's an easy habit to fall into when you work on commission—treating those enormous commission checks like Monopoly money and assuming there are plenty more growing on that money tree in the backyard.

I haven't seen a $23,500 month in a while! Neither has anyone I know.

We Old Fogie agents developed some poor spending habits during the days of prosperity, habits which are hard to break. But break them we must. We need to practice using that dirty little word...NO.

I can proudly admit that I have curtailed my lifestyle, although it took a while to admit to myself that I needed to do so, and then some more time to actually listen to myself when I told myself NO. I'm far from perfect, and I still spend money I probably shouldn't, but I can promise you, when those $50,000 months return, I intend to maintain my frugal lifestyle (although I really miss those weekly massages)!

Many of my Old Fogie agent friends are giving lip service to the idea of cutting back. But they aren't doing it. They're so used to the good life they don't see that many of what they consider "necessities" are actually ridiculous luxuries: New Year's Eve in Aspen, a ski pass to Vail, season tickets to the Nuggets, gourmet coffee imported from Costa Rica, monthly facials and weekly visits to the acupuncturist.

Hey, I understand how hard it is to sacrifice in response to what we hope is a temporary downturn in the economy. And I hope with all my heart that my current state of frugality soon becomes a choice, rather than a necessity. But in the meantime, I can almost feel that character building!

Seriously, Is It Time to Hit PAUSE on Your Real Estate Career?

originally posted: December 2008

While I don't advertise it, I do some one-on-one consulting for Very Special People. By VSP, I mean people who buy into the Sell with Soul philosophy (yeah, I discriminate) and who are intelligent and self-aware enough to: 1) be willing to play outside the box and forego traditional wisdom most of the time; and 2) are willing, even eager, to ask, "How did I contribute to this problem?" rather than simply whine about how everyone else on the planet sucks.

Anyway, wanna guess what's the most common consultation I'm doing these days? Seducing a Sphere of Influence? Nope. Writing a Non-Dorky Announcement or Reconnection letter? Nope. Getting a difficult listing sold? No again.

"I'm thinking of quitting. Can you help me decide?"

Sounds kind of grim, doesn't it? And yeah, most agents who contact me with this question are, frankly, out of time. Either something has to happen RIGHT NOW or they're in deep doo-doo. Or, rather, deeper doo-doo.

What I'm about to say here may not be popular, but the answer many of these consultees have gotten from me is: "Yes, I suspect you need to quit, at least for now. Maybe not forever, but for now it's probably the right thing."

Are you asking yourself this question, or some version of it? You don't have to answer me out loud, but if you're at this point in your career, please don't be afraid to explore your options. There is no shame in redirecting your career if that career is putting you and your family at risk of financial ruin. This is a tough business! Yeah, we all know that, but sometimes we forget the reality of that statement. When something is "tough," that means a whole lot of people aren't going to make a go of it—maybe even you or me!

I'm not saying that giving up is the only option; of course it isn't. But it IS an option. Don't let your pride, ego or fantasies get in the way of making the right decision for you.

Is It Okay to Blame the Market for Your Lower Production?
originally posted: December 2008

In my consulting business, I refuse to work with agents if their only explanation for their struggles is to blame the Other Guy. If someone isn't willing to first look in the mirror to find the solutions to their dilemma, I know I'll be of no use to them!

But let's talk about blame for a moment...rational blame vs. irrational blame.

I think it's pointless to "blame" our clients for our troubles. Oh, we real estate agents are experts in doing this. After all, the phrase "Buyers are Liars" is deeply ingrained in our industry, as obnoxious as it is (don't get me started). We ridicule our sellers for wanting Top Dollar for their home in Less-than-Top condition, or for "needing" a certain sales price in order to sell. Well, guess what? The ability to resolve these transaction-specific issues is our job and the reason we're paid the way we are. If we can't empathize, thus effectively communicate with our clients, then that's our fault, not theirs.

That's a topic for a different day.

Today I want to talk about the other thing we blame for our struggles: The Market. And y'know what? I'll buy that. I do think it's perfectly reasonable to blame the market and/or the economy for a failing (or frustrated) real estate career. Hey, if buyers aren't buying, there's NOTHING we can do about that. We certainly can't manufacture buyers if none exist!

So, what if YOUR market sucks? And some certainly do. I've been contacted by agents in most of the infamously sucky markets, including Las Vegas, Florida, Michigan and Phoenix, wanting to know if I can help them. Well, frankly, I'm not sure I can, at least not in the time-frame they need in order to survive.

Here's what I ask these struggling agents:

"In your market...

...is there business to be had, if you could figure out how to get it?" (One agent I spoke with said that the very top producers are selling no more than a dozen homes per year. If this is true, I'd say that no, there is NOT much business to be had at this time.)

....are there buyers?" (Of course, this is related to the first question but a bit more specific. In some markets or specific market areas, there simply may not be a buyer on the planet right now. Again, there's nothing that can be done about that.)

...are houses selling?" (Many agents ask me for help getting listings, but when I ask this question and the answer is "no, not really," I have to wonder why one would want listings!)

If you work in an unviable market, then you need to make some tough decisions, decisions that may conflict mightily with your gut. Here are your options as I see them:

1. Focus on the future. Stop fretting about the NOW, and strive to increase the number of raving fans in your Sphere of Influence. When good times return (and they will), you'll be one of the few still standing. Of course, this requires that you have an alternative source of income or that you drastically curtail your lifestyle.

2. Back off...slow down...take a deep breath. ARE you doing what you know needs to be done to generate business, or are you so scared and frustrated that you're spending most of your time bon-bonning on the couch (or behind the keyboard)? Don't declare the market dead if you haven't given it a good effort. Even if your good efforts fail, at least you'll know you tried. Re-evaluate your business plan and review (or create a list of) your activity goals. Are you holding up your end of the bargain? If you can honestly say that you aren't, give it a few more über-focused months and see if things turn around.

3. Quit. Yeah, quit. There's no shame in throwing in the towel and moving onto something else that pays the bills and allows you to sleep peacefully at night. I know lots of agents, great ones even, who have chosen this path, and they're actually proud of themselves for making this very tough decision.

But...if your market is okay (and many are), stop blaming the Other Guy for your troubles, and let's get you back in the saddle!!!

*I sincerely hope that by the time you're reading **Lessons from a Recession** you can smile to yourself and say "Whew, I'm sure glad THOSE days are behind us," and are again enjoying the heck out of this career you fell in love with. Or, if you began your career during the recession, you're realizing how much more FUN it is to sell real estate in a stable economy. If we aren't there yet (I seem to have misplaced my crystal ball), just know that good times will return and yes, we all have a lot of FUN to look forward to!*
Jennifer Allan, October 2009

appendix

Sample Competitive Market Analysis (CMA)

Sample Reconnection Letters

"What to Expect When on the Market"

Contributors

Resources

Excerpt from Prospect With Soul: *The Story of Joe*

Jennifer Allan-Hagedorn's Sample CMA

www.SellwithSoul.com

Your Property

Property Profile - Denver County
Report Date: February 3, 2009

PROPERTY INFORMATION
Property Address: ▓▓▓ ▓▓▓▓▓ ▓▓
DENVER, CO 80211-4023
Owner Occupied: N

Parcel Identification Number:
▓▓▓▓▓▓▓▓▓▓▓▓
County PIN: ▓▓▓▓▓▓▓▓▓▓
Assessor: ▓▓▓▓▓ ▓▓▓▓

OWNER INFORMATION
Owner: ▓▓▓▓ ▓▓▓
Co-Owner: ▓▓▓▓▓ ▓▓▓
Owner Address: ▓▓▓ ▓▓▓ ▓▓
BOULDER, CO 80304-2506

Sale Price: ▓▓▓▓▓▓
Sale Date: ▓▓ ▓▓▓ ▓▓▓
Previous Price: ▓▓▓▓▓▓
Previous Date: ▓▓ ▓▓▓ ▓▓▓▓

LAND INFORMATION
Subdivision Name: ▓▓▓▓ ▓ ▓▓▓▓▓▓ ▓▓▓▓▓▓▓
Legal: L 3 & S 1/2 OF L 2 BLK 1 KEEL
& ELLISONS ADD
Property Type: RESIDENT
Improvement Code: 11.2
Land Code: 11.7
Zoning: R2

Subdivision Number: ▓▓▓▓▓
Schedule Number: ▓▓▓▓▓▓▓▓▓▓
Census Tract: ▓▓▓▓▓▓▓▓▓
Latitude: ▓▓ ▓▓▓▓▓
Longitude: ▓▓▓ ▓▓▓▓▓
Acres: ▓ ▓▓▓
Lot Size: ▓▓▓▓

PROPERTY CHARACTERISTICS
Year of Construction: 1910
Style: RANCH
Bedrooms: 2
Baths: 2.00
Roof Cover:
Stories: 1.0
Square Feet: 1045
Fireplace:

Garage Type: DET GAR
Garage Sq Ft: 480
Heat Type: HOT WATER
Heat Fuel: GAS
Construction: BRICK
Basement Type:
Basement Sq Ft: 1045
Basement Finished Sq Ft: 900

Tax Year: ▓▓▓▓
Taxes Paid: ▓▓▓▓▓ ▓▓
Annual Taxes: ▓▓▓▓▓ ▓▓

Land Value: $162800
Assessed Total: $24830
Value Total: $311900

Photo Date: ▓▓▓▓▓

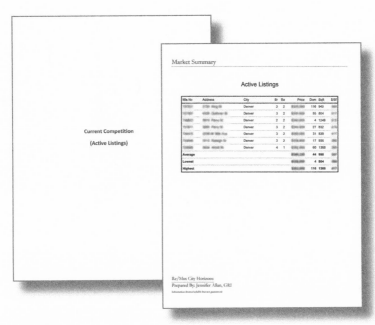

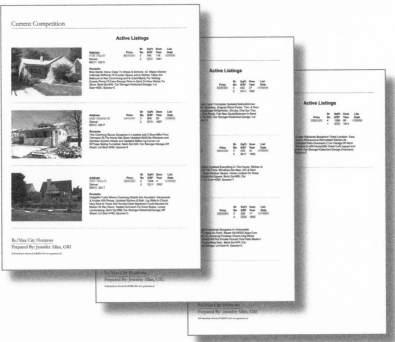

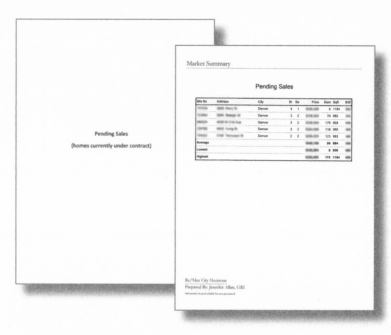

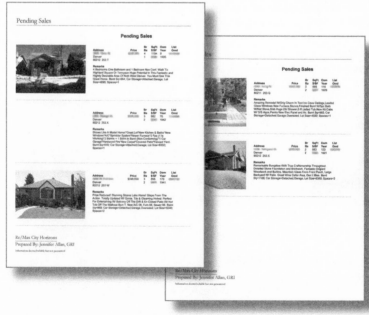

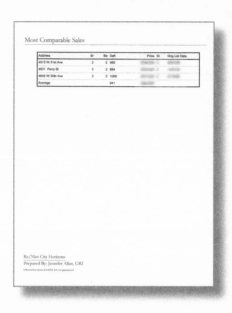

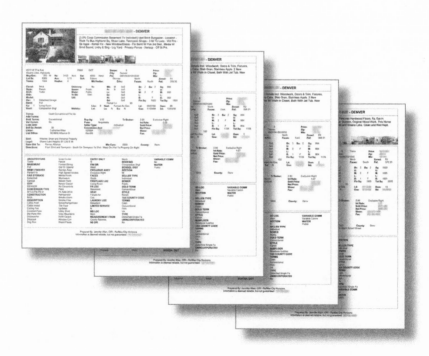

Estimated Cost of Sale

Sellers Net Sheet

Sale Price:	⬚⬚⬚
Loan Balance:	⬚⬚⬚
Total Gross Equity:	⬚⬚⬚
Listing Fee	⬚⬚⬚
Buyer Agent Fee	⬚⬚⬚
Title Insurance (worst case)	⬚⬚⬚
Miscellaneous Closing Costs	⬚⬚⬚
Water Escrow (unused portion refunded)	⬚⬚⬚
Prorated Tax (refunded from escrow acct)	⬚⬚⬚
Total Estimated Costs:	⬚⬚⬚
Total Gross Equity:	⬚⬚⬚
Total Estimated Costs:	⬚⬚⬚
Total Estimated Net Proceeds:	⬚⬚⬚

Agent:_____ Seller:_____ Date:_____

I understand that the above is an ESTIMATE and cannot be guaranteed in any way.

Re/Max City Horizons
Prepared By: Jennifer Allan, GRI
Information deemed reliable but not guaranteed

Sample Reconnection Letters

A "reconnection letter" is what a real estate agent writes to reconnect with his (or her) sphere of influence after a period of silence. Usually that silence is the time between when the agent sent out his new agent announcement letter... and a few years later when he realizes he's completely lost touch with this incredibly valuable source of business.

There are many approaches to writing an effective reconnection letter, but what isn't effective is to attempt to reconnect with any sort of sales pitch. Take a look at the following real-world letters submitted by fellow SWS'ers and see if they inspire you to write your own fabulous one!

Dear Friends,

Remember those Perception vs Reality ads launched originally by Rolling Stone magazine? They are classic. I like the analogy.

As you may know, I have been practicing real estate for a while, and I love it.

"So, Jim," you want to ask, "How's business?" But then again you may be thinking, "The market is not so hot, maybe it's better to be gracious and not ask."

The Reality is I have been busy. With the arrival of spring, things are blossoming, both for me and the Charlotte real estate market.

Now as far as this letter to you, I want to keep in touch with people I know and care about. That whole perception versus reality thing going on again here — please don't think that my lack of contact is lack of interest (wrong perception). The reality is I'm just reluctant to do what all the gurus tell us real estate agents to do to the people we know, that is, to hound you for referrals!

So I have committed, with some help from a mentor, to approach this business in a non-salesy way, which, as you know, is really my personality (non-salesy). Doesn't mean that when doing real estate I don't negotiate, act business-like or work hard as the dickens; just that my approach to growing my business is to first gain your trust and good will.

How does a real estate agent (me) gain the trust and good will of people he knows and cares about? I don't know all the answers, but my thinking is that, as in any venture, respect, integrity and resourcefulness go a long way. Hopefully we have a good start. Staying in touch and providentially working together will only strengthen this reality.

I do need to do some house-keeping, which includes updating my contact information for you. But don't worry, it's safe with me...no flooding you with annoying advertising pieces or calls during dinner. You have my promise. So, I do appreciate your passing any missing information along.

I will give you a call soon to say HI. I'm looking forward to catching up.

Thanks for your support.

Happy New Year!

As many of you know, about two years ago, I decided to become a rich and famous real estate writer. I chucked my City life, moved to the country and set up a sweet little office for myself so I could write, write, write to my heart's content. Ah... bliss. No schedules, no real deadlines, no need to even shower if I didn't feel like it. I could work from anywhere... or not work, as the mood struck.

And I've enjoyed the heck out of it. In two years, I've written five books and even have a little fan club! I've been told more than once that my writing has changed lives. Wow. It's been one of the most rewarding things I've ever done in my almost 41 years on this planet.

However... the life of a writer is... lonely. That surprised me – I didn't realize how much of a recluse I would become and how much I'd miss my friends. But a few months ago, I got a major case of Writer's Block which wouldn't go away. Where it used to be easy to bang out a chapter or article or blog, I was utterly stuck. Where'd my MoJoGo?

After some soul searching, I came to the conclusion that it's time to re-enter the real world... including the real world of real estate. Go, me!

So, here I am, at your service once again. All fired up with an arsenal of tools created to SELL HOUSES, even in today's less–than-stellar marketplace. Oh yeah, I wrote the book on it!

I'll be in touch. I can't wait to reconnect.

All my best,

Hello there!

I hope you're doing well, and everything's good in your part of the world.

Me? I've been around, but due to some major changes in life, have lost touch with a lot of folks these past few years. One of those changes was getting married in 2005. Integrating a new husband (that would be Gregg) and 2 new step-kitties into our lives has been challenging, to say the least!

Another exciting change that some of you know about; I've put together a new business for myself, one I've always "known" was right for me. I'm selling houses...and I absolutely love it! I should have been doing this years ago. I've always had an interest in real estate, but family commitments came first. As they should. And then I thought maybe I was "too old" to start over. Ironically, it was my wonderful family who helped convince me that you're never too old to follow your dreams!

So that's exactly what I'm doing. Last summer, I joined Gentry Real Estate Company and am very proud to be on their team. Their support and marketing tools are top-notch. I remember watching the "Gentry TV Showcase of Homes" almost 20 years ago, and now one of my listings will actually be on it! How cool is that??

Both kids are now in high school...Andy's a freshman, and Kelly will be graduating in June. My baby...going to college. Wow! As always, I'm very proud of them both.

Thankfully, the family's being very supportive of my new career. I'm not home quite as much, but I know they're enjoying the fact that I have Marco's Pizza on my cell phone's speed-dial. :)

I'd love to find out what you've been up to...what changes have come your way. Let's do some catching up!

Bye for now,

Dear Friend,

I'm on the move...and want to make sure you can find me the next time you wake up in the middle of the night and desperately want to talk real estate (well, if it can wait til morning, that would be great).

I recently changed real estate offices and even though most of my contact information is the same, I'm sending you my new business card, just in case. Same great service you expect and deserve, with even MORE company support behind me! I'm excited to take advantage of all my new company offers.

Did you know that most real estate agents spend the vast majority of their time looking for NEW business? Prospecting, networking, advertising, etc.? I didn't know that - and it certainly doesn't sound right to me. If an agent is spending all his or her time prospecting... how much time and energy does he have left over for his current clients?

I don't work that way. I intend to spend my time working for the clients I am honored to serve today, not searching for clients I hope to have tomorrow. It just makes more sense, and, frankly, sounds like a whole lot more fun.

My goal as a real estate agent is to ensure that my clients have such a pleasant real estate experience that they find themselves naturally recommending me to others. I do this by being a trusted advisor, a patient listener, a knowledgeable practitioner and a great negotiator. Pretty simple, really.

Enclosed is a little brochure about the tax advantages of owning a home. I think you'll find it interesting, if you already own your home, and inspiring, if you're thinking about owning your home!

Yours sincerely,

What to Expect When on the Market

A Seller's Guide to What to Do, How to Help and When to Stay Out of the Way

What to Expect While on the Market

Dear Home Seller,

First, allow me to thank you for inviting me into your life and for offering me the opportunity to interview for the honor of selling your home. I'm looking forward to a mutually satisfying relationship for both of us.

With that goal in mind, I have created this packet of information designed to give you an overview of the home-selling process. I find that in all the confusion of choosing the right agent, determining an asking price and developing a marketing strategy for their home, sellers almost always forget to ask (and their agents neglect to explain) what exactly is going to happen to them during the home sale process!

And you need to know...your life is about to change!

Your real estate agent needs your help to sell your home; we can't do it alone. We need you to understand why we do things the way we do and why we give the advice we give. We need your support and commitment to get the job done.

I find that the best way to get the support and commitment I need from my sellers is to be upfront and honest about HOW you can help me...get the highest price for your home...in the shortest amount of time...with the least amount of hassle.

So...with that said...please enjoy "What to Expect While On the Market!"

Jennifer Allan-Hagedorn

Showings

As soon as your home shows up for sale on the Multiple Listing Service (MLS), other real estate agents will expect to be able to show your home. The agent will call our office or showing service to schedule the showing and receive any special instructions. Showings are typically scheduled a few hours in advance within a certain time frame, for example between 2:00 and 4:00 on Tuesday. However, there are no strict guidelines on how much notice agents provide; sometimes they will call the day before; sometimes one hour before.

We will take the agent's information, call you to confirm that the showing time will work for you, and then call back to the agent's office with the approval and special instructions. This procedure ensures that only active real estate agents gain access to your home.

WHAT TO DO DURING THE SHOWING WINDOW

Tidy up and LEAVE!! Many sellers understandably believe that because they know and love their home, they can best sell it to potential buyers. However, in reality, most buyers and their agents are uncomfortable looking at a home when the owner is there. They will tend to give only a cursory look to the home, and will have trouble imagining themselves in what is so obviously YOUR home.

When I am acting as Buyers Agents with my clients, I cringe when I realize that the owner is home and intends to show us the house himself.

How tidy does the home need to be?

As tidy and de-personalized as reasonably possible. Potential buyers need to imagine themselves living in your home, which is difficult if it is messy, crowded or overly personal.

Strive for an odor free environment.

Smell has enormous impact on buyers, even "pleasant" smells such as potpourri or baking bread may evoke negative feelings for some. Almost all buyers react negatively to pet smells, smoke and incense.

- Do not leave food cooking during showings - dinner is highly personal and will make buyers feel that they're intruding on your privacy.

- While you're on the market, try to prepare meals that don't produce strong odors.

- Thoroughly clean your refrigerator. Out of habit, buyers will open the refrigerator door. Most refrigerators do not smell fresh and leave a lingering odor in the air.

- Clean out the litter box frequently. Cat odors can be a strong deterrent to sale. Ask a friend you can trust if your home has any pet odor at all.

A LAST LOOK AROUND AS YOU LEAVE EACH DAY...

- Make all beds
- Wash dishes
- Put away dirty (and clean) clothes
- Clean the sinks and mirrors
- Straighten newspapers
- Turn on lights
- Close toilet lids

Yes, it is inconvenient, but clean, tidy homes sell at higher prices, period. Isn't it worth the extra effort?

CAN I TURN DOWN A SHOWING?

Of course - it's your home and you have a right to privacy. HOWEVER, please understand how Buyer Agents work with their clients.

Typically, the agent and buyer schedule some time together to look at homes - perhaps 2 -3 hours once or twice a week. They may look at many homes in various parts of town. The agent may want to show your home between 1:00 and 2:00 on Saturday, along with other homes nearby.

If that time slot is inconvenient for you, and you turn down the showing, chances are that the buyer will never see your home. Unfortunately, it won't work to ask the buyer to come at a different time, because they'll already be in another part of town, or finished looking. Or, perhaps writing an offer on a competing home...

Try not to risk losing the Perfect Buyer by declining showings unnecessarily.

AGENT PREVIEWS

Sometimes we will call you to schedule an "agent preview". This means that an agent will come alone to your home (with no buyer) for a quick run through. There are three reasons agents preview:

1. They have busy buyers who want their agent to screen all properties before showing,

2. They specialize in your area and like to keep up on the market,

3. They have a new listing coming up and are checking out the competition.

The same guidelines for tidiness apply during previews, but it's not really necessary to leave.

Previewing agents are usually just trying to get a feel for the home, so will probably just breeze through quickly. Don't be offended or concerned if they are only in your home a few minutes.

Will I show or sell your home?

Maybe...but don't be surprised if I don't. There are thousands of real estate agents in our area so the chances of my selling your home personally are small. Of course, if I have, or find, buyer clients who might like your home, I'll certainly show it to them first.

Offers

QUICK OFFERS

Even in a buyer's market, we may receive an offer right away. Buyer agents with active buyers are on a daily watch for new listings. Well priced and well presented homes still can sell quickly and if your home meets the needs of an active buyer, his or her agent will show it to them as soon as possible.

If this happens, it does not mean that your home was underpriced. Do NOT beat yourself up that you should have asked more. Overpriced homes that sit on the market get stale and the best way to obtain the highest price is to sell quickly.

LOW OFFERS
Everyone wants a DEAL. Most buyers want to try a "low ball" offer to see what happens. Don't be offended. If your home is reasonably priced, we'll simply counter back. If you're a little high, you'll probably need to give a little. We'll discuss your options thoroughly and you will make the final decision.

CONTINGENT OFFERS

A contingent offer is one where the buyer needs to sell a home to qualify to buy yours. Responses to a contingent offer include the following:

1. Reject it, who needs the hassle?
2. Accept it, hopefully they'll be able to sell their home.
3. Counter with a First Right of Refusal.

Home Sale Contingencies definitely add a wrinkle to the process. Instead of one inspection, one loan approval, one appraisal, we have to deal with TWO. Any real estate deal, contingent or not, can fall apart at any time prior to closing, but it is slightly more likely to happen with a contingency.

So why would you ever accept a contingency? A few reasons:

- **More money**

A good Buyer Agent knows that a contingent contract is not as appealing as a clean contract; therefore, the offer should be as attractive as possible in other respects. If you accept a contingent offer, you should expect a great price and reasonable terms.

- **Market Realities**

As real estate prices move higher, it will become more and more difficult for first time buyers to purchase a home. Therefore, the buyer for your home will likely already be a homeowner who needs to sell their home to qualify to buy a new home. Bridge loans are not easy or cost effective to get.

If you are committed to a specific moving date, it is probably a good idea to avoid contingent offers; however, in reality, I don't know if a contingent contract (or any, for that matter) will close on time, or at all. Neither do I know if a clean offer will come along soon. Whether or not to accept a contingent offer is a judgment call. If we do agree to accept a contingent offer, I will work diligently to make the process as smooth as possible for you.

NO OFFERS

I will be providing feedback to you from agents who show the home, so we may already know what the problem is (price, condition, location, etc.). Some homes simply take longer to sell than others, but in today's market, many homes don't sell at all. If we aren't seeing second showings or receiving inquiries from showing agents within a reasonable amount of time, we need to discuss alternative strategies, including price.

Inspection

The first hurdle after contract acceptance is the inspection. The buyer will hire a professional inspector to thoroughly go over your home looking for major and minor defects (no home is perfect!). Areas of specific concern are: roof, furnace, structure, electrical and plumbing.

It's not a bad idea to hire your own inspector prior to marketing the home. For $200 - $300, you can eliminate most surprises, and know up front if your roof or furnace will need to be replaced. If your furnace is unsafe or your roof is damaged, you will probably be asked to fix or replace it. You might as well know these things up front; possibly we can recapture the cost of repair or replacement in the listing price. When I act as buyer agents, I insist that the roof and furnace be safe and functional for our clients.

Another advantage to pre inspection is that many minor irritants can be fixed. The more "nickel and dime" problems that an inspector points out to a buyer, the more nervous the buyer becomes that the home hasn't been maintained. When a home comes through inspection with a short punch list, the buyer feels good about the home, and is excited to move forward. Obviously, a lengthy punch list creates the opposite emotion.

What should I expect to fix?

A defective roof, furnace or sewer line will almost always need to be repaired/replaced. Otherwise, there are no rules. The buyer can ask for anything, and you can respond any way you want.

Unless your home is truly in poor repair, the buyer should not give us a laundry list of minor repairs, but it happens every day. The inspection is simply a second negotiation.

What I Need From You

When you hire me to sell your home, you have certain expectations from me that I hope to fulfill and exceed. I also have expectations from my sellers that will make the process go smoothly and more profitably for all...

- A clean home, ready and available to show with reasonable notice

- Sellers out of the house during most showings

- No smoking in the home during the marketing period

- Lawn care & snow removal if your home is vacant

- A willingness to ensure a safe and working furnace, and an insurable roof to the new buyers, even if that means repairs or replacement (unless your home is marketed as a 'fix up')

- An open mind to our suggestions and recommendations

What You Can Expect From Me

WEEK ONE

- MLS entry
- Lockbox & sign installed
- Brochures delivered to home
- Web Sites activated
- Virtual Tour created and distributed
- First market report
- Feedback reports
- Review our first week on market (showing procedures, any feedback, general observations)

WEEKS TWO - THREE

- Continued feedback reports
- Weekly check in phone calls
- Second market report (at three weeks)
- Brochures re stocked (as necessary)
- Discuss price adjustment
- Open house, if desired and appropriate

WEEKS FOUR - SIX

- Thorough review of the market and re evaluation of our strategy
- Continued feedback reports
- Weekly check in phone calls
- Evaluation of feedback
- Third market report (at six weeks)

WEEKS SIX - ONWARD

- Continued feedback reports
- Weekly check in phone calls
- Periodic market reports (if desired)
- Exterior photo re-taken (as the season changes)

I Work For You

If you have additional needs, or suggestions for improving my service to you, please share them! I want your experience with me to be one of the best customer service experiences you've ever had. My goal is to provide 100% Customer Satisfaction.

Help Me Make That Happen

Contributors

A big THANK YOU to my friends who graciously contributed to this book! It just wouldn't have been the same without you. Hugs to you all.

- **Broker Bryant Tutas**, Broker/Owner Tutas Towne Realty
  Poinciana, Florida www.brokerbryant.com

- **Scott Nordby**, Broker/Owner Innovative Real Estate Group
  Denver, Colorado www.iregroup.com

- **Loretta Hughes**, Broker/Owner Exit Realty Fusion
  Regina, Saskatchewan, Canada

- **Jackie Leavenworth**, Real estate speaker, teacher, trainer
  www.coachjackie.com

- **Tupper Briggs**, REALTOR
  Evergreen, Colorado www.tuppersteam.com

- **Susan Haughton**, REALTOR
  Alexandria, Virginia www.novapropertyshop.com

- **Kim Brown**, REALTOR
  Keene, New Hampshire

- **Meyer Leibovitch**, REALTOR
  Montgomery County, Maryland www.meyerl.com

- **John MacArthur**, REALTOR,
  Olney, Maryland www.jmacsays.com

- **Sue Gabriel**
  North Olmsted, Ohio

- **Jim Swanger**, REALTOR
  Charlotte, North Carolina

Resources

Free Stuff @ www.SellwithSoul.com

Like any good website, I offer lots of free stuff at mine... to draw you in, get you addicted to me and then sell you all my goodies... well, that's the plan anyway! But whether or not you ever buy anything from me, I thought you might like to know what's there for the taking[1]...

FREE NEWSLETTERS

- The Daily Seduction - Tips & Strategies for Generating Business & Referrals from the Very Important People Who Know You (Your Sphere of Influence)

- The Reluctant Prospector - Sanity Savers for Introverts & other Reluctant Prospectors

- Confidence-Builders for Rookie Real Estate Agents

- So, You Wanna be a Real Estate Agent?

LOUNGES & FORUMS

- The VIP Lounge - This is where you'll find checklists, a sample listing presentation, sample client communications & more

- The Sell with Soul Forum - Where the smartest, coolest, funniest people in real estate hang out

Just visit www.SellwithSoul.com to access these resources.

---

[1] *These offerings are subject to change, of course.*

Want More?

JENNIFER WRITES ...

If you enjoyed "The More Fun You Have Selling Real Estate" and want more, you're in luck! Jennifer loves to write, so you can find hours and hours of soulful material all over the WWW. Of course, you can purchase her other books, including her first, "*Sell with Soul: Creating an Extraordinary Career in Real Estate without Losing Your Friends, Your Principles or Your Self-Respect*" on her website or at Amazon. com. But if you're not in the mood to spend your dollars today, here is a link to the Searchable Soul blog archive where you will find years of Jennifer's writings all organized and categorized for your reading enjoyment!

www.SearchableSoul.com

JENNIFER SPEAKS ...

Yes, Jennifer writes about real estate. But she speaks about it, too! Out loud - to your office, group or association. Help us spread the word that there is an alternative to cheesy Old School tactics & techniques; that serving one's current clients is the highest and best use of a real estate agent's time and that it is possible to succeed in a real estate career without sacrificing one's soul to do so.

Jennifer speaks on a variety of topics, including "Selling to Your Sphere of Influence: No Sales Pitch Required," "For Sale Signs Don't Pay the Bills," "Selling Real Estate is Not a Numbers Game," and "The Art of Pricing." Some of her presentations are approved for Continuing Education credit in several states.

To learn more or to request a proposal, just contact Jennifer at Jennifer@sellwithsoul.com

JENNIFER COACHES ...

Want to implement something you just read about in "The More Fun You Have Selling Real Estate...?" Talk to Jennifer. Whether you're just starting out or taking it to the next level, she can probably help you figure out what to do now, what to do next, and what to do after that. She doesn't have a formal coaching program in place, and that's by design. She evaluates and advises each client as an individual, according to his or her personality, lifestyle, goals and budget. No long-term contracts or condescending sales pitches; just a sincere desire to help agents reach their goals - no matter how lofty or down-to-earth they may be.

Interested? Just contact Jennifer at Jennifer@sellwithsoul.com.

The Story of Joe

As told to the author
by Dennis J. Giannetti

Joe was at a crossroads in his real estate career.

Business was okay...not great by any means, but it paid the bills, most months anyway. Joe couldn't really complain since many of his associates had no idea where their next mortgage payment was coming from and more than a few were on the verge of leaving the business altogether.

While Joe hadn't reached that point, he frequently felt discouraged and wasn't having nearly as much fun selling real estate as he'd had in the past. In fact, lately he'd had to drag himself into the office to do the three hours of focused prospecting his new coach recommended. He usually spent these hours calling expired listings and FSBOs, with occasional calls to friends to remind them to send referrals his way.

Even though Joe didn't really enjoy all this focused prospecting, he knew it had to be done. Especially in today's market, where buyers and sellers weren't found on every street corner, it was even more necessary than it had been in years past to devote a significant amount of time and energy to prospecting for new business.

So, as much as Joe dreaded his daily three-hour prospecting routine, he told himself that the end goal was worth the pain—that eventually he'd have a more consistent stream of business coming in the door and then he wouldn't have to worry so much about where his next client would come from.

Because he did worry a lot about that. Some days the worry consumed him, to the point where he couldn't think about anything else. He knew the stress was

Prospect with Soul for Real Estate Agents

affecting his business and his health, not to mention his marriage, and that he needed to make a change.

But...what?

One day, instead of going in to the office at 8:00 a.m. as was his habit, he found himself driving to the beach, almost as if a force beyond his control was steering the car.

When he arrived, there was no one else there. Well, almost no one. Standing along the water's edge, amidst the waves crashing into the shore, was a woman moving in place, slowly, with grace and fluidity. To Joe, it was almost as if she were one with the ocean. She seemed completely at peace and, in a moment of clarity, Joe realized that more than anything else, he too wanted that peace. He waited patiently for the woman to complete the exercise and, as she headed toward the steps leaving the beach, Joe hesitantly waved at her.

"Sorry, can I ask what you were doing out there?"

"Sure," she answered, "I was doing a little moving meditation. Is it something you want to learn?"

"Um, not really," Joe admitted. He paused. "But I would really love to be at peace like that--you know focused, flowing, clear."

"I see," said the woman. "May I ask why you don't have this feeling now?"

"That's the thing," said Joe, "I don't really know."

"Well, I have some time this morning. Would you like to join me for a cup of tea and talk about it?"

About 10 minutes later, they were sitting in a small café.

Joe asked the woman what she did for a living.

"Oh, I'm retired now, but I was a real estate agent for years," the woman responded.

It was like music to Joe's ears. Could this woman hold the answers to his questions?

The Story of Joe

As the woman took her first sip of peppermint tea, Joe told her he also was a real estate agent.

"Ah," said the woman, "and that is where your confusion is coming from?"

The woman's soft voice and calm demeanor opened the floodgates for Joe. For over an hour, he poured out his frustrations and fears, his hopes and dreams. The woman listened quietly, occasionally taking notes on her napkin.

When Joe ran out of steam, he smiled sheepishly and apologized for monopolizing the conversation.

"Not at all," the woman assured him. "I have to go now, but I'd like to meet you again. I think I can help you find what you're looking for. Meet me at the beach tomorrow morning and I will share with you how what you saw me doing on the beach today relates to what you need to do to change your business."

"Can't wait," Joe said sincerely.

The next morning, Joe arrived at the beach and found the woman already there, in movement as she'd been the morning before. Fluid, purposeful, and peaceful. In a few minutes, she concluded her exercise and smiled at Joe.

"Ready?" she asked.

"Absolutely," answered Joe.

"Tell me, what was I doing just then?"

"Um, meditating? Tai chi?" Joe guessed.

"That's what it's called, but what was I *doing*?"

Pausing for a moment, Joe took a shot at going deep. "Um, connecting? Becoming one with your environment? Finding yourself from the inside out?"

The woman laughed softly. "Close enough, Joe, close enough. Now, let me ask you this—when you're prospecting, do you feel any of those things? Do you feel connected? Are you acting in a way that makes you peaceful from the inside out?"

"Well, no," Joe admitted, "but I'm just doing what I was taught. Is that wrong?"

Prospect with Soul for Real Estate Agents

"Does it feel right?"

"Well, to be honest, no," Joe answered.

"Why not?"

Joe paused.

"I feel like...I feel like I'm pushing people to do things they don't want to do. Like I'm trying to be someone I'm not in order to make things happen."

"Go on," said the woman.

"Well, I don't know how to explain it, but you know how you move so gracefully and effortlessly on the beach? I feel nothing like that day to day. I feel like I'm stumbling on my own efforts. I'm not excited about what I do anymore, or how I do it."

"I see," said the woman. "So, what do you think would make you feel more at peace? What do you want to change?"

"I want...I want to feel that I'm bringing real value to my clients. I want to feel confident when I prospect that I'm truly the best man for the job, not just a man who needs a paycheck. I want the people I know to think of me as an exceptional real estate agent who is deserving of their business and referrals. I want to build a successful real estate business without, well, without selling my soul, if you know what I mean."

"Excellent," said the woman. "Now here's the good news. Everything you say you want; everything you are seeking, is within your reach. It's already inside you. The problem is that you are ignoring your own quiet voice and, instead, you're listening to all those louder, more insistent voices on the outside telling you to do it their way. That emptiness and confusion you feel is just your soul trying to get your attention.

"Sounds kind of new-agey," Joe protested, but without conviction.

"Maybe," agreed the woman. "But it's true. To experience the success you dream of, you need to be in touch with who you are. You need to let *who you are* define *what you do*, not *what you do* define *who you are*."

The Story of Joe

"Wow," said Joe. "That makes sense. I think it does, anyway."

The woman smiled and continued. "Let's end today's lesson this way. You have been working for a commission check. You are attached to the outcome. But you feel empty inside. You seek to fill that emptiness by pursuing more and bigger commission checks. But the reality is that a commission check is simply the reward for doing a great job, not a definition of who you are. If you want to increase the balance in your bank account and your life, you need to listen to your soul and trust what it is telling you."

Joe took a moment to ponder this.

"Ok," he said. "I'm in. What do I have to do?"

"Meet me tomorrow, same place, same time. I will show you how to find people to serve and provide value to. I will teach you how to prospect from the inside out."

"Kind of like prospecting with soul," Joe said, trying to be witty.

"Exactly," said the woman. "Now, go enjoy your day. I'll see you tomorrow."

Prospect with Soul for Real Estate Agents